AUTOMATION IN THE AGE OF ARTIFICIAL INTELLIGENCE

Automation in the Age of Artificial Intelligence draws on historical and contemporary debates to examine the future of work in the age of artificial intelligence.

While automation is often portrayed as an inevitable technological force driving economic progress or job loss, this book reframes it as a socially constructed discourse that is shaped by competing beliefs, interests and narratives about human labor, progress and value. It situates current anxieties about AI within a longer trajectory of industrial transformation by identifying four distinct ways of understanding automation: the activist, resigned, status quo and futurist discourses. By analyzing how these discourses emerge in policy debates, media coverage and academic research, this book reveals how language and ideology influence the adoption and governance of new technologies.

This book offers conceptual framework for scholars in sociology, political economy and science and technology studies, as well as for policymakers and labor advocates seeking to navigate automation's social impacts. In doing so, it moves beyond deterministic narratives of job loss to uncover the deeper cultural meanings attached to technological change and the uncertain future of work.

Larry Liu is Assistant Professor in the Department of Sociology and Anthropology at Morgan State University, USA.

Routledge Studies in the Sociology of Work, Professions and Organisations

This series presents the latest sociological and social scientific research on professions, work and organisations, welcoming studies of careers, professional motivations, organisational change, entrepreneurship, workplace issues, working lives and identities, labour relations and the transformation of work in a changing economy.

Titles in this series

Scrutinizing Polarization
Patterns and Consequences of Occupational Transformation in the Swedish Labour Market
Ylva Ulfsdotter Eriksson and Thomas Berglund

Governing Street-level Bureaucracies
The Organizational Shaping of Caseworkers
Kerstin Jacobsson and Håkan Johansson

Workers without Companies
Towards a New Way of Working
Sylvie Célérier and Alberto Riesco-Sanz

Automation in the Age of Artificial Intelligence
The Social Construction of the Future of Work
Larry Liu

For more information about this series, please visit: https://www.routledge.com/Routledge-Studies-in-the-Sociology-of-Work-Professions-and-Organisations/book-series/RSSWPO

Larry Liu dissects the rhetoric regarding the future of work as the AI drumbeat grows ever louder. He insightfully analyzes the competing narratives that are likely to shape our understanding of the role AI and other emerging technologies will play in our society. Liu effectively brings the rich history of debates about automation to bear on current conversations. Rather than assuming technology is an irresistible force, Liu helps the reader ask, 'Whose vision of emerging technologies will prevail?'

Jerry Jacobs, *Professor of Sociology, University of Pennsylvania*

In *Automation in the Age of Artificial Intelligence*, Larry Liu conceptualizes automation as a socially constructed discourse shaped by competing ideological orientations and institutional interests. Synthesizing historical analysis with contemporary case studies across labor, policy and media domains, Liu delineates four dominant frameworks – activist, resigned, status quo and futurist – that structure public understanding of technological change and its implications for the future of work. By theorizing automation through the lenses of sociotechnical imaginaries, expectations and power, this highly informative, easily accessible and sufficiently nuanced book offers scholars and policymakers a rigorous framework for interpreting how societies negotiate the political, economic and normative stakes of AI-driven transformation.

Richard K. Caputo, *PhD, Professor Emeritus of Social Policy & Research, Yeshiva University*

Treating AI as a twenty-first century version of the steam engine, Larry Liu brilliantly analyzes how we are reacting to automation and its challenges. Beginning with a succinct account of where we are now, Liu defines the different perspectives from fears to aspirations and provides a guidebook as to the rhetoric and the reality of our new "industrial revolution."

Miguel Centeno, *Professor of Sociology, Princeton University*

This book addresses what is perhaps the fundamental problem of our time – the advance of artificial intelligence and the possibility that it will substitute human labor and, eventually, humans themselves. Liu outlines four alternative positions on this issue and documents them with a wealth on examples.

Early forms of class struggle are being substituted by a novel form in which the powers-that-be in the capitalist world pit the incredible advances in technology against living humans and their chances for survival in the future. Liu has rendered us a great service by documenting this struggle and the forms it is now taking head on.

Alejandro Portes, *Professor of Sociology, Princeton University and University of Miami*

The consequences of technologies such as AI and automation are not inevitable but are socially constructed based on competing narratives. This timely and historically grounded book identifies and evaluates four competing perspectives about how these technologies have shaped work in the past and might do so in the future.

Arne L. Kalleberg, *Kenan Distinguished Professor of Sociology, University of North Carolina at Chapel Hill*

Larry Liu reminds us that our choices, not "impersonal" technology, drive automation, artificial intelligence and work's future. This is empowering and scary.

Cory Isaacs, *Postdoctoral Fellow at Harvard University, City Manager of Hillsboro, Wisconsin*

AUTOMATION IN THE AGE OF ARTIFICIAL INTELLIGENCE

The Social Construction of the Future of Work

Larry Liu

Routledge
Taylor & Francis Group
LONDON AND NEW YORK

Designed cover: Getty Images

First published 2027
by Routledge
4 Park Square, Milton Park, Abingdon, Oxon OX14 4RN

and by Routledge
605 Third Avenue, New York, NY 10158

Routledge is an imprint of the Taylor & Francis Group, an informa business

British Library Cataloguing-in-Publication Data
A catalogue record for this book is available from the British Library

ISBN: 9781041316848 (hbk)
ISBN: 9781041316831 (pbk)
ISBN: 9781003780236 (ebk)

DOI: 10.4324/9781003780236

Typeset in Gaillard
by codeMantra

CONTENTS

INTRODUCTION

Automation as a Sociological Project

In 2016, an AI (artificial intelligence) robot called Benjamin wrote a script for the ten-minute short film "Sunspring". Four years later, an AI bot developed by Calamity AI wrote a three-and-half minute short film titled "Solicitors." The capabilities of AI in the film industry are not confined to screenwriters. Filmmakers use CGI (computer-generated imagery) to bring dead actors back to the movie screen. Actors who passed away before finishing their performance could have their TV episodes and movies completed. The company ScriptBook has created an AI-based script analysis to automate recommendations on what scenes to promote commercially. AI developed by the University of Edinburgh has created forty trailers for existing films, which were rated better than human-created trailers. Improvements in AI translation generate automated subtitles which increases the international reach of movies.[1] The company Deepdub is also creating AI for dubbing movies.[2] Particle6 is an AI production studio that produces AI-generated movies, TV shows and commercials end-to-end. OpenAI's Sora 2 can generate high-quality, coherent video sequences.[3]

In the meantime, Hollywood writers in the Writers Guild of America are not just passively accepting their fate but have engaged in a months-long labor strike totaling 148 days between May and September 2023. The panoply of grievances went beyond the bread and butter bargaining issues like wages and benefits or the share of residuals to collect. It also covered the legitimate use of AI. In the agreement reached between the studio owners and the writers, AI cannot be credited as a writer, cannot write literary material and cannot be used as a source material. Writers cannot be forced to use AI in their work but may do so if they wish to use it. Thus, human writers should remain important actors in the film-writing process.[4] While the negotiated outcome looks

DOI: 10.4324/9781003780236-1

quite promising, how effective is the union going to be in sustaining their human-centric business model? Will it not be possible for independent studios to increase their use of AI and more cheaply generate popular and highly profitable movie scripts, thus circumventing the studios that stuck to more rigid union contracts? Would the movie viewers be able to tell the difference between AI and human-generated movies, and do they care?

The movie industry is only one example of what automation could mean for workers in the industry. There is still uncertainty about whether AI exists primarily to *assist* or to *replace* screenwriters, actors, translators, or marketers. CGI has so far only been used to complete unfinished movie projects of dead actors, but it is conceivable that these popular dead actors could be inserted into new movies, and it might no longer be necessary to hire any actors. As for living actors, once the person's voice and body movements/ appearance are trained into the algorithm, CGI could work without further live actor input. Talent agencies that represent top Hollywood actors have attacked OpenAI's effort to generate clips based on the likeness to major actors. United Talent Agency issued the statement,

> There is no substitute for human talent in our business, and we will continue to fight tirelessly for our clients to ensure that they are protected. When it comes to OpenAI's Sora or any other platform that seeks to profit from our clients' intellectual property and likeness, we stand with artists.[5]

Perhaps, intellectual property lawsuits will slow down AI companies' push to promote AI in the movie industry, but can it be stopped?

Would movie viewers care about sustaining a film industry of human actors? After all, actors are not just adored on the screen but are also celebrities that attend red carpet film festivals and are the fodder for the entertainment industry (paparazzi, celebrity magazines and TV shows) and their consumers. On the other hand, there is a desire among film executives to increase their profit margin by sharing the revenues with fewer people, e.g., other managers, shareholders and AI programmers, so the temptation to rely more on AI is enormous, especially as its abilities continue to improve. To the extent, that movies pass the Turing test (i.e., AI is indistinguishable from humans), movie viewers might welcome fully AI-produced movies. Perhaps, human actors will be enjoyed like ballet or opera: by cinema connoisseurs rather than the masses.[6] Consider also that AI is only the most recent iteration of automation technology coming at the end of a long line of inventions that have changed human lives and reshaped how we work.

The resistance of the Hollywood writers, which I call an "activist" perspective, is only one of the possible societal views vis-à-vis automation. What I refer to as the activists argue that social actors such as labor unions protecting their jobs or politicians advocating for job creation/protection policies can actively shape the trajectory of social change and mold the technologies according to the needs and interests of society. A more passive perspective is that technological change produces a deeply dystopian vision including an increase in technological unemployment, more economic instability for the displaced workers and growing societal and political instability. I consider academics and political actors that focus on these negative ramifications of technology as the "resigned" group. A third perspective is the most conservative in that it asserts that AI and other forms of automation technology are no different than previous innovations. Most politicians, businesspeople and consultancies take on a largely neoliberal framework, according to which these new technologies will assist businesses in the accumulation of more capital. Displaced workers are assured that training and workforce development programs will maintain full employment, and that the capitalist status quo can be maintained in the future. Hence, I label this view the "status quo" view. A fourth group within automation discourse asserts that humans are in a fast trajectory toward the replacement of jobs but are not at all pessimistic about the future direction of humanity. They envision a workless future and a leisure society which comes with a combination of universal basic income (UBI) or services. Most people will no longer have to work for a living, so there is a general redefinition of people's identity. I call this group the "futurists."

This above description implies that there is not a single prevalent discourse in automation and how the future of work will look like. There are really four different perspectives, and often these four perspectives happen within their own networks and social bubbles. The key contribution of this book is to analyze the four societal perspectives on automation and the future of work, contributing to the broad literatures in economic, political, historical, labor sociology and technology studies.

What Is Automation?

One of the mysteries of contemporary life under capitalism is whether automation is going to substantially reduce employment opportunities. Technically, automation is "the creation and application of technology to monitor and control the production and delivery of products and services." It involves AI, robotics, telemetry, communications, electro-optics, cybersecurity, process measurement, sensors, wireless applications, system integration and test measurement, among others.[7] But where are the humans in this highly technical definition? Sociologically, automation is the "act or process of replacing human workers with machines so that tasks can be performed automatically."[8] There is an important distinction between mechanization and automation. Mechanization is about specialized machinery that does a task at superhuman speed with human supervision, while automation is the use of computers and electronic data processing to replace human workers.[9] The salience of the automation discourse comes precisely from fears that mechanization (reduced labor use) will end up in automation (no labor use).

Automation is primarily about labor replacement due to technology and can but does not necessarily result in technological unemployment, i.e., an elevation in unemployment due to technological change. Automation is distinct from deskilling, reskilling and changes to the content and intensity of the work experience due to the introduction of technology. On the other hand, technology does all these things. It results in work intensification, deskilling, in some cases reskilling and causing job loss, but at different rates in different time periods in different social contexts. Oftentimes, capitalists driven by the profit motive introduce technology to cause intensification and deskilling, where human workers have to adjust to the whims of the machines or algorithms to allow the production of goods or delivery of services to proceed smoothly, and once they perform well enough without human assistance, these workers lose their jobs eventually.

To complicate matters further, the labor impacts of technology are not restricted to the workplace but extend into the social discourse. Here, what matters is not so much job displacement itself but the talk about job displacement. How serious will job displacement be? What if anything should be done about job displacement? What is a desirable future of work? The discourse of automation is an imagination of a workless future with corresponding attitudes of derision ("technological unemployment is unlikely or will never happen"), fear ("technological unemployment is coming and we will suffer"), determination ("technological unemployment is controllable by worker resistance"), indifference ("we don't know whether technological unemployment will happen and are not concerned about it") and excitement ("technological unemployment will liberate humanity from the drudgery of wage work"). In short, automation is not an exclusively technical-instrumental process but has profound social meanings, causes and consequences. As I argue in this book, it is also shaped by human actors.

The pervading fear about the wide-scale displacement of jobs has long antecedents and has been covered in many published works. As far ago as the 1930s, the renowned British economist John Maynard Keynes predicted that there will be a future where humans will only be working 15-hour weeks, largely because technological progress will have made many jobs obsolete.[10] Unfortunately, the overall trend is that working hours in the US have declined from the beginning of the twentieth century but stagnated since the early-1980s at about 1,800 annual hours on average.[11] The subjective experience of many workers is the sense of 'overwork' due to rising cost of living and declining purchasing power of middle-class occupations.[12] Nonetheless, the long-term historical experience has been a shift from an agricultural to a manufacturing economy, and from manufacturing to a service-based economy, which suggests that technical innovation has been resulting in shifts in employment, involving both displacement as well as the creation of new jobs in other sectors.

In this context, I find that there are four major perspectives in the automation discourse. Mainstream neoliberal responses to automation are focused on traditional policy levers that shore up job training and education programs (status quo), while activists want the protection of existing jobs or more public sector job creation. A more left-utopian futurist approach is to advocate for less dependence on wage-work as a defining social identity and the pursuit of a leisure-oriented society via a universal basic income or improved welfare programs (futurist). The most pessimistic analysis comes from the resigned group, who primarily identify the problematic social, political and psychological outcomes of existing automation trends.

Thus, the potential political, economic, social and normative implications of automation are wide-ranging, offering social scientists a lot of discourses to analyze. Next, I turn to the plan for the book.

Plan for the Book

Chapter 1 lays out the current landscape of automation. This involves discussing current published research on automation, which involve the technological effects on past employment and predictions on future employment. I also review the literature on the economic and social causes of automation. This book makes the case that there is a fourth strand of research that is relevant, covering the discourses of automation. This is an important sociological contribution to the technology studies literature.

Chapter 2 frames automation discourse in the context of sociotechnical imaginary and the sociology of expectations. The former is about a social vision of technological projects, and the latter is about the social vision of how work will be structured given recent technological advances. I identify four discourses in automation, which I call the activist, resigned, status quo and futurist perspectives. Activists seek to resist automation or create collective bargaining agreements that preserve as many jobs as possible. The resigned lament and critique the negative societal effects of automation. The status quo view claims that automation is reinforcing the present economic system focused on capital accumulation and that it is necessary to reskill and retrain workers that are temporarily displaced. Futurists believe that automation will bring material abundance, reduce work hours and bring leisure via increased welfare programs and redistributive government programs or institutional changes. I relate these four discourses to their normative/ positivist commitments, their position in the utopia/dystopia continuum and their views on agency and social change. The rest of the book covers these four discourses.

Chapter 3 describes the activist discourse using the British Luddites, the American longshoremen, vehicle drivers and various other contemporary labor struggles as examples for the forms of labor resistance. In the most extreme cases, labor unions attempt to block automation altogether, and if they fail to do so they want other favorable collective bargaining clauses such as guaranteed retraining, first preference for other internal jobs or early retirement programs. Some politicians have also engaged in the anti-automation discourse. Legislation and lawsuits express those sentiments in policymaking. The national job guarantee is a policy idea that can be linked to the activist discourse.

Chapter 4 covers the resigned discourse, which are mainly academics that point to the worsening social mobility, populist electoral politics, declining political legitimacy of the present order, societal instability, communal disorder and poor mental health. The resigned view wage work as an essential human identity conferring purpose and self-confidence. I discuss various cultural accounts of technological unemployment in novels and movies that most closely reflect the resigned discourse.

Chapter 5 presents the status quo discourse, where automation is essential for the competitiveness of a nation's businesses and where technological unemployment is at best a brief, temporary phenomenon that can easily be handled by job training. It is the responsibility of the workers to be flexible and keep up with new technologies. The discourse is promoted by business leaders, consultancies, international organizations close to businesses, labor unions and mainstream politicians like US presidents from both political parties. There is a slight difference in emphasis between liberal presidents that focus on job training to address unemployment while conservative presidents have faith in free markets to create new jobs.

Chapter 6 reveals the futurist discourse that sees automation as a liberator from human wage work. They regard wage work as oppressive rather than essential. They desire a workless future or leisure society as final aim, while a shorter work week and UBI are the intermediate tools in that direction. The leading representatives of the futurist discourse are the Silicon Valley tech company leaders, progressive academics and political leaders advocating these two policies. I also present cultural depictions in movies and novels of a utopian future without work which contrasts the dystopian cultural accounts of technological unemployment.

The conclusion summarizes the four discourses and offers potential ways how these perspectives evaluate each other's arguments. I speculate on how various AI futures might impact the validity or salience of these four discourses and explain why Marx' and Weber's frameworks of technology in the context of capitalism and rationalization still matter to us moderns.

Notes

1 Krishna, Sri. "How AI Is Used in Filmmaking." *Analytics India Magazine*, May 12, 2022.

2 Perez, Sarah. "Deepdub Raises $20M for AI-Powered Dubbing that Uses Actors' Original Voices." *TechCrunch*, February 10, 2022.

3 Maddaus, Gene. "AI Actress Tilly Norwood Has Hollywood Fuming. Is She a Threat or a Stunt?" *Variety*, October 8, 2025.
4 Coyle, Jake. "In Hollywood Writers' Battle against AI, Humans Win (for Now)." *AP*, September 27, 2023.
5 Hayden, Erik. "Major Talent Agencies Circle the Wagons as Sora 2 Destabilizes Hollywood." *The Hollywood Reporter*, October 9, 2025.
6 Guardian. "'It's Too Late to Be Scared': Readers on the Controversial Rise of AI 'Actors'." October 1, 2025. https://www.theguardian.com/film/2025/oct/01/tilly-norwood-ai-actress-reaction
7 International Society of Automation. "What Is Automation?" https://www.isa.org/about-isa/what-is-automation
8 Open Education Sociology Dictionary. "Automation" https://sociologydictionary.org/automation/ 2025. https://www.theguardian.com/film/2025/oct/01/tilly-norwood-ai-actress-reaction
9 Steinhoff, James. *Automation and Autonomy: Labour, Capital and Machines in the Artificial Intelligence Industry*. New York: Palgrave, 2021.
10 Keynes, John Maynard. "Economic Possibilities of Our Grandchildren." In *Essays in Persuasion*, 358–73. New York: W.W. Norton, 1963.
11 OECD. Retrieved May 2022. https://data.oecd.org/emp/hours-worked.htm
12 Schor, Juliet. *The Overworked American: The Unexpected Decline of Leisure*. New York: Basic Books, 2008.

References

Coyle, Jake. "In Hollywood Writers' Battle Against AI, Humans Win (for Now)." *AP*, September 27, 2023.

Guardian. "'It's Too Late to Be Scared': Readers on the Controversial Rise of AI 'Actors'." October 1, 2025. https://www.theguardian.com/film/2025/oct/01/tilly-norwood-ai-actress-reaction

Hayden, Erik. "Major Talent Agencies Circle the Wagons as Sora 2 Destabilizes Hollywood." *The Hollywood Reporter*, October 9, 2025.

International Society of Automation. "What Is Automation?" https://www.isa.org/about-isa/what-is-automation

Keynes, John Maynard. *Essays in Persuasion*, 358–373. New York: W.W. Norton, 1963.

Krishna, Sri. "How AI Is Used in Filmmaking." *Analytics India Magazine*, May 12, 2022.

Maddaus, Gene. "AI Actress Tilly Norwood Has Hollywood Fuming. Is She a Threat or a Stunt?" *Variety*, October 8, 2025.

OECD. Retrieved May 2022. https://data.oecd.org/emp/hours-worked.htm

Open Education Sociology Dictionary. "Automation" https://sociologydictionary.org/automation/

Perez, Sarah. "Deepdub Raises $20M for AI-Powered Dubbing that Uses Actors' Original Voices." *TechCrunch*, February 10, 2022.

Schor, Juliet. *The Overworked American: The Unexpected Decline of Leisure*. New York: Basic Books, 2008.

Steinhoff, James. *Automation and Autonomy: Labour, Capital and Machines in the Artificial Intelligence Industry*. New York: Palgrave, 2021.

1

THE AUTOMATION LANDSCAPE

The rise of AI has unknown consequences on the general labor market. It is the latest in a long line of technological progress within human history. AI has produced renewed anxieties about the mass replacement of jobs or at least a fundamental shift in job tasks and power dynamics in the workplace. In this chapter, I describe the landscape of automation. What do we know about the state of automation? I review empirical studies on automation. Automation research can be divided into four categories: the technological effects on past employment; its potential effects on future employment; the social and economic causes of automation; and the discourses of automation. The key contribution in this book is focused on the discourses of automation. This chapter reviews the literature on the first three, while the latter is presented in Chapter 2.

Automation and Past Employment

Agricultural Automation

Automation has been a long-running characteristic of market-based capitalist economies. The history of technology holds so many innovations that cannot be fully covered in this book. The early seeds of industrialization were laid with the mechanization of agriculture via the invention of the seed drill, which was invented in 1701, to save on labor to distribute seeds to grow crops and increase agricultural output.[1] The invention of the threshing machine in 1786, quintupled the speed of cutting wheat and saved on farm labor costs.[2] Agricultural mechanization releases a significant amount of human labor to be used in urban factories and offices. The increase in the urban population increases demand for farm products, which further increases agricultural

DOI: 10.4324/9781003780236-2

mechanization.[3] Between 1840 and 2015, the US agricultural employment share declined from 63.1% to 1.4%.[4]

Textile and Manufacturing Automation

Another socially consequential example of automation was in the textile industry. The invention of the cotton gin in 1794 increased cotton production, which increased slave employment in the US South temporarily.[5] While the transatlantic slave trade was prohibited in 1808, and slavery itself was abolished at the end of the Civil War in 1865, sharecropping was a continuation of the southern economic model based on African American cotton labor. The introduction of the mechanical harvester in the 1940s, displaced these sharecroppers from cotton harvesting and caused the Great Migration to the northern industrial cities.[6] The northern industrial cities had faced labor shortages from the more restrictive immigration laws imposed in the 1920s. Prior to that from 1880 to 1920, more than half of the employment growth in the manufacturing sector originated from immigration, first from Northwestern Europe, and later from Southern and Eastern Europe.[7] The industrial heartland included the iron ore mines in Minnesota, Wisconsin, and Michigan, the coal mines in the Appalachian Basin in Pennsylvania and West Virginia; and the factory belt in the major manufacturing cities Chicago, Buffalo, Detroit, Milwaukee, Cincinnati, Toledo, Cleveland, St. Louis, Youngstown and Pittsburgh.[8] By the late-1970s, US industrial employment had peaked and declined with increasing automation in the manufacturing industry. Thereafter, nearly all the employment growth came from the personal and professional services industry.[9]

Automation and Employment

Automation can wipe out jobs, reduce the content of jobs/job tasks, or change skill requirements, which impacts worker control.[10] Past-oriented studies of economists have shown that US regions with more industrial robots have lost jobs and incomes between 1990 and 2007.[11] An analysis of French data shows that more automation is associated with more jobs, as productivity increases lower the cost of consumer goods and aggregate demand, which favors more employment.[12] In Germany, robots have displaced manufacturing workers, but new service sector jobs compensated for these job losses.[13] In Japan, cheaper robots result in more robot adoption and an increase in employment.[14] Across countries, rapid aging is connected to secular stagnation as older people tend to consume and work less, but rapid aging is counteracted by more automation.[15] From the 1970s to 2007, increasing technological intensity has not diminished the employment share, but has resulted in a declining labor share of income, which generates more economic inequality.[16] The US labor market is increasingly exhibiting job polarization. Automation replaces medium-skilled jobs (e.g., office and administration) while boosting the number of low-skilled people (e.g., delivery, warehousing) and a smaller number of high-skilled jobs (e.g. data science and engineering).[17]

Automation and Job Polarization

Job polarization is reinforced during an economic downturn because that is when automation in the middle-skill routine occupations occurs, and once the economy recovers, it takes longer to restore full employment. This suggests that substituted workers are no longer needed, even if the financial pressures on the firm are relieved. US recessions in the 1970s and 1980s restored aggregate employment within a year, but beginning in the 1990s, net employment has not been restored within two years of the trough of a recession.[18] One qualification to the job polarization argument among high-skilled workers is that the college wage premium has declined since 2000.[19] The college wage gap is the gap in wages between college-educated and high school – educated workers. This finding implies that high-skilled labor demand has not increased while more college-educated workers compete for ever scarce high-skilled jobs.

Hiding Technological Unemployment

Descriptively, the unemployment rate does not suggest that robots have mass-displaced workers, because unemployment has been reduced after every recession, reaching 4.3% in the US in 2025.[20] However, the unemployment rate only captures individuals looking for work, not the total available population that could be part of the workforce. The employment-population ratio for men has been declining continuously since the 1950s. It was 85% in 1950 and is 65% in 2025.[21] Overall increases in the employment-population ratio came from women joining the workforce in greater numbers, which increased from 31% in 1950 to 57% in 2000. However, since 2000 female labor participation has been stagnant, and as of 2025 it declined to 54%.[22] A declining employment-population ratio is somewhat linked to demographic aging and the retiring baby boomers. But the labor market number for prime-age workers is not increasing either. Among persons aged 25–54, that employment-population ratio increased from 62 to 80% from 1950 to 2000, but it has been about stagnant ever since and is recovering from a sharp drop during the 2008 recession.[23]

Furthermore, for the youngest workers, fast food and retail jobs, which tended to be the popular entry-level jobs, are getting rarer, as the employment-population ratio of people aged 16–19 declined from 45% to 30% from 2000 to 2025.[24] While young people tend to be increasingly well-educated (and thus not available in the labor force[25]), a recent trend among young men has been a shift to leisure activities, such as video and computer games.[26] Considering that computer games are a cheaper form of entertainment than traveling or collecting rare items, they can be pursued without the earning of extra income, especially if well-off parents are indulgent to their offspring. Japanese society has a phenomenon called "hikikomori," or extreme social withdrawal of adult children living in their parents' home. They neither work nor are in school and are enabled by their parents to live that lifestyle.[27] For Abraham and Kearney, the decline of the employment-population ratio for young and prime-age adults is linked to international trade competition (–1.04 percentage points) and exposure to robots (–0.55), i.e., automation.[28]

Automation of work is not an abstract vision of the future but the present reality of millions of displaced manufacturing workers, who must shift to low-wage service work or drop out of the labor force altogether, taking advantage of social insurance programs for the disabled. The number of Social Security Disability Insurance recipients tripled from 3 million in the early-1990s to 9 million in 2013, before receding slightly to 8.7 million in 2017, as new awards declined after 2009 and termination increased, primarily because these people reached the full retirement age and shifted to regular Social Security benefits.[29] Hence, the declining size of disability insurance does not imply an improvement in the labor market more broadly but simply a shift to a different part of the welfare state apparatus.

Job Destruction and Job Creation

Mainstream economists tend to take the view that innovation, cheaper goods and more purchasing power in other sectors or the same sector of the economy can compensate for any job losses due to automation in one sector. James Bessen's case study of the effect of ATM machines in the 1990s on bank teller employment shows that the number of bank tellers continued to expand, because lower upkeep costs for bank branches allowed banks to open new branches.[30] Another example is the elevator operator that was automated in 1950. This innovation followed a labor strike of elevator operators in prior years.[31] The disappearance of the elevator operator was compensated by the growth of other service-based jobs.

Occupations that use more computers experienced an increase in employment, while less computer-intensive industries tend to lose employment.[32] In a different paper, Bessen examined long-term employment patterns in the textile, steel and auto industries and found an inverted U-shape of employment over time. In the initial period, new machines increased the total demand for the product, which led to more hiring, but once the market becomes saturated (e.g., most people own enough clothes or have a car), output stabilizes and employment declines. As a result, once demand saturated, only by shifting workers to other sectors that have more labor demand can full employment be maintained.[33]

For Autor, the account of automation misses the labor complementariness of new technology, even though he admits that technology contributes to job polarization and more inequality. Autor found that in the period from 2007 to 2012, most of the employment growth occurred in the very low-skill occupations, while the high-skill occupations are stagnating, which could suggest that automation is encroaching on highly paid professionals or that slower computer investment growth is linked to less demand for these high-skilled professionals.[34] Economists generally define skill by the worker's level of education.[35] There is a gradient of job displacement by level of education. College-educated workers displaced from middle-skill occupations in the 1980s and 1990s slotted equally into high- and low-skilled occupations, though from 2000 to 2016, they slot exclusively into low-skilled occupations. For non-college educated workers displaced in middle-skilled occupations, virtually the entire growth of jobs is in low-skilled service work in all periods.[36] Overall, nearly all of the recent job growth occurred in the low-wage sector, while middle and high-wage jobs have not increased.[37] A counterpoint to the labor-complementarity of technology is that since the late-1980s technology has been, on-balance, labor-displacing rather than labor-complementing.[38]

Automation and Productivity

Mainstream economists argue that the productivity impact of technology is limited. This argument is in line with the stagnation thesis. Gordon argues that productivity growth has been declining compared to earlier decades. This suggests that computers might be less productivity-enhancing forms of innovation than the steam engine.[39] Larry Summers revived Alvin Hansen's idea from the 1930s that the global economy is suffering from "Secular Stagnation" because of an aging population, demand saturation (people not buying more commodities), lessening capital intensity in modern industries (e.g., IT, Airbnb, Uber, etc.) and the growth of internet monopolies, which results in fewer investment opportunities and a savings glut. This savings glut is reflected in incredibly low interest rates and financial/real estate asset price inflation.[40]

Brynjolfsson et al. counter that it takes time for technological effects on productivity to be measured. New technology needs complementarities to be used on a wide scale, and that process takes time.[41] In a similar vein, Kurzweil counters that productivity growth statistics only narrowly measure value arising from the sale value of goods, which could decline with advancing automation. This explains the lower productivity growth, while ignoring the rising utility benefits for technology users.[42] Capitalism is about increasing sale value (what Marx called "Exchange Value"), not utility benefits (or "use value").[43]

The widely observed productivity growth slowdown may reflect not the failure of automation, but its very success. Once manufacturing and production workers get replaced by robots, these laid off workers get absorbed into low-productivity sectors like security services, cleaning, childcare, social care, entertainment, food service and retail, where productivity growth is limited. The depressed median wages then have a negative ripple effect on aggregate demand, business investment and productivity growth. Unless low-productivity workers get a substantial bump in pay subsidized by the capitalists in productive sectors, it will be difficult to reproduce the "golden period" of high productivity and economic growth in the post-World War II era.[44] Ironically, if wages are pushed too low, it could reduce the firm's incentives to automate.[45] Fast food restaurants rely on low-wage workers, but they might be more inclined to automate, when the minimum wage increases or their workers unionize.[46] Perhaps continued advances in AI, such as self-driving cars, automated customer service calls, security guard robots, robot retail assistants and other sectors will change the automation calculation to also involve workers in the expanding industries, which are in the low-wage service sector.

Growing productivity in "progressive" sectors where unit labor costs decline, contrasting with stagnant productivity in the employment-growing service sector, where unit labor costs rise, is known as "Baumol's cost disease."[47] As entertainment, education and healthcare sectors expand employment and keep their productivity unchanged, these services become more expensive and consume a bigger share of the household budget. The implication for automation is that it is those stagnant sectors where the pressure and desire to automate is the greatest, while the likelihood is the smallest.

Automation and Bullshit Jobs

Another explanation for the apparent disconnect between rapid automation and the low unemployment rate is the rise of bullshit jobs.[48] In Graeber's account, automation has eliminated many production jobs (agriculture, manufacturing and the useful service sector), but clerical/ administrative/ managerial jobs continue to proliferate, and workers occupying these jobs think that their job is pointless for society.[49] The jobs exist not to maximize firm output but because the organizations operate according to a feudal logic, where elevated status is dependent on having a large subordinate staff.[50] 37% of British workers and 40% of Dutch workers think that their job makes no meaningful contribution to society.[51] In a similar qualitative account based in Sweden, white-collar workers engage in "empty" labor, i.e. the time spent at work not performing work duties, such as online shopping, social media usage, conversing with co-workers on non-work matters. One of the most commonly cited reasons for empty labor is the feeling of not being needed and not being given enough tasks by the supervisors.[52] Walo's statistical analysis of the American Working Conditions Survey shows that office, sales, business and managerial workers are most likely to perceive their job as socially useless.[53]

The bullshit job thesis is not uncontested. Drawing on the *European Working Conditions Survey, Soffia et al.* argue that only less than 5% of workers believe that their work makes no meaningful contributions to society. The survey reports a much lower incidence of useless jobs than in the polls. In their account, worker perception of the low utility of the job is linked to worker alienation, low autonomy/skill use, poor management and toxic workplace environments rather than the low social utility of the job.[54] Similarly, neoclassical economists find the bullshit job argument unconvincing, because utility theory blocks the notion that anyone would shell out money or resources to hire people without satisfying a utility-enhancing human need in exchange. In fact, in their mind any level of compensation *reflects* the workers' marginal productivity of labor or contribution to the output.[55] In other words, if a worker gets paid, he/she delivers value to the employer or society. One counterpoint to the alienation and utility-focused accounts is that they do not directly deal with political economy considerations that favor the rise of bullshit jobs; in an industrial setting characterized by a few major companies in each industry, there is no price competition. Big companies become price setters and, thus, generate revenues large enough to create big bureaucracies that do not operate on maximizing efficiency while production lines for the creation of the final output to subsidize these bureaucracies still operate based on efficiency metrics.[56]

One of the empirical complications of measuring bullshit jobs is that there is a distinction between subjective and objective measurement. That involves the distinction of whether people think their own job is useless vs. whether the job is objectively useless to society. Subjective measurements, while being informative for researchers of work, cannot ultimately resolve whether bullshit jobs exist, because two individuals working the identical job could say the opposite about the utility of their job.

Objective measures are empirically more useful, but harder to come by. Two studies give an indication that there is a hierarchy in the usefulness of jobs. *Lawlor et al.* examined occupations by their usefulness and found that city of London bankers destroy 7 pounds of social value for every pound they earn, implying its bullshit nature, while nursery workers produce 7 pounds in social value for every pound paid.[57] Similarly, Bregman examined a six-month strike among Irish bankers in 1970 and found no negative ramifications to society, as people began to write each other checks on napkins for payment. For Bregman, bankers pass the bullshit test. In contrast, the garbage collectors of New York went on strike in 1968, for only ten days and had all their demands for pay raises met as the city was buried in garbage and became dysfunctional. Garbage collection is clearly not a bullshit job.[58]

Automation in the Pandemic Era

The COVID-19 pandemic has also resulted in the spelling out of a hierarchy of jobs, namely between what the government called 'essential' workers in health care, energy, agriculture, food retail, construction, or transportation.[59] Non-essential workers include, among others, most white-collar workers, whose work activities were moved to the home office. Non-essential is not the same as useless, and many home office and other workers also create a useful product. On the other hand, non-essential could have bullshit occupations. Regardless of the precise magnitude of bullshit jobs, their very presence bears a direct relationship to automation. The greater the economic surplus due to automation, the greater the number of non-productive occupations.[60]

The COVID-19 pandemic was also an exogenous shock that impacted employer decisions to automate. For instance, warehouses introduced disinfecting robots, circumventing the hassle of hiring human cleaners that risk infection.[61] Aerial drones were used to deliver medical supplies, monitor social distancing and body temperatures of crowds in public.[62] The pandemic lockdown has favored the reshaping of customer shopping behavior via the rising popularity of online retail, which has been made possible by warehouse automation.[63] The fact that employers adopt automation during the pandemic means that long-term employment effects could be negative. Employers are unlikely to re-employ labor in tasks that were automated as a result of the pandemic. Furthermore, the growth of telecommuting for white-collar workers that could extend beyond the end of the lockdown could reduce employment in dense urban areas which support these white-collar workers. These include workers in shops, restaurants and public transit.[64] White-collar workers can work from home an average of one working day per week, which has been persistent between 2023 and 2025.[65] In Stockholm, post-pandemic office vacancy has increased, while public transportation use has decreased.[66] This suggests a significant shift and displacement in downtown urban economies.

Automation and Future Employment

Automation Forecasts

Future-oriented research on automation produced widely differing accounts on how many occupations are likely to be automated. Organisation for Economic Co-operation and Development forecasters estimate that 9% of the jobs in OECD countries can be automated,[67] while US-specific forecasters Frey and Osborne suggest that 47% of jobs can be automated.[68] The different findings come from different assumptions. The OECD study uses a task-based approach for automation, which generates a lower automation estimate because they assume, it is unlikely that all the tasks within an occupation can be automated. They also make more restrictive assumptions about technological abilities, and they think that human skills will evolve with technology. In comparison, Frey and Osborne use an occupation-based approach based on robotics and technology expert surveys to generate high automation scores for different occupations. McKinsey confirms the divergent assumptions inherent to occupational vs. task displacement, predicting that 50% of tasks are automatable, but only 15% of jobs.[69] Another noteworthy study found that jobs with low prior automation are more likely to be automated in the future compared to high prior automation jobs, which suggests that professional jobs that were safe from prior automation may not be in the future.[70] World Economic Forum is convinced that the world will create 170 million jobs in the second half of the 2020s while eliminating 92 million jobs from automation and assumes net job growth of 78 million.[71]

Thus, automation forecasts are highly dependent on measurement criteria, although the precision of these forecasts is further reduced if we include institutional factors such as the presence of labor unions to protect jobs, societal attitudes toward technology, or the overall wealth level of a country that could impact how many occupations are ultimately replaced, not just replaceable. How many jobs will be automated is an empirical question and depends on the technological affordance, social context and the skills profile of the workforce.

AI Automation

Future automation most likely affects people in low-wage jobs and with low levels of education,[72] although improvements in AI push the boundaries on what activities can be automated. Medical diagnostics is a very high-skilled operation for which algorithms are programmed to automate that portion of the medical profession, even as doctors are still needed to verify diagnoses and communicate with patients.[73] Big consulting firms, banks and firms in various industries had carried out significant cuts in white-collar work, claiming that AI allows for more work rationalization. Here are a brief list of 2025 layoff announcements:

- **Accenture:** The consulting giant announced layoffs for 11,000 employees in September 2025 who could not be retrained for AI skills.[74]
- **Fiverr:** The freelancing platform is cutting 30% of its workforce (about 250 employees) to become a leaner, 'AI-first company'. The CEO stated that employees must know how to use AI to avoid being left behind.[75]
- **Indeed, and Glassdoor:** These job sites, owned by the same parent company (Recruit Holdings), are eliminating approximately 1,300 jobs as part of a restructuring to combine operations and focus on AI.[76]
- **Intel:** The chipmaker began laying off more than 5,000 employees in July 2025, with plans to reduce its core workforce by 15%–20% by early 2025. The company said the cuts would help it become a "leaner, faster and more efficient company" and reinvest in AI development.[77]

- **Just Eat:** Europe's largest food delivery company is eliminating around 450 jobs by shifting many manual customer service tasks to automated and AI-powered systems.[78]
- **Microsoft:** In July 2025, Microsoft announced a round of layoffs affecting about 4% of its total workforce (9,000 employees) to shift resources toward funding AI development and infrastructure. This followed earlier cuts in January and May of 2025.[79]

In *Felten et al.'s* estimation, the highly educated white-collar workers will be most impacted by AI automation. They expect that 80% of the workforce will have at least 10% of their work tasks automated by AI.[80] AI can take on more non-routine occupational tasks.[81] The introduction of generative AI has reduced job postings and incomes for online contractors.[82] Along with globalization and outsourcing of work, the rise of robots and AI competes for jobs of workers in the rich industrialized countries.[83]

AI is considered a general-purpose technology in the sense that it can increase labor productivity in many different industries and domains. It is part of the "Fourth Industrial Revolution." The first three revolutions originate from steam, electricity and ICT (information and communication technology).[84] In Restrepo's pessimistic account, AGI (artificial general intelligence) will take on more routine intellectual tasks, shrink wages and increase inequality, as the AI owners will be the main economic beneficiaries in this new economy. He only sees a human advantage in "accessory" jobs where the human touch is nice to have but the economy does not depend on it. These occupations include nannies or live musicians.[85] Thus, a "world without work" is possible in principle, even if the prospect is still remote.[86]

A more critical forecast argues that occupations with high AI exposure may still be growing, e.g., statisticians.[87] According to Bureau of Labor Statistics (BLS), translators are strongly impacted by AI translation services, but due to increasing globalization, the rising demand for translators is expected to make up for the reduced labor demand from AI translations, thus increasing total employment for translators. The important qualification is that BLS had been wrong on some projections: landscapers were forecast to grow 18% between 2000 and 2018 but remained stagnant from 2008 to 2018. In addition, some expected job declines are attributable to offshoring rather than automation, e.g., computer programmers, so job projections are not exclusively related to technology. The overall BLS conclusion is that job losses in occupations experiencing job losses "are more than offset by growth in other occupations, which is to say those jobs are not representative of a broader trend."[88] Economic job forecasts must be critically evaluated against the empirical trends. Despite limitations to forecasts, society and policymakers are asking for such job forecasts to mentally and practically prepare for the labor market implication of automation.

Economic and Social Causes of Automation

Wages and Labor Costs

What are the economic and social factors behind automation? Economic forces behind automation are regulated by the change in wages compared to the cost of introducing the technology. The first impetus to automate comes from the high cost of labor, as labor and capital (or technology) are the major inputs to generate economic output. Rising economic output depends on rising total factor productivity, which is predicated on improvements in technology, according to the Solow-Swan growth model and Cobb-Douglas production function.[89] The higher relative cost of one input (labor) implies the lower relative cost of the other (capital), which incentivizes investment in the lower cost option (capital). Capitalists deploying more technology could result in worker displacement, which increases the competition for remaining jobs. For instance, downsized car manufacturing workers apply for a warehouse or delivery job. This competition for remaining jobs results in lower wages in that sector. These low wages compete against the high cost of robots, which should deter further automation. However, in a platform monopoly model, where profits are enormous or investor capital is abundant, it is still possible to advance automation even if the sector is dominated by low-wage, unstable, gig work.[90]

In the more traditional, neoclassical model, Say's Law, which is named after the French economist Jean-Baptiste Say, predicts that automation cheapens goods for consumers, whose higher savings translate into more consumption of the same product, which means more jobs in the same field.[91] It could also mean more consumption of a different product, which reduces jobs in the automated sector but creates new, non-existing jobs. For instance, food is a diminishing share of the average household budget. Farming employs less than 2% of the US workforce.[92] In contrast, social media content moderators who filter out violence and pornographic material on Facebook and Twitter is a completely new and increasing job category.[93]

Automation also increases corporate profits, which increases corporate savings, which can increase investments. Higher corporate profits could also increase loanable funds in the banking system, which can induce general consumption growth even without wage growth, though it results in more economic inequality and increases the risk of a financial crash.[94] In each case, technology favors job creation, which means more job vacancies and employer competition for labor. This pushes up wages and cheapens the relative cost of technology, which means more automation. Thus, the relationship between technology and wage/job growth is complex and can point in either direction.

Within economic history, wages and labor scarcity are important explanations for the British Industrial Revolution aside from the cheap availability of coal that fired the coal plants, a patent system to reward innovators, and high agricultural productivity to sustain city populations. In contrast, labor and coal were more expensive in continental Europe, so there were fewer incentives to automate. What explained the high wages in Britain? It was not due to a labor shortage emanating from a lack of childbirth as the population increased in the eighteenth century. Rather Britain was a leader in international trade and colonial plunder, so the British could purchase a greater variety and higher quality diet and consumer goods than their continental counterparts. Initial steam engine technology was geared to the local context. It was not until the middle of the nineteenth century that British steam engine technology was repurposed to be universally applicable and could spread worldwide, initiating the spread of global capitalism.[95]

The Effects of Stagnation

The wage-based model of explaining automation does not account for macroeconomic factors affecting automation. Benanav points out that rather than ever-accelerating automation, we are facing a slowdown in new automation, which is explained by the stagnation in overall output, especially in manufacturing.[96] Ironically, economic stagnation may favor more automation. Manufacturers facing tighter profit margins in the 1970s embraced quick innovation in numeric control machine tools to produce them at lower cost. Numeric control, in turn, allowed for more factory automation, where fewer people were needed to produce machine tools.[97]

Labor Union Power

The purely economic mechanism of automation neglects what Marx called the "social relations of production."[98] Capital-labor relations are driven by the contestation for social power, in which capitalists' ownership of the means of production, including the use or non-use of technology, means an asymmetric power balance favoring capital over labor.[99] Workers regain some discretion over their conditions of work by banding together in trade unions. The presence of unions can temporarily stabilize labor relations. Higher union wages attract higher quality and reliable labor, resulting in less turnover. Union training programs produce a steady supply of skilled workers. But unions are viewed as irritation for employers, who use technology and outsourcing to bypass and erode union power. Various empirical studies have shown that capitalists favor automation to weaken organized labor.[100] Workplaces where employee voice is greater have a higher technological uptake, presumably because of the buy-in from workers.[101]

Governments and States

The state is another influential social actor in the context of automation. Sociologists have recognized the power of the state in predicting social revolutions,[102] conducting war,[103] or moving up the value chain in the global economy.[104] Similarly, the state provides the supportive environment for the private sector to adopt technology.[105] For new technology to enter the pipeline, basic and applied research is needed: the state promotes both by providing research and development tax credits or subsidy programs for private labs and companies (primarily for applied research) and research grants to universities (primarily for basic research, some of which become commercialized). Once the product is developed with the help of public funds, the state protects the intellectual property via patents or foreign trade enforcement. That means ensuring trade partners respect one's intellectual property standards. Because the US economy is highly reliant on rents drawn from intellectual property, the US government is very keen to protect its intellectual property against attempts by foreign countries to steal it.[106]

The state plays a vital role in mediating labor relations. These include laws that promote or hinder unions. States set the minimum wage. A substantial increase could make automation a more cost-effective solution for businesses.[107] Overtime rules enable higher pay for workers beyond set work hours. Non-compete clauses limit employees' ability to switch their employer. Their presence weakens employee rights, while their absence strengthens them. Health and safety work standards limit the exploitability of workers. Tripartite Wage Agreements involve the state in the collective bargaining agreements among employers and workers, which are not common in Anglo-Saxon countries, but are common in Scandinavia and Central Europe. Automation is most likely to happen in a context where employers impose few barriers to job duty reassignment.[108] Labor-friendly labor relations or strong unions generate more employer incentives to carry out automation, as shown by the earlier discussion. In the Marxist framework, the state is the "executive committee of the bourgeoisie,"[109] which implies that the state will commonly side with employers and against workers. For example, the 1894 Pullman strike in Chicago culminated in the US army breaking up the strike. But states can also side with workers by expanding labor rights like the passage of the US Wagner Act of 1935, during the New Deal.

States also sponsor workforce training and education programs (including K-12 to college) to create the workforce that employers use to operate technology, which requires technical and computer skills. In the phenomenon of education credential inflation, the value of the college degree is declining as the number of college graduates rises faster than college-requiring jobs. Thus, the state's secondary function in subsidizing the education system is to reduce the size of the labor force. 22+ year olds compete for jobs rather than age 18–21.[110] Similarly, early retirement, welfare, or disability insurance pensions are government programs to minimize the size of the labor force, and, thus, hide technological unemployment.[111] In the US, the mass incarceration of primarily poor Black people has been another state response to hide the displaced victims of deindustrialization.[112] The state promotes technology to aid capital accumulation, but it also has to fund welfare programs to retain the legitimacy of the capitalist economy and automation.[113]

Finally, the state retains an open regulatory environment to promote technology development. For example, the state allows trials with drones, or self-driving cars long before they were commercially introduced. The US government promised a hands-off regulatory approach to advance self-driving vehicles.[114] Companies like Amazon, who are automating package deliveries via the development of drones, have to work closely with the government regulators, even if there are occasional conflicts between companies and regulators.[115] The European Union is much more aggressive in its regulation of AI, citing the precautionary principle of preventing possible harm rather than undoing harm already incurred.[116]

There are many reasons for the failure of any of these state technology promotion strategies; Insufficient research funding, weak intellectual property and a restrictive regulatory environment. These failures could undermine technological development. Because states act in response to global competition, they must keep and attract top talent and industries into their jurisdictions.[117] Their incentive is to promote more technology. Countries lower down the value chain of the world system via the export of cheap raw material struggle to move up the value chain via the export of expensive finished goods. Wealthy countries and their companies hold control over intellectual property that keeps them high up in the value chain.[118] While strong state capacity is not a sufficient condition for technological innovation, Evans points out that it is a necessary condition.[119]

Late-developing countries have the disadvantage of being relatively backward technologically, but they can industrialize faster as they can leapfrog technologies from the early developing states. Late-developing countries are also more dependent on large-scale enterprises, powerful banks and states to provide capital and direction, which substitutes for missing private initiatives and markets. Late developers like Germany or Russia have much more powerful states than early developing UK and US.[120]

Acemoglu and Robinson argue that authoritarian countries like China do not offer enough space for individual freedom and creativity, which could limit future innovation in China compared to the more open US society.[121] On the other hand, lack of innovation is not problematic for all forms of new technology. The Chinese and American businessman and computer scientist Kai-Fu Lee argues that China holds the key advantage over the US in artificial intelligence because Chinese society is more embedded in big data and electronic payment via apps. That data is fed into improving the predictive power of the algorithms. The presence of big data, not innovation per se, is at the heart of better algorithmic models.[122] The US has attempted to limit China's access to advanced semiconductors, so the Chinese tech companies developed the LLM DeepSeek AI, which uses a smaller number of parameters that are computationally cheaper than US models while retaining high predictive power.[123] Nonetheless, the US retains a significant advantage in AI investment in infrastructure and compute capacity via private venture capital and it still attracts foreign research talent into university programs and AI companies, while China has an advantage in the energy infrastructure to power the AI data centers.[124]

While a capitalist state can be expected to promote new technologies, rent-seeking states who protect vested interests via restrictive laws can block the introduction of new technologies.[125] More broadly, Acemoglu and Robinson point out that states pursuing inclusive economic institutions experience more innovation and economic development. In inclusive institutions, property rights cover a broad segment of society, and the political institutions tend to be liberal and democratic. In extractive economic institutions, elites exclude broader segments of society from innovating, reserve power in their hands via authoritarian systems, and concentrate significant rents from more productive actors in the economy.[126] Thus, states play an important role in promoting technological innovation, but not all states are developmentalist, and some states may be explicitly rent-seeking and anti-developmentalist.

Demographics

Demographic forces are correlated with technological trends. A declining and aging society is one of the main explanations for secular stagnation in the absence of sufficient technological productivity growth.[127] *Park et al.* argue that rapidly aging societies *on average* exhibit less productivity growth (which also means less output growth), although, on the flip side, they partially compensate for aging-related productivity declines by training old workers to operate robots. These workers are still more productive than old workers without robots, but each are less productive than a young workforce operating robots.[128]

The reverse causation also applies. In other words, technological changes can also impact demographic choices. Wei and Xie believe that as automation increases incomes, couples will presumably find it easier to afford babies and have more of them,[129] though this logic is quite questionable given that even with rising productivity, average incomes have stagnated in the neoliberal era and the cost of living for essentials like housing, energy and health care keep rising. Annelli and co-authors find that while US regions exposed to more automation do not have a lower fertility rate, nonmarital birth and divorce rates are higher while marriage rates are lower. The presumed mechanism is that past automation has disproportionately replaced male workers, whose lowered relative incomes expressed in a lower gender wage gap make them less desirable marital partners.[130] The lack of automation impacting fertility negatively could change if future automation is more likely to affect female workers; *Egana-Delsol et al.* estimate that in Latin America, women are less likely to work in Science, Technology, Engineering and Mathematics (STEM) occupations which have a lower likelihood of displacement.[131] Higher female unemployment could deter child-rearing assuming the high economic cost of raising children, but it could also encourage child-rearing as women have more time to raise children.

In Japan, automation has increased work insecurity and reduced the marriage rate, similar to the US, but also impinged on family formation,[132] which suggests that the alternative to marriage and in-wedlock birth in the Japanese cultural context is not out-of-wedlock births but singlehood or, more rarely, childless cohabitation. These trends explain reduced fertility. Furthermore, shifting industrial needs from industrialization/ technological change have boosted education credentialing, which delays and reduces overall fertility in Confucian East Asian countries that heavily emphasize education. The excessive cost of education for potential children also reduces the desire to have children.[133] The outcome is that Japan's fertility rate is lower than in the US and other Western countries. Japan also has 390 robots per 10,000 workers in 2020, which is the third highest rate in the world behind South Korea and Singapore.[134] Thus, automation implies reduced fertility, while the direction of causality is unclear. In whatever ways demography and technology affect each other, it is conceivable that they are mutually reinforcing. A shrinking population increases the pressure to automate. Displaced workers, who remain unemployed or work lower paid jobs might be less inclined to reproduce, which further shrinks the population.

Migration is another demographic variable in relation to automation. US regions with more immigrants experience less automation, which suggests that it is extreme scarcity of (immigrant) labor that promotes automation, as in the case of low-migrant societies like Japan with high intensity of robots and automation.[135] As with fertility trends, reverse causation is also plausible, at least with respect to popular opinion: people who are threatened by automation are more likely to favor restrictive immigration laws, presumably to reduce labor competition with migrant workers that reduces the wages of domestic workers. Native workers are also more likely to favor layoffs among immigrant workers first.[136] Ironically, to the extent that governments respond to nativist pressure to restrict migration, it would make automation more attractive, like in Japan and in that way, this still hurts the economic interest of displaceable native workers.

Social Norms and Culture

Microsociological factors also explain technological adoption. Social norms/ practices constrain to what extent automation gets adopted. Tele-medicine is the delivery of medical services via video calls, and E-learning involves massive open online courses (MOOCs) and online lectures. This modality of service delivery has been frowned upon prior to the coronavirus pandemic but has become a necessity during the pandemic. Because of the value of in-person medicine and education, these steps toward automation could be reversed post-pandemic, although some economists argue that COVID-19 has accelerated automation.[137] The pandemic is an exogenous shock that re-frames acceptable work practices such as remote work.[138]

Remote work, tele-medicine and online education may be considered technological intermediation and is labor-enhancing and not meet the classic definition of automation. But to the extent that the delivery of such services becomes standardized and captured in data via the online interactions, it opens the door for algorithms to produce automated service delivery at a later stage. Currently, AI services are marketed to physicians in recommending treatment options for patients, which raises the question to what extent doctors are embracing the AI and whether patients are interested in pursuing AI-only consultations to meet their health care needs.[139] Open AI introduced ChatGPT Health that uses patients' medical record to help them how to prepare for their next doctor's appointment and customize diet plans or workout routines.[140] Online education was supposed to be labor-saving, taking the form of MOOCs. MOOCs enroll a large number of students in courses and offer them recorded lectures and automated student assessments. But the MOOCs have not displaced regular instruction, indicating the persistent value of in-person education.[141] But to the extent that online enrollment is elevated compared to the pre-pandemic period and there are improvements in AI instruction, there could be new pressure to accredit individualized AI instruction.[142]

Public opinion that opposes algorithms in making decisions like screening job applicants or storing consumer financial data can affect to what extent automation gets adopted.[143] Government agencies do not operate in a competitive market logic and can afford to retain obsolete forms of technology.[144] Poor government IT infrastructure during the COVID-19 pandemic hampered the timely distribution of relief economic payments.[145] Hence, civil servants who become comfortable using old technology, defend their old turf and refuse to go with the times can limit automation.[146] Deloitte pointed out that between 96 million and 1.2 billion employee hours could be saved if the federal government adopted automation.[147] Even in private sector engineering firms, the lack of fast product cycles can slow down technology adoption.[148]

Public acceptability of automation hinges on the economic vulnerabilities of the survey respondents: people who think they are relatively safe from displacement favor more automation with some redistribution of the technological gains, while people who think they are vulnerable to displacement want restrictions on technology.[149] Another study shows that workers that are very susceptible to automation prefer economically redistributive policies.[150]

Ideological obstacles to technological change have been common in history. For instance, the Romans embraced animism, which made them skeptical of developing technologies to alter nature. Only after the rise of Christianity has animism been overcome, which made possible the view that humans could control nature with their tools.[151] On the other hand, Christian theology in Europe has reinforced the social and technological conservatism in the feudalist era. There were limited pockets of science that formed the basis of Enlightenment. The peasant-based feudal order could only be overcome with external pressure; the growth of cities favored commerce and resulted in the growth of the money economy and the drive to produce more goods and services.[152] Mokyr argues that the foundation of the Industrial Revolution was Europe's enlightenment culture valuing curiosity, challenging tradition and rewarding innovators.[153]

Professional norms affect technological adoption. Different professional logics responding to different perceived needs produce different willingness among engineers to welcome technology. In Bailey and Leonardi's study of engineers, structural engineers tended to minimize the computer's role because they intended to avoid errors due to stringent government regulations; have an inability to test the soundness of their design virtually; and regard the technology as intransparent (black box). Hardware engineers tend to embrace computer technology, because of their perception of competition with other firms that incentivize the quick turnaround of products to market via automation. Automotive engineers preferred computer solutions in developing the product because of product competition *and* more restrictive technology solutions using physical testing because of government testing regulations.[154]

In Vertesi's research on the Rover Mars Mission, engineers and scientists have different approaches in handling spacecraft equipment, as scientists request too much equipment without understanding what it does, while engineers are protective of the equipment and want to use it sparingly.[155] Barley used the computerized tomography (CT) scanner as an example to argue that the introduction of the same new technology could have different status effects on different workers due to the organization of the workplace: in one hospital, radiologists lost their high status relative to experienced technologists, whom the radiologists treat as lower-ranked assistants. The hospital administration feared patient lawsuits from the poor handling of the Computed Tomography (CT) scanner and only wanted experienced technologists, while the radiologists assumed CT duty without much first training. In another hospital, radiologists kept their high status because the administrators only hired inexperienced technologists, because the administrators favored insiders to become technologists.[156]

Conclusion

Many empirical studies attempt to establish how past automation has affected jobs, occupational structure and societal inequality. Other studies in economic forecasting generate estimates on future occupational trends based on assumptions around the ability of AI or other technologies to automate labor tasks. A third set of historically oriented studies examines what causes automation. Automation as a research field is a broad landscape that has affected different groups of workers in different regions in different times and distinct social context. Automation is also a discourse by different social actors. This statement forms the thesis of this book and is covered in detail in Chapter 2.

Notes

1 Ricci, Tom. "Jethro Tull." *The American Society of Mechanical Engineers*, June 25, 2012. https://www.asme.org/topics-resources/content/jethro-tull
2 Van der Heyden, Peter. "11.14. Threshing Machines." *The Industrial Revolution in England Was Not All Bad*, February 26, 2020. https://history.pictures/2020/02/26/11-14-threshing-machines/
3 Diao, Xinshen, Jed Silver, and Hiroyuki Takeshima. "What's Driving the Growth of Agricultural Mechanization in Africa?" *International Food Policy Research Institute*, December 20, 2017.
4 Roser, Max. "Employment in Agriculture." https://ourworldindata.org/employment-in-agriculture
5 Martin, Lyn. "Eli Whitney and the Cotton Gin – A Mixed Legacy." *Freedom Center Voices*, December 8, 2020.
6 Rifkin, Jeremy. *The End of Work*. New York: Putnam, 1995.
7 Hirschman, Charles, and Elizabeth Mogford. "Immigration and the American Industrial Revolution from 1880 to 1920." *Social Science Research* 38, no. 4 (2009): 897–920.
8 McClelland, Ted. *Nothin' but Blue Skies: The Heyday, Hard Times, and Hopes of America's Industrial Heartland*. New York: Bloomsbury Press, 2013.
9 Harris, Katelynn. "Forty Years of Falling Manufacturing Employment." *Beyond the Numbers, Bureau of Labor Statistics* 9, no. 16 (2020). https://www.bls.gov/opub/btn/volume-9/forty-years-of-falling-manufacturing-employment.htm
10 Killingsworth, Charles C. "Industrial Relations and Automation." *The Annals of the American Academy of Political and Social Science* 340 (1962): 69–80.
11 Acemoglu, Daron, and Pascual Restrepo. "Robots and Jobs: Evidence from US Labor Markets." *NBER Working Paper* w23285 (2017).
12 Aghion, Philippe, Céline Antonin, Simon Bunel, and Xavier Jaravel. "What Are the Labor and Product Market Effects of Automation? New Evidence from France." *CEPR Discussion Paper* No. DP14443 (2020).
13 Dauth, Wolfgang, Sebastian Findeisen, Jens Suedekum, and Nicole Woessner. "The Adjustment of Labor Markets to Robots." *Journal of the European Economic Association* 19, no. 6 (2021): 3104–53.
14 Adachi, Daisuke, Daiji Kawaguchi, and Yukiko Saito. "Robots and Employment: Evidence from Japan, 1978–2017." Discussion Papers 20051, Research Institute of Economy, Trade and Industry (RIETI) (2020).
15 Acemoglu, Daron, and Pascual Restrepo. "Secular Stagnation? The Effect of Aging on Economic Growth in the Age of Automation." *American Economic Review* 107, no. 5 (2017): 174–79.

16 Autor, David, and Anna Salomons. "Is Automation Labor-Displacing? Productivity Growth, Employment, and the Labor Share." *Brookings Papers on Economic Activity* (2018).
17 Autor, David. "Why Are There Still So Many Jobs? The History and Future of Workplace Automation." *Journal of Economic Perspectives* 29, no. 3 (2015): 3–30.
18 Jaimovich, Nir, and Henry E. Siu. "Job Polarization and Jobless Recoveries." *National Bureau of Economic Research*, No. w18334 (2012).
19 Valletta, Robert G. "Recent Flattening in the Higher Education Wage Premium Polarization, Skill Downgrading, or Both?" *NBER* Working Paper, w22935 (2016).
20 Bureau of Labor Statistics (BLS). "Civilian Unemployment Rate." https://www.bls.gov/charts/employment-situation/civilian-unemployment-rate.htm
21 Employment-Population Ratio: Men, FRED: https://fred.stlouisfed.org/series/LNS12300001
22 Employment-Population Ratio: Women, FRED: https://fred.stlouisfed.org/series/LNS12300002
23 Employment-Population Ratio: 25–54 Years, FRED: https://fred.stlouisfed.org/series/LNS12300060
24 Employment-Population Ratio: 16–19 Years, FRED: https://fred.stlouisfed.org/series/LNS12300012
25 Krueger, Alan B. "Where Have All the Workers Gone? An Inquiry into the Decline of the US Labor Force Participation Rate." *Brookings Papers on Economic Activity*, No. 2 (2017): 1–87, pp. 12–3.
26 Aguiar, Mark, Mark Bils, Kerwin Kofi Charles, and Erik Hurst. "Leisure Luxuries and the Labor Supply of Young Men." *National Bureau of Economic Research*, No. w23552 (2017). Parshakov, Petr, Sofiia Paklina, Dennis Coates, and Aleksei Chadov. "Does Video Games' Popularity Affect Unemployment Rate? Evidence from Macro-Level Analysis." *Journal of Economic Studies* 48, no. 4 (2021): 817–35.
27 Malagón-Amor, Ángeles, Luis Miguel Martín-López, David Córcoles, Anna González, Magda Bellsolà, Alan R. Teo, Antoni Bulbena, Víctor Pérez, and Daniel Bergé. "Family Features of Social Withdrawal Syndrome (Hikikomori)." *Frontiers in Psychiatry* 11 (2020): 138.
28 Abraham, Katharine G., and Melissa S. Kearney. "Explaining the Decline in the US Employment-to-Population Ratio: A Review of the Evidence." *National Bureau of Economic Research*, No. w24333 (2018).
29 Li, Zhe. "Trends in Social Security Disability Insurance Enrollment." *Congressional Research Service*, November 30, 2018.
30 Bessen, James E. "How Computer Automation Affects Occupations: Technology, Jobs, and Skills." *Boston University School of Law, Law and Economics Research Paper*, No. 15-49 (2016).
31 Greenidge, Henry Lawson. "How a Historic Strike Paved the Way for the Automated Elevator and What Those Lessons Could Mean for Self-Driving Cars." *Medium*, May 12, 2020.
32 Bessen, James E. "How Computer Automation Affects Occupations: Technology, Jobs, and Skills." *Boston University School of Law, Law and Economics Research Paper*, No. 15-49 (2015).
33 Bessen, James E. "Automation and Jobs: When Technology Boosts Employment." *Boston University School of Law, Law and Economics Research Paper*, No. 17-09 (2018).
34 Autor, David H. "Why Are There Still So Many Jobs? The History and Future of Workplace Automation." *Journal of Economic Perspectives* 29, no. 3 (2015): 3–30.
35 Ingram, Beth F., and George R. Neumann. "The Returns to Skill." *Labour Economics* 13, no. 1 (2006): 35–59.

36 Autor, David. "Work of the Past, Work of the Future." *National Bureau of Economic Research*, No. w25588 (2019).
37 Mishel, Lawrence, Heidi Shierholz, and John Schmitt. "Don't Blame the Robots: Assessing the Job Polarization Explanation of Growing Wage Inequality." Working Paper no. 295. Washington, DC: Economic Policy Institute–Center for Economic and Policy Research, 2013.
38 Acemoglu, Daron, and Pascual Restrepo. "Automation and New Tasks: How Technology Displaces and Reinstates Labor." *Journal of Economic Perspectives* 33, no. 2 (2019): 3–30.
39 Gordon, Robert J. "The Demise of US Economic Growth: Restatement, Rebuttal, and Reflections." *NBER Working Paper*, No. w19895 (2014).
40 Summers, Lawrence H. "Accepting the Reality of Secular Stagnation." *IMF Finance and Development* 57, no. 1 (2020).
41 Brynjolfsson, Erik, Daniel Rock, and Chad Syverson. "Artificial Intelligence and the Modern Productivity Paradox: A Clash of Expectations and Statistics." *NBER Working Paper*, No. w24001 (2017).
42 Kurzweil, Ray. *The Singularity Is Nearer: When We Merge with AI.* New York: Penguin, 2024.
43 Marx, Karl. *Capital, Volume 1.* London: Penguin, 1990, ch.1.
44 Storm, Servaas. "The New Normal: Demand, Secular Stagnation, and the Vanishing Middle Class." *International Journal of Political Economy* 46, no. 4 (2017): 169–210.
45 Avent, Ryan. "Take My Job (Please)." *Medium*, November 8, 2017.
46 Taylor, Kate. "America's Fast-Food Chains Are Contemplating Replacing Minimum Wage Workers with Robots - and It Could Lead to a Crisis." *Business Insider*, January 11, 2018.
47 Baumol, William J. *The Cost Disease.* New Haven, CT: Yale University Press, 2012.
48 Graeber, David. *Bullshit Jobs: A Theory.* New York: Simon and Schuster, 2018.
49 Graeber, *Bullshit Jobs*, p. 265.
50 "Corporations are less and less about making, building, fixing, or maintaining things and more and more about political processes of appropriating, distributing, and allocating money and resources." Graeber, *Bullshit Jobs*, p. 127.
51 Graeber, *Bullshit Jobs*, p. XXIV.
52 Paulsen, Ronald. *Empty Labor.* Cambridge: Cambridge University Press, 2014.
53 Walo, Simon. "'Bullshit' After All? Why People Consider Their Jobs Socially Useless." *Work, Employment and Society* 37, no. 5 (2023): 1123–46.
54 Soffia, Magdalena, Alex J. Wood, and Brendan Burchell. "Alienation Is Not 'Bullshit': An Empirical Critique of Graeber's Theory of BS Jobs." *Work, Employment and Society* 36, no. 5 (2022): 816–40.
55 Mankiw, N. Gregory. "Defending the One Percent." *Journal of Economic Perspectives* 27, no. 3 (2013): 21–34.
56 Baran, Paul, and Paul Sweezy. *Monopoly Capital: An Essay on the American Economic and Social Order.* New York: Monthly Review Press, 1966. Critique in Tiratelli, Matteo. "Where Did the Bullshit Jobs Go?" *Jacobin*, March 8, 2023.
57 Lawlor, Eilis, Helen Kersley, and Susan Steed. *A Bit Rich: Calculating the Value to Society of Different Professions.* London: New Economics Foundation, 2009. https://neweconomics.org/2009/12/a-bit-rich
58 Bregman, Rutger. *Utopia for Realists: The Case for Universal Basic Income, Open Borders, and a 15-Hour Workweek.* New York: Bloomsbury Publishing, 2017.
59 National Conference of State Legislatures. "Covid-19: Essential Workers in the United States." January 11, 2021. https://www.ncsl.org/research/labor-and-employment/covid-19-essential-workers-in-the-states.aspx
60 Marx classified workers as 'unproductive' if they did not directly participate in value creation, e.g. circulation labor (sales, accounting, advertising, finance). Moseley, Fred.

"Marx's Concepts of Productive Labor and Unproductive Labor: An Application to the Postwar US Economy." *Eastern Economic Journal* 9, no. 3 (1983): 180–89.
61 Gordon, Rachel. "CSAIL Robot Disinfects Greater Boston Food Bank." *MIT News*, June 28, 2020.
62 Williams, Alex. "The Drones Were Ready for This Moment." *New York Times*, May 23, 2020.
63 Laber, Joshua, Ravindra Thamma, and E. Daniel Kirby. "The Impact of Warehouse Automation in Amazon's Success." *International Journal of Innovative Science, Engineering & Technology* 7, no. 8 (2020): 63–70.
64 Autor, David, and Elisabeth Reynolds. "The Nature of Work After the COVID Crisis: Too Few Low-Wage Jobs." *The Hamilton Project, Brookings* (2020).
65 Aksoy, Cevat Giray, Jose Maria Barrero, Nicholas Bloom, Steven J. Davis, Mathias Dolls, and Pablo Zarate. "The Global Persistence of Work from Home." *Proceedings of the National Academy of Sciences* 122, no. 27 (2025): e2509892122.
66 Hassan, Navita. "Work from Home: Impacts on Public Transportation and Commercial Real Estate Vacancies." Master's Thesis, KTH Royal Institute of Technology, School of Architecture and the Built Environment (ABE), Stockholm (2024).
67 Arntz, Melanie, Terry Gregory, and Ulrich Zierahn. "The Risk of Automation for Jobs in OECD Countries." *OECD Working Paper* (2016).
68 Frey, Carl Benedikt, and Michael A. Osborne. "The Future of Employment: How Susceptible Are Jobs to Computerisation?" *Technological Forecasting and Social Change* 114 (2017): 254–80.
69 Manyika, James, and Kevin Sneader. "AI, Automation, and the Future of Work: Ten Things to Solve for." *McKinsey* (2018).
70 Sampson, Scott. "Predicting Job Automation: What Have We Observed?" *Proceedings of the 57th Hawaii International Conference on System Sciences* (2024).
71 World Economic Forum. "The Future of Jobs Report 2025." https://www.weforum.org/publications/the-future-of-jobs-report-2025/digest/
72 Frey, Carl Benedikt, and Michael A. Osborne. "The Future of Employment: How Susceptible Are Jobs to Computerisation?" *Technological Forecasting and Social Change* 114 (2017): 254–80.
73 Mukherjee, Siddhartha. "A.I. versus M.D." *New Yorker*, March 27, 2017. Pendyala, V. S., and S. Figueira. "Automated Medical Diagnosis from Clinical Data." In *2017 IEEE Third International Conference on Big Data Computing Service and Applications (BigDataService)*, 185–90. San Francisco, CA, 2017.
74 NDTV. "Accenture Lays Off 11,000 Employees, CEO Reveals Why It's Necessary." September 30, 2025. https://www.ndtv.com/world-news/accenture-lays-off-11-000-employees-ceo-julie-sweet-reveals-why-its-necessary-9368776
75 Reuters. "Online Marketplace Fiverr to Lay Off 30% of Workforce in AI Push." September 15, 2025.
76 Golden, Ryan. "Glassdoor and Indeed Announce Layoffs, Reportedly Due to AI." *HR Dive*, July 11, 2025.
77 Owens, Nathan. "Intel Layoffs Exceed 5,000 across US." *Manufacturing Dive*, July 11, 2025.
78 Kacher, Alban. "Just Eat to Lay Off Around 450 Employees, Partly Automating Operations." *Reuters*, September 25, 2025.
79 Novet, Jordan. "Microsoft Laying Off about 9,000 Employees in Latest Round of Cuts." *CNBC*, July 2, 2025.
80 Felten, Edward W., Manav Raj, and Robert Seamans. "Occupational Heterogeneity in Exposure to Generative AI." *SSRN no. 4414065* (2023).
81 Brynjolfsson, Erik and Andrew McAfee. *The Second Machine Age: Work, Progress, and Prosperity in a Time of Brilliant Technologies.* New York: W.W. Norton & Company, 2014.

82 Hui, Xiang, Oren Reshef, and Luofeng Zhou. "The Short-Term Effects of Generative Artificial Intelligence on Employment: Evidence from an Online Labor Market." (July 31, 2023). Available at SSRN: https://ssrn.com/abstract=4527336
83 Baldwin, Richard. *The Globotics Upheaval: Globalization, Robotics, and the Future of Work*. Oxford: Oxford University Press, 2019.
84 Crafts, Nicholas. "Artificial Intelligence as a General-Purpose Technology: An Historical Perspective." *Oxford Review of Economic Policy* 3, no. 37 (2021): 521–36.
85 Restrepo, Pascual. "We Won't Be Missed: Work and Growth in the Era of AGI." *NBER*, September 18-10, 2025. https://www.nber.org/books-and-chapters/economics-transformative-ai/we-wont-be-missed-work-and-growth-era-agi
86 Susskind, Daniel. *A World without Work: Technology, Automation, and How We Should Respond*. New York: Macmillan, 2020.
87 Wynne, Mark A., and Lillian Derr. "Will AI Replace Your Job? Perhaps Not in the Next Decade." *Dallas Fed*, June 3, 2025.
88 Handel, Michael. J. "Growth Trends for Selected Occupations Considered at Risk from Automation." *Monthly Labor Review* (2022).
89 Solow, Robert M. "A Contribution to the Theory of Economic Growth." *Quarterly Journal of Economics* 70, no. 1 (1956): 65–94. Cobb, C. W., and P. H. Douglas. "A Theory of Production." *American Economic Review* 18, no. Supplement (1928): 139–65.
90 Vertesi, Janet A., Adam Goldstein, Diana Enriquez, Larry Liu, and Katherine T. Miller. "Pre-Automation: Insourcing and Automating the Gig Economy." *Sociologica* 14, no. 3 (2020): 167–93.
91 Named after the French economist Say, Jean-Baptiste. *Traité d'économie politique ou simple exposition de la manière dont se forment, se distribuent et se composent les richesses*, 1re éd., Crapelet, 1803. Newman, Jonathan. "Why Robots Won't Cause Mass Unemployment." Mises Institute (2017). Autor, David, H. "Why Are There Still so Many Jobs? The History and Future of Workplace Automation." *Journal of Economic Perspectives* 29, no. 3 (2015): 3–30.
92 United States Department of Agriculture. "Ag and Food Sectors and the Economy." Economic Research Service. Accessed November 2, 2024. https://www.ers.usda.gov/data-products/ag-and-food-statistics-charting-the-essentials/ag-and-food-sectors-and-the-economy/
93 Elliott, Vittoria, and Tekendra Parmar. "The Despair and Darkness of People Will Get to You." *Rest of the World*, July 22, 2020.
94 Lin, Ken-Hou, and Megan Tobias Neely. *Divested: Inequality in Financialized America*. New York: Oxford University Press, 2020.
95 Allen, Robert. "Why Was the Industrial Revolution British?" *VoxEU*, May 15, 2009. Hickel, Jason. "How Britain Stole $45 Trillion from India." *Al Jazeera*, December 19, 2018.
96 Benanav, Aaron. *Automation and the Future of Work*. New York: Verso, 2020.
97 Arnold, Heinrich. "The Recent History of the Machine Tool Industry and the Effects of Technological Change." *Münchner Betriebswirtschaftliche Beiträge* 14 (2001).
98 Marx, Karl. *Wage Labour and Capital*, in *Karl Marx and Friedrich Engels Collected Works, 9*. London: Lawrence & Wishart, 1977, p. 212.
99 Braverman, Harry. 1974. *Labor and Monopoly Capital: The Degradation of Work in the Twentieth Century*. New York: Monthly Review Press. Wright, Erik Olin. *Class Counts: Comparative Studies in Class Analysis*. Cambridge: Cambridge University Press, 1997.
100 Liu, Larry. "Labor Unions and Robots: The Logic of Automation Given the Power of Organized Labor." Unpublished manuscript. Hanley, Caroline. "Putting the Bias in Skill-Biased Technological Change? A Relational Perspective on White-Collar Automation at General Electric." *American Behavioral Scientist* 58,

no. 3 (2014): 400–15. However, the evidence is the strongest for the US, while in Germany and Finland, union members have a greater say in industrial automation, so the relationship between union and automation is weaker there. Haapanala, Henri, Zachary Parolin, and Ive Marx. "Blame the Robots? Routine-Biased Technological Change and the Recent Decline of Union Membership in Europe and the United States." *University of Antwerp* (2022). https://medialibrary.uantwerpen.be/files/57001/fdb41032-25dc-4f4a-b13c-eb4f1502c191.pdf

101 Belloc, Filippo, Gabriel Burdin, and Fabio Landini. "Advanced Technologies and Worker Voice." *Economica* 90, no. 357 (2023): 1–38.

102 Skocpol, Theda. *States and Social Revolutions: A Comparative Analysis of France, Russia and China*. New York: Cambridge University Press, 1979.

103 Tilly, Charles. *Coercion, Capital and European States, AD 990–1992*. Oxford: Basil Blackwell, 1990.

104 Evans, Peter. *Embedded Autonomy: States and Industrial Transformation*. Princeton, NJ: Princeton University Press, 1995.

105 Mazzucato, Mariana. *The Entrepreneurial State: Debunking Public vs. Private Sector Myths*. London: Anthem Press, 2013.

106 Reuters. "USTR Nominee Tai Says New Tools Needed to Protect U.S. Intellectual Property." February 25, 2021.

107 Karsten, Jack and Darrell M. West. "Rising Minimum Wages Make Automation More Cost-Effective." *Brookings*, September 30, 2015.

108 Killingsworth, Charles C. "Industrial Relations and Automation." *The Annals of the American Academy of Political and Social Science* 340 (1962): 69–80.

109 Marx, Karl. "Manifesto of the Communist Party." *Marxists.org*, 1848. https://www.marxists.org/archive/marx/works/1848/communist-manifesto/ch01.htm

110 Collins, Randall. *The Credential Society: An Historical Sociology of Education and Stratification*. New York: Academic Press, 1979. In the US context, colleges are increasingly funded by federally backed student loans, which is economically and socially dysfunctional, because due to credential inflation the payoff for graduates is either not happening or it takes a long career to pay off the debt. On the other hand, by allowing student loan deferrals and forgiving portions of the debt, the government is effectively providing free college through the backdoor, which functionally supports a credential society.

111 Esping-Andersen, Gøsta. "Welfare States without Work: The Impasse of Labor Shedding and Familialism in Continental European Social Policy." Instituto Juan March de estudios y investigaciones, 1995. Yashiro, Naomitsu, Tomi Kyyrä, Hyunjeong Hwang, Juha Tuomala. "Technology, Labour Market Institutions, and Early Retirement." *VoxEU*, March 12, 2021. Stettner, Andrew. "Mounting a Response to Technological Unemployment." *The Century Foundation*, April 26, 2018.

112 Wacquant, Loic. *Punishing the Poor: The Neoliberal Government of Social Insecurity*. Durham, NC: Duke University Press, 2009. Western, Bruce, and Christopher Wildeman. "The Black Family and Mass Incarceration." *The ANNALS of the American Academy of Political and Social Science* 621, no. 1 (2009): 221–42.

113 The accumulation and legitimation function of the state is discussed in O'Connor, James. *The Fiscal Crisis of the State*. New Brunswick: Transaction Publishers, 1973.

114 Short, Aaron. "Trump Administration Keeps Hands Off Self-Driving Cars." *Streets Blog*, January 8, 2020.

115 New York Times quotes a former Amazon drone executive, "The attitude was 'we're Amazon. We'll convince the F.A.A…The F.A.A. wants companies to come in with great humility and great transparency. That is not a strength of Amazon." Streitfeld, David. "Watch the Skies! Your Soup Is Here." *New York Times*, November 9, 2023.

116 Pöysti, Tuomas. "The Precautionary Approach Design Pattern." *Digital Society* 3, no. 1 (2024): 5.
117 Ricardo, David. *On the Principles of Political Economy and Taxation*. London: John Murray, 1817.
118 Chang, Ha-Joon. *Kicking away the Ladder: Development Strategy in Historical Perspective*. New York: Anthem Press, 2002.
119 Evans, *Embedded Autonomy*.
120 Gerschenkron, Alexander. *Economic Backwardness in Historical Perspective: A Book of Essays*. Cambridge: Harvard University Press, 1962.
121 Acemoglu, Daron, and James A. Robinson. *Why Nations Fail: The Origins of Power, Prosperity, and Poverty*. New York: Crown Publishing, 2012.
122 Lee, Kai-Fu. *AI Superpowers: China, Silicon Valley, and the New World Order*. Boston, MA: Houghton Mifflin Harcourt, 2018.
123 Liu, Aixin, Bei Feng, Bin Wang, Bingxuan Wang, Bo Liu, Chenggang Zhao, Chengqi Dengr et al. "Deepseek-v2: A Strong, Economical, and Efficient Mixture-of-Experts Language Model." *arXiv preprint arXiv:2405.04434* (2024).
124 Haag, Alex. "The State of AI Competition in Advanced Economies." *FEDS Notes*, October 6, 2025. https://www.federalreserve.gov/econres/notes/feds-notes/the-state-of-ai-competition-in-advanced-economies-20251006.html
125 Acemoglu, Daron, and James A. Robinson. "Political Losers as a Barrier to Economic Development." *American Economic Review* 90, no. 2 (2000): 126–30.
126 Acemoglu, Daron, and James A. Robinson. *Why Nations Fail: The Origins of Power, Prosperity, and Poverty*. New York: Crown Business, 2012.
127 Jimeno, J.F. "Fewer Babies and More Robots: Economic Growth in a New Era of Demographic and Technological Changes." *SERIEs* 10 (2019): 93–114.
128 Park, Cyn-Young, Kwanho Shin, and Aiko Kikkawa. "Aging, Automation, and Productivity in Korea." *Journal of the Japanese and International Economies* 59 (2021): 101–9.
129 Wei, Wenshi, and Danxia Xie. "Can AI Help to Raise the Fertility Rate?" Available at SSRN 4171328 (2022).
130 Anelli, Massimo, Osea Giuntella, and Luca Stella. "Robots, Marriageable Men, Family, and Fertility." *Journal of Human Resources* (2021): 1020–11223R1.
131 Egana-delSol, Pablo, Monserrat Bustelo, Laura Ripani, Nicolas Soler, and Mariana Viollaz. "Automation in Latin America: Are Women at Higher Risk of Losing Their Jobs?" *Technological Forecasting and Social Change* 175 (2022): 121333.
132 Piotrowski, Martin, Arne Kalleberg, and Ronald R. Rindfuss. "Contingent Work Rising: Implications for the Timing of Marriage in Japan." *Journal of Marriage and Family* 77, no. 5 (2015): 1039–56.
133 Cheng, Yen-hsin Alice. "Ultra-Low Fertility in East Asia: Confucianism and Its Discontents." *Vienna Yearbook of Population Research* 18 (2020): 83–120.
134 International Federation of Robotics. "Robot Density Nearly Doubled Globally." December 14, 2021.
135 Liu, Larry and Alejandro Portes. "Immigration and Robots: Is the Absence of Immigrants Linked to the Rise of Automation?" *Racial and Ethnic Studies*, 44, no. 15 (2021): 2723–51; Wu, Nicole. "Automation, Not Immigration?" In *Culture, Sociality, and Morality: New Applications of Mainline Political Economy*, edited by Paul Dragos Aligica, Ginny Seung Choi, Virgil Henry Storr, 153–74. Lanham: Rowman and Littlefield, 2022.
136 Gamez-Djokic, Monica, and Adam Waytz. "Concerns about Automation and Negative Sentiment toward Immigration." *Psychological Science* 31, no. 8 (2020): 987–1000.
137 Chernoff, Alex W., and Casey Warman. "COVID-19 and Implications for Automation." No. w27249. National Bureau of Economic Research, 2020.
138 McKinsey Global Institute. "The Future of Work after COVID-19." February 18, 2021.

139 Sun, Paul. "How AI Helps Physicians Improve Telehealth Patient Care in Real-Time." *Arizona Telemedicine Program*, June 23, 2022. https://telemedicine.arizona.edu/blog/how-ai-helps-physicians-improve-telehealth-patient-care-real-time The former orthopedic surgeon, Shawn Baker, promotes a future of AI doctors replacing human doctors. X. Dr. Shawn Baker. January 12, 2024. https://x.com/SBakerMD/status/1745800070019293377

140 Beaty, Artie. "This Might Be the Best Way to Get Medical Advice from ChatGPT - and It's Free to Use." *ZDNet*, January 23, 2026.

141 Laaser, Wolfram. "The Rise and Fall of the "Massively Open Online Courses"." *South Eastern European Journal of Public Health* (2023).

142 Zimmerman, Alex. "AI's New Role in NYC Schools? Chancellor Banks Teases Personalized Learning and College Counseling." *Chalkbeat*, September 17, 2024.

143 Smith, Aaron. "Public Attitudes Toward Computer Algorithms." *Pew Research Center*, November 16, 2018.

144 GAO Watch Blog. "A Look at the Federal Government's Aging Computer Systems." August 6, 2019. https://blog.gao.gov/2019/08/06/a-look-at-the-federal-governments-aging-computer-systems/

145 Wilner, Michael, and Sophia Bollag. "Tech Problems Mire Gavin Newsom's COVID Fight in CA." *Sacramento Bee*, August 12, 2020.

146 See for example librarians: Rajput, P.S., and J.N. Gautam. "Automation and Problems in their Implementation: An Investigation of Special Libraries in Indore, India." *International Journal of Library and Information Science* 2, no. 7 (2010): 143–47.

147 Eggers, William D., David Schatsky, and Peter Viechnicki. "How Artificial Intelligence Could Transform Government." *Deloitte*, April 26, 2017.

148 Bailey, Diane E., and Paul M. Leonardi. *Technology Choices: Why Occupations Differ in Their Embrace of New Technology*. Cambridge: MIT Press, 2015.

149 Lee, Jaewook. "Luddite or Technophile?—Policy Preferences for Governing Technology-Driven Economic Change." *Socio-Economic Review* 22, no. 3 (2024): 1019–46.

150 Thewissen, Stefan, and David Rueda. "Automation and the Welfare State: Technological Change as a Determinant of Redistribution Preferences." *Comparative Political Studies* 52, no. 2 (2019): 171–208.

151 Forbes, R.J. "Power." In *A History of Technology*, vol. 2, edited by Charles Singer, E.J. Holmyard, A.R. Hall, and Trevor I. Williams, 589–628. Oxford: Oxford University Press, 1957.

152 Sengupta, Ramprasad. "Technology and Social Dynamics: Feudalism and Its Decline." *Economic and Political Weekly* 10, no. 38 (1975): 1504–10.

153 Mokyr, Joel. *A Culture of Growth: The Origins of the Modern Economy*. Princeton, NJ: Princeton University Press, 2016.

154 Bailey, Diane E., and Paul M. Leonardi. *Technology Choices: Why Occupations Differ in Their Embrace of New Technology*. Cambridge: MIT Press, 2015.

155 Vertesi, Janet. *Seeing Like a Rover: How Robots, Teams, and Images Craft Knowledge of Mars*. Chicago, IL: Chicago University Press, 2014, p. 40.

156 Barley, Stephen R. "Technology as an Occasion for Structuring: Evidence from Observations of CT Scanners and the Social Order of Radiology Departments." *Administrative Science Quarterly* 31, no. 1 (1986): 78–108.

References

Abraham, Katharine G., and Melissa S. Kearney. "Explaining the Decline in the US Employment-to-Population Ratio: A Review of the Evidence." *National Bureau of Economic Research* Working Paper no. w24333, 2018.

Acemoglu, Daron, and James A. Robinson. "Political Losers as a Barrier to Economic Development." *American Economic Review* 90, no. 2 (2000): 126–30.

Acemoglu, Daron, and James A. Robinson. *Why Nations Fail: The Origins of Power, Prosperity, and Poverty.* New York: Crown Business, 2012.

Acemoglu, Daron, and Pascual Restrepo. "Robots and Jobs: Evidence from US Labor Markets." *NBER* Working Paper no. w23285, 2017.

Acemoglu, Daron, and Pascual Restrepo. "Secular Stagnation? The Effect of Aging on Economic Growth in the Age of Automation." *American Economic Review* 107, no. 5 (2017): 174–79.

Acemoglu, Daron, and Pascual Restrepo. "Automation and New Tasks: How Technology Displaces and Reinstates Labor." *Journal of Economic Perspectives* 33, no. 2 (2019): 3–30.

Adachi, Daisuke, Daiji Kawaguchi, and Yukiko Saito. "Robots and Employment: Evidence from Japan, 1978–2017." Discussion Papers 20051, Research Institute of Economy, Trade, and Industry (RIETI), 2020.

Aghion, Philippe, Céline Antonin, Simon Bunel, and Xavier Jaravel. "What Are the Labor and Product Market Effects of Automation? New Evidence from France." *CEPR* Discussion Paper no. DP14443, 2020.

Aguiar, Mark, Mark Bils, Kerwin Kofi Charles, and Erik Hurst. "Leisure Luxuries and the Labor Supply of Young Men." *National Bureau of Economic Research* Working Paper no. w23552, 2017.

Aksoy, Cevat Giray, Jose Maria Barrero, Nicholas Bloom, Steven J. Davis, Mathias Dolls, and Pablo Zarate. "The Global Persistence of Work from Home." *Proceedings of the National Academy of Sciences* 122, no. 27 (2025): e2509892122.

Allen, Robert. "Why Was the Industrial Revolution British?" *VoxEU*, May 15, 2009.

Anelli, Massimo, Osea Giuntella, and Luca Stella. "Robots, Marriageable Men, Family, and Fertility." *Journal of Human Resources* (2021): 1020–11223R1.

Arnold, Heinrich. "The Recent History of the Machine Tool Industry and the Effects of Technological Change." *Münchner Betriebswirtschaftliche Beiträge* 14 (2001).

Arntz, Melanie, Terry Gregory, and Ulrich Zierahn. "The Risk of Automation for Jobs in OECD Countries." *OECD* Working Paper, 2016.

Autor, David. "Why Are There Still So Many Jobs? The History and Future of Workplace Automation." *Journal of Economic Perspectives* 29, no. 3 (2015): 3–30.

Autor, David. "Work of the Past, Work of the Future." *National Bureau of Economic Research* Working Paper no. w25588, 2019.

Autor, David, and Anna Salomons. "Is Automation Labor-Displacing? Productivity Growth, Employment, and the Labor Share." *Brookings* Papers on Economic Activity, 2018.

Autor, David, and Elisabeth Reynolds. "The Nature of Work after the COVID Crisis: Too Few Low-Wage Jobs." *The Hamilton Project,* Brookings, 2020.

Avent, Ryan. "Take My Job (Please)." *Medium*, November 8, 2017.

Bailey, Diane E., and Paul M. Leonardi. *Technology Choices: Why Occupations Differ in Their Embrace of New Technology.* Cambridge, MA: MIT Press, 2015.

Baker, Shawn. X tweet, January 12, 2024. https://x.com/SBakerMD/status/1745800070019293377

Baldwin, Richard. *The Globotics Upheaval: Globalization, Robotics, and the Future of Work.* Oxford: Oxford University Press, 2019.

Baran, Paul, and Paul Sweezy. *Monopoly Capital: An Essay on the American Economic and Social Order.* New York: Monthly Review Press, 1966.

Barley, Stephen R. "Technology as an Occasion for Structuring: Evidence from Observations of CT Scanners and the Social Order of Radiology Departments." *Administrative Science Quarterly* 31, no. 1 (1986): 78–108.

Bastani, Aaron. *Automation and the Future of Work*. New York: Verso, 2020.
Baumol, William J. *The Cost Disease*. New Haven, CT: Yale University Press, 2012.
Beaty, Artie. "This Might Be the Best Way to Get Medical Advice from ChatGPT – and It's Free to Use." *ZDNet*, January 23, 2026.
Belloc, Filippo, Gabriel Burdin, and Fabio Landini. "Advanced Technologies and Worker Voice." *Economica* 90, no. 357 (2023): 1–38.
Benanav, Aaron. *Automation and the Future of Work*. New York: Verso, 2020.
Bessen, James E. "How Computer Automation Affects Occupations: Technology, Jobs, and Skills." *Boston University School of Law*, Law and Economics Research Paper no. 15–49, 2015.
Bessen, James E. "Automation and Jobs: When Technology Boosts Employment." *Boston University School of Law*, Law and Economics Research Paper no. 17–09, 2018.
Braverman, Harry. *Labor and Monopoly Capital: The Degradation of Work in the Twentieth Century*. New York: Monthly Review Press, 1974.
Bregman, Rutger. *Utopia for Realists: The Case for Universal Basic Income, Open Borders, and a 15-Hour Workweek*. New York: Bloomsbury Publishing, 2017.
Brynjolfsson, Erik, and Andrew McAfee. *The Second Machine Age: Work, Progress, and Prosperity in a Time of Brilliant Technologies*. New York: W. W. Norton & Company, 2014.
Brynjolfsson, Erik, Daniel Rock, and Chad Syverson. "Artificial Intelligence and the Modern Productivity Paradox: A Clash of Expectations and Statistics." NBER Working Paper no. w24001, 2017.
Bureau of Labor Statistics. "Civilian Unemployment Rate." https://www.bls.gov/charts/employment-situation/civilian-unemployment-rate.htm.
Chang, Ha-Joon. *Kicking Away the Ladder: Development Strategy in Historical Perspective*. New York: Anthem Press, 2002.
Cheng, Yen-Hsin Alice. "Ultra-Low Fertility in East Asia: Confucianism and Its Discontents." *Vienna Yearbook of Population Research* 18 (2020): 83–120.
Chernoff, Alex W., and Casey Warman. "COVID-19 and Implications for Automation." *National Bureau of Economic Research* Working Paper no. w27249, 2020.
Cobb, C. W., and P. H. Douglas. "A Theory of Production." *American Economic Review* 18, Supplement (1928): 139–65.
Collins, Randall. *The Credential Society: An Historical Sociology of Education and Stratification*. New York: Academic Press, 1979.
Crafts, Nicholas. "Artificial Intelligence as a General-Purpose Technology: An Historical Perspective." *Oxford Review of Economic Policy* 37, no. 3 (2021): 521–36.
Dauth, Wolfgang, Sebastian Findeisen, Jens Suedekum, and Nicole Woessner. "The Adjustment of Labor Markets to Robots." *Journal of the European Economic Association* 19, no. 6 (2021): 3104–53.
Diao, Xinshen, Jed Silver, and Hiroyuki Takeshima. "What's Driving the Growth of Agricultural Mechanization in Africa?" *International Food Policy Research Institute*, December 20, 2017.
Ebsco. "Eli Whitney and the Cotton Gin – A Mixed Legacy." *Freedom Center Voices*, December 8, 2020.
Egana-Delsol, Pablo, Monserrat Bustelo, Laura Ripani, Nicolas Soler, and Mariana Viollaz. "Automation in Latin America: Are Women at Higher Risk of Losing Their Jobs?" *Technological Forecasting and Social Change* 175 (2022): 121333.
Eggers, William D., David Schatsky, and Peter Viechnicki. "How Artificial Intelligence Could Transform Government." *Deloitte*, April 26, 2017.
Elliott, Vittoria, and Tek Endra Parmar. "The Despair and Darkness of People Will Get to You." *Rest of the World*, July 22, 2020.

Esping-Andersen, Gøsta. "Welfare States without Work: The Impasse of Labor Shedding and Familialism in Continental European Social Policy." *Instituto Juan March de Estudios y Investigaciones*, 1995.
Evans, Peter. *Embedded Autonomy: States and Industrial Transformation*. Princeton, NJ: Princeton University Press, 1995.
Felten, Edward W., Manav Raj, and Robert Seamans. "Occupational Heterogeneity in Exposure to Generative AI." SSRN Working Paper no. 4414065, 2023.
Forbes, R. J. "Power." In *A History of Technology*, vol. 2, edited by Charles Singer, E. J. Holm yard, A. R. Hall, and Trevor I. Williams, 589–628. Oxford: Oxford University Press, 1957.
Frase, Peter. *Four Futures: Life after Capitalism*. London: Verso, 2016.
FRED. Employment-Population Ratio: 16 to 19 Years. Federal Reserve Bank of St. Louis. https://fred.stlouisfed.org/series/LNS12300012.
FRED. Employment-Population Ratio: 25–54 Years. Federal Reserve Bank of St. Louis. https://fred.stlouisfed.org/series/LNS12300060.
FRED. Employment-Population Ratio: Men. Federal Reserve Bank of St. Louis. https://fred.stlouisfed.org/series/LNS12300001.
FRED. Employment-Population Ratio: Women. Federal Reserve Bank of St. Louis. https://fred.stlouisfed.org/series/LNS12300002.
Frey, Carl Benedikt, and Michael A. Osborne. "The Future of Employment: How Susceptible Are Jobs to Computerisation?" *Technological Forecasting and Social Change* 114 (2017): 254–80.
Gamez-Djokic, Monica, and Adam Waytz. "Concerns about Automation and Negative Sentiment toward Immigration." *Psychological Science* 31, no. 8 (2020): 987–1000.
GAO. "A Look at the Federal Government's Aging Computer Systems." *GAO Watch Blog*, August 6, 2019.
Gerschenkron, Alexander. *Economic Backwardness in Historical Perspective: A Book of Essays*. Cambridge, MA: Harvard University Press, 1962.
Golden, Ryan. "Glassdoor and Indeed Announce Layoffs, Reportedly Due to AI." *HR Dive*, July 11, 2025.
Gordon, Rachel. "CSAIL Robot Disinfects Greater Boston Food Bank." *MIT News*, June 28, 2020.
Gordon, Robert J. "The Demise of US Economic Growth: Restatement, Rebuttal, and Reflections." *NBER* Working Paper no. w19895, 2014.
Graeber, David. *Bullshit Jobs: A Theory*. New York: Simon and Schuster, 2018.
Greenidge, Henry Lawson. "How a Historic Strike Paved the Way for the Automated Elevator and What Those Lessons Could Mean for Self-Driving Cars." *Medium*, May 12, 2020.
Haag, Alex. "The State of AI Competition in Advanced Economies." *FEDS Notes*, October 6, 2025.
Haapanala, Henri, Zachary Parolin, and Ive Marx. "Blame the Robots? Routine-Biased Technological Change and the Recent Decline of Union Membership in Europe and the United States." *University of Antwerp*, 2022.
Handel, Michael J. "Growth Trends for Selected Occupations Considered at Risk from Automation." *Monthly Labor Review*, 2022.
Hanley, Caroline. "Putting the Bias in Skill-Biased Technological Change? A Relational Perspective on White-Collar Automation at General Electric." *American Behavioral Scientist* 58, no. 3 (2014): 400–15.
Harris, Katelynn. "Forty Years of Falling Manufacturing Employment." *Beyond the Numbers: Bureau of Labor Statistics* 9, no. 16 (2020).

Hassan, Navita. "Work from Home: Impacts on Public Transportation and Commercial Real Estate Vacancies." Master's Thesis, KTH Royal Institute of Technology, School of Architecture and the Built Environment (ABE), Stockholm (2024).

Hickel, Jason. "How Britain Stole $45 Trillion from India." *Al Jazeera*, December 19, 2018.

Hirschman, Charles, and Elizabeth Mogford. "Immigration and the American Industrial Revolution from 1880 to 1920." *Social Science Research* 38, no. 4 (2009): 897–920.

Hui, Xiang, Oren Reshef, and Luofeng Zhou. "The Short-Term Effects of Generative Artificial Intelligence on Employment: Evidence from an Online Labor Market." SSRN Working Paper, 2023.

Ingram, Beth F., and George R. Neumann. "The Returns to Skill." *Labour Economics* 13, no. 1 (2006): 35–59.

International Federation of Robotics. "Robot Density Nearly Doubled Globally." December 14, 2021.

Jaimovich, Nir, and Henry E. Siu. "Job Polarization and Jobless Recoveries." *NBER* Working Paper no. w18334, 2012.

Jimeno, J.F. "Fewer Babies and More Robots: Economic Growth in a New Era of Demographic and Technological Changes." *SERIEs* 10: 93–114 (2019).

Kacher, Alban. "Just Eat to Lay Off Around 450 Employees, Partly Automating Operations." *Reuters,* September 25, 2025.

Karsten, Jack, and Darrell M. West. "Rising Minimum Wages Make Automation More Cost-Effective." *Brookings*, September 30, 2015.

Killingsworth, Charles C. "Industrial Relations and Automation." *The Annals of the American Academy of Political and Social Science* 340 (1962): 69–80.

Krueger, Alan B. "Where Have All the Workers Gone? An Inquiry into the Decline of the US Labor Force Participation Rate." *Brookings Papers on Economic Activity*, no. 2 (2017): 1–87.

Kurzweil, Ray. *The Singularity Is Nearer: When We Merge with AI.* New York: Penguin, 2024.

Laaser, Wolfram. "The Rise and Fall of the 'Massively Open Online Courses.' " *South Eastern European Journal of Public Health* (2023).

Laber, Joshua, Ravindra Thamma, and E. Daniel Kirby. "The Impact of Warehouse Automation in Amazon's Success." *International Journal of Innovative Science, Engineering & Technology* 7, no. 8 (2020): 63–70.

Lawlor, Eilis, Helen Kersley, and Susan Steed. *A Bit Rich: Calculating the Value to Society of Different Professions.* London: New Economics Foundation, 2009.

Lee, Jaewook. "Luddite or Technophile? Policy Preferences for GoverningTechnology-Driven Economic Change." *Socio-Economic Review* 22, no. 3 (2024): 1019–46.

Lee, Kai-Fu. *AI Superpowers: China, Silicon Valley, and the New World Order.* Boston: Houghton Mifflin Harcourt, 2018.

Li, Zhe. "Trends in Social Security Disability Insurance Enrollment." *Congressional Research Service*, November 30, 2018.

Lin, Ken-Hou, and Megan Tobias Neely. *Divested: Inequality in Financialized America.* New York: Oxford University Press, 2020.

Liu, Aixin, Bei Feng, Bin Wang, Bingxuan Wang, Bo Liu, Chenggang Zhao, Chengqi Dengr, et al. "DeepSeek-V2: A Strong, Economical, and Efficient Mixture-of-Experts Language Model." arXiv preprint arXiv:2405.04434, 2024.

Liu, Larry. "Labor Unions and Robots: The Logic of Automation Given the Power of Organized Labor." Unpublished manuscript.

Liu, Larry, and Alejandro Portes. "Immigration and Robots: Is the Absence of Immigrants Linked to the Rise of Automation?" *Ethnic and Racial Studies* 44, no. 15 (2021): 2723–51.

Malagón-Amor, Ángeles, Luis Miguel Martín-López, David Córcoles, Anna González, Magda Bellsolà, Alan R. Teo, Antoni Bulbena, Víctor Pérez, and Daniel Bergé. "Family Features of Social Withdrawal Syndrome (Hikikomori)." *Frontiers in Psychiatry* 11 (2020): 138.

Mankiw, N. Gregory. "Defending the One Percent." *Journal of Economic Perspectives* 27, no. 3 (2013): 21–34.

Manyika, James, and Kevin Sneader. "AI, automation, and the future of work: Ten things to solve for." *McKinsey* (2018).

Martin, Lyn. "Eli Whitney and the Cotton Gin – A Mixed Legacy." *Freedom Center Voices,* December 8, 2020.

Marx, Karl. "Manifesto of the Communist Party." 1848. https://www.marxists.org/archive/marx/works/1848/communist-manifesto/ch01.htm.

Marx, Karl. "Wage Labour and Capital." In Karl Marx and Friedrich Engels, *Collected Works, vol. 9,* 197–228. London: Lawrence & Wishart, 1977.

Marx, Karl. *Capital, Volume 1.* London: Penguin, 1990.

Mason, Paul. *PostCapitalism: A Guide to Our Future*. London: Allen Lane, 2016.

Mazzucato, Mariana. *The Entrepreneurial State: Debunking Public vs. Private Sector Myths.* London: Anthem Press, 2013.

McClelland, Ted. *Nothin' but Blue Skies: The Heyday, Hard Times, and Hopes of America's Industrial Heartland.* New York: Bloomsbury Press, 2013.

McKinsey Global Institute. "The Future of Work after COVID-19." February 18, 2021.

Mishel, Lawrence, Heidi Shierholz, and John Schmitt. "Don't Blame the Robots: Assessing the Job Polarization Explanation of Growing Wage Inequality." Working Paper no. 295. Washington, DC: Economic Policy Institute–Center for Economic and Policy Research, 2013.

Mokyr, Joel. *A Culture of Growth: The Origins of the Modern Economy.* Princeton, NJ: Princeton University Press, 2016.

Moseley, Fred. "Marx's Concepts of Productive Labor and Unproductive Labor: An Application to the Postwar US Economy." *Eastern Economic Journal* 9, no. 3 (1983): 180–89.

Mukherjee, Siddhartha. "A.I. versus M.D." *New Yorker,* March 27, 2017.

National Conference of State Legislatures. "COVID-19: Essential Workers in the United States." January 11, 2021.

NDTV. "Accenture Lays Off 11,000 Employees, CEO Reveals Why It's Necessary." September 30, 2025. https://www.ndtv.com/world-news/accenture-lays-off-11-000-employees-ceo-julie-sweet-reveals-why-its-necessary-9368776

Newman, Jonathan. "Why Robots Won't Cause Mass Unemployment." *Mises Institute*, 2017.

Novet, Jordan. "Microsoft Laying Off About 9,000 Employees in Latest Round of Cuts." *CNBC,* July 2, 2025.

O'Connor, James. *The Fiscal Crisis of the State.* New Brunswick, NJ: Transaction Publishers, 1973.

Owens, Nathan. "Intel Layoffs Exceed 5,000 across US." *Manufacturing Dive*, July 11, 2025.

Park, Cyn-Young, Kwanho Shin, and Aiko Kikkawa. "Aging, Automation, and Productivity in Korea." *Journal of the Japanese and International Economies* 59 (2021): 101–9.

Parshakov, Petr, Sofiia Paklina, Dennis Coates, and Aleksei Chadov. "Does Video Games' Popularity Affect Unemployment Rate? Evidence from Macro-Level Analysis." *Journal of Economic Studies* 48, no. 4 (2021): 817–35.

Paulsen, Roland. *Empty Labor.* Cambridge: Cambridge University Press, 2014.

Pendyala, V. S., and S. Figueira. "Automated Medical Diagnosis from Clinical Data." In *2017 IEEE Third International Conference on Big Data Computing Service and Applications (BigDataService)*, 185–90. San Francisco, CA: IEEE, 2017.

Piketty, Thomas. *Capital in the Twenty-First Century.* Cambridge, MA: Harvard University Press, 2014.

Piotrowski, Martin, Arne Kalleberg, and Ronald R. Rindfuss. "Contingent Work Rising: Implications for the Timing of Marriage in Japan." *Journal of Marriage and Family* 77, no. 5 (2015): 1039–56.

Pöysti, Tuomas. "The Precautionary Approach Design Pattern." *Digital Society* 3, no. 1 (2024): 5.

Pugh, Allison J. *The Tumbleweed Society: Working and Caring in an Age of Insecurity.* New York: Oxford University Press, 2015.

Rajput, P. S., and J. N. Gautam. "Automation and Problems in Their Implementation: An Investigation of Special Libraries in Indore, India." *International Journal of Library and Information Science* 2, no. 7 (2010): 143–47.

Restrepo, Pascual. "We Won't Be Missed: Work and Growth in the Era of AGI." In *The Economics of Transformative AI.* NBER, 2025.

Reuters. "USTR Nominee Tai Says New Tools Needed to Protect U.S. Intellectual Property." February 25, 2021.

Reuters. "Online Marketplace Fiverr to Lay Off 30% of Workforce in AI Push." September 15, 2025.

Ricardo, David. *On the Principles of Political Economy and Taxation.* London: John Murray, 1817.

Ricci, Tom. "Jethro Tull." *The American Society of Mechanical Engineers*, June 25, 2012.

Rifkin, Jeremy. *The End of Work.* New York: Putnam, 1995.

Roser, Max. "Employment in Agriculture." Our World in Data. https://ourworldindata.org/employment-in-agriculture.

Sampson, Scott. "Predicting Job Automation: What Have We Observed?" In *Proceedings of the 57th Hawaii International Conference on System Sciences*, 2024.

Say, Jean-Baptiste. *Traité d'économie politique ou simple exposition de la manière dont se forment, se distribuent et se composent les richesses.* Paris: Crapelet, 1803.

Sengupta, Ramprasad. "Technology and Social Dynamics: Feudalism and Its Decline." *Economic and Political Weekly* 10, no. 38 (1975): 1504–10.

Short, Aaron. "Trump Administration Keeps Hands Off Self-Driving Cars." *Streetsblog*, January 8, 2020.

Skocpol, Theda. *States and Social Revolutions: A Comparative Analysis of France, Russia, and China.* New York: Cambridge University Press, 1979.

Smith, Aaron. "Public Attitudes Toward Computer Algorithms." *Pew Research Center*, November 16, 2018.

Soffia, Magdalena, Alex J. Wood, and Brendan Burchell. "Alienation Is Not 'Bullshit': An Empirical Critique of Graeber's Theory of BS Jobs." *Work, Employment and Society* 36, no. 5 (2022): 816–40.

Solow, Robert M. "A Contribution to the Theory of Economic Growth." *Quarterly Journal of Economics* 70, no. 1 (1956): 65–94.

Stettner, Andrew. "Mounting a Response to Technological Unemployment." *The Century Foundation*, April 26, 2018.

Storm, Servaas. "The New Normal: Demand, Secular Stagnation, and the Vanishing Middle Class." *International Journal of Political Economy* 46, no. 4 (2017): 169–210.

Streitfeld, David. "Watch the Skies! Your Soup Is Here." *New York Times*, November 9, 2023.

Summers, Lawrence H. "Accepting the Reality of Secular Stagnation." *Finance and Development* 57, no. 1 (2020).

Sun, Paul. "How AI Helps Physicians Improve Telehealth Patient Care in Real-Time." *Arizona Telemedicine Program*, June 23, 2022.

Susskind, Daniel. *A World without Work: Technology, Automation, and How We Should Respond*. New York: Macmillan, 2020.

Taylor, Kate. "America's Fast-Food Chains Are Contemplating Replacing Minimum-Wage Workers with Robots—and It Could Lead to a Crisis." *Business Insider*, January 11, 2018.

Thewissen, Stefan, and David Rueda. "Automation and the Welfare State: Technological Change as a Determinant of Redistribution Preferences." *Comparative Political Studies* 52, no. 2 (2019): 171–208.

Tilly, Charles. *Coercion, Capital, and European States, AD 990–1992*. Oxford: Basil Blackwell, 1990.

Tiratelli, Matteo. "Where Did the Bullshit Jobs Go?" *Jacobin*, March 8, 2023.

United States Department of Agriculture. "Ag and Food Sectors and the Economy." *Economic Research Service*. Accessed November 2, 2024. https://www.ers.usda.gov/data-products/ag-and-food-statistics-charting-the-essentials/ag-and-food-sectors-and-the-economy/.

Valletta, Robert G. "Recent Flattening in the Higher Education Wage Premium: Polarization, Skill Downgrading, or Both?" *NBER Working Paper* no. w22935, 2016.

Van der Heyden, Peter. "11.14. Threshing Machines." *The Industrial Revolution in England Was Not All Bad*, February 26, 2020. https://history.pictures/2020/02/26/11-14-threshing-machines/

Vertesi, Janet. *Seeing Like a Rover: How Robots, Teams, and Images Craft Knowledge of Mars*. Chicago: University of Chicago Press, 2014.

Vertesi, Janet A., Adam Goldstein, Diana Enriquez, Larry Liu, and Katherine T. Miller. "Pre-Automation: Insourcing and Automating the Gig Economy." *Sociologica* 14, no. 3 (2020): 167–93.

Wacquant, Loïc. *Punishing the Poor: The Neoliberal Government of Social Insecurity*. Durham, NC: Duke University Press, 2009.

Walo, Simon. "'Bullshit' After All? Why People Consider Their Jobs Socially Useless." *Work, Employment and Society* 37, no. 5 (2023): 1123–46.

Wei, Wenshi, and Danxia Xie. "Can AI Help to Raise the Fertility Rate?" *SSRN Working Paper* no. 4171328, 2022.

Western, Bruce, and Christopher Wildeman. "The Black Family and Mass Incarceration." *The ANNALS of the American Academy of Political and Social Science* 621, no. 1 (2009): 221–42.

Williams, Alex. "The Drones Were Ready for This Moment." *New York Times*, May 23, 2020.

Wilner, Michael, and Sophia Bollag. "Tech Problems Mire Gavin Newsom's COVID Fight in CA." *Sacramento Bee*, August 12, 2020.

World Economic Forum. "The Future of Jobs Report 2025." 2025.
Wright, Erik Olin. *Class Counts: Comparative Studies in Class Analysis.* Cambridge: Cambridge University Press, 1997.
Wu, Nicole. "Automation, Not Immigration?" In *Culture, Sociality, and Morality: New Applications of Mainline Political Economy*, edited by Paul Dragos Aligica, Ginny Seung Choi, and Virgil Henry Storr, 153–74. Lanham, MD: Rowman and Littlefield, 2022.
Wynne, Mark A., and Lillian Derr. Will AI Replace Your Job? Perhaps Not in the Next Decade. *Dallas Fed*, June 3, 2025.
Yashiro, Naomitsu, Tomi Kyyrä, Hyunjeong Hwang, and Juha Tuomala. "Technology, Labour Market Institutions, and Early Retirement." *VoxEU*, March 12, 2021.
Zimmerman, Alex. "AI's New Role in NYC Schools? Chancellor Banks Teases Personalized Learning and College Counseling." *Chalkbeat*, September 17, 2024.

2

AUTOMATION DISCOURSE(S)

From a broader sociological lens, automation is a discourse in which different actors formulate different understandings of what the likely impact of automation is on the workforce and whether a workless future is desirable. This discourse of automation changes from period to period. It also reveals the biases, preferences and interests of various social actors that have different stakes in shaping the direction of technological change. In this chapter, I present the automation discourse as a part of the sociotechnical imaginary and the sociology of expectations and then build the main argument in the book. There is not only one discourse of automation but four. The representatives in each discourse argue for different goals and pay attention to different problems.

Automation Discourse as Sociotechnical Imaginary

Automation and the future of work discourse can be seen within the framework of the socio-technical imaginary. Imaginaries of a future of technology are labeled "sociotechnical imaginary," which, following Jasanoff and Kim, are "collectively imagined forms of social life and social order reflected in the design and fulfillment of nation-specific scientific and/or technological projects."[1] Following this definition, the imaginary is an instrument of the state to realize a certain vision, such as building nuclear power plants to project energy independence and economic power.[2] A government's science and technology policies are embedded in political cultures and practices that stabilize imaginaries and mobilize resources in the name of 'national interest'.[3]

However, the imaginary is not limited to the nation-state but can encompass a broader societal vision. It is a "collectively held, institutionally stabilized and publicly performed vision of desirable futures, animated by shared

DOI: 10.4324/9781003780236-3

understandings of forms of social life and social order attainable through, and supportive of, advances in science and technology."[4] This imaginary is more than a fashion or idea, because it is "collective, durable, capable of being performed; yet they are also temporally situated and culturally particular."[5] This collective imagination produces a system of meanings that enable actors to collectively interpret social reality and work toward technological goals.[6] Such imagination creates the basis for a shared sense of belonging and it enables people's attachment to a political community.[7] A collective imagination facilitates a more standardized governance and control of human subjects.[8] It also produces a social order that is shaped by cultural flows and many imagined worlds.[9] Imaginaries are instrumental and futuristic because they project a future vision of what is good and desirable to achieve for a political community. They also warn against social risks that come with innovation if the society advances too rapidly. They create the national political will to resolve problems caused by technology or have not been resolved by the technology.[10]

Socio-technical imaginaries implicitly assume that technical artifacts are political in their design, implementation and effects on various constituencies. Technologies are not politically neutral but are socially impactful by favoring certain groups and lifestyles over others. Langdon Winner described how the New York City planner Robert Moses had designed low bridges that excluded buses from accessing parks and beaches in Long Island that are reserved to the middle class that had private cars. Low-income people and people of color, who did not own cars and were reliant on public buses for mobility, could not visit the parks and beaches and were socially excluded from these public goods. In another example, the invention of the atom bomb centralized political control, even more so than prior military technologies that offer tactical discretion to low-ranking military officers and soldiers. The use and deployment of atom bombs lie with the leader of the nation state that has such weapons.[11] Thus, a socio-technical vision can produce winners and losers and establish or reinforce political hierarchies.

Because technology shapes collective futures, Jasanoff advocated for bringing uncertainties and value conflicts in technologies and their social visions from elite discourse or lack of discourse into the public sphere, allowing citizens to participate in deciding technological pathways rather than leaving it solely to experts or markets. Fundamental political questions about justice, power and the good life are continuously debated and enacted, though not everyone has an equal voice.[12]

The sociotechnical imaginary framework can be applied in different industries and domains. The South Korean government had framed the obtaining of nuclear power plants in the early 1970s as a state-building project that would enable the country to achieve technological self-reliance.[13] Technology companies like International Business Machines (IBM) and Cisco Systems, Inc (Cisco) have promoted the smart city imaginary, where they can sell overcrowded cities their sensors, computers, cameras and algorithms to deliver public services in resource-constrained municipalities.[14] The energy transition toward renewable energy that are less carbon-intensive is framed as a form of socio-technical imaginary, because of an envisioned end point of carbon emissions at a definite point in the future. This end point is reached as net zero emissions by 2050.[15] The self-driving car automates driving and is considered a socio-technical imaginary because it is ideologically undergirded by the normative desire to improve road safety and reduce road accidents.[16] Another form of socio-technical imaginary is the deference of government officials to scientists in managing social problems, i.e., the techno-scientific viewpoint of policy-making.[17] This elite deference can come at the expense of tolerance, open-mindedness, the limits of evidence, willingness to entertain uncertainty and a commitment to the entire truth.[18] Artificial intelligence (AI) in the visual arts is viewed as a tool to enhance creativity, increase productivity and democratize art, but also as a cause of job displacement, the marginalization of human artists and the rise of industrial art, thus containing positive and negative imaginations.[19]

The last example reveals that the future of work discourse and labor market instability is an important aspect of the sociotechnical imaginary. It can be situated within a broader historical and cultural context and is not purely a reliable forecast of what type of technologies will appear in the future. The Fourth Industrial Revolution (FIR) has been most prominently promoted by the World Economic Forum (WEF) and allied business consultancies, policy organizations and technology firms. Within this imaginary, rapid advances in artificial intelligence, robotics and digital platforms are framed as ushering in an unprecedented transformation of work, which is both global in scope and inevitable in trajectory. The FIR narrative emphasizes large-scale shifts in skill requirements, occupational structures and employer labor needs across virtually all industries, positioning continuous reskilling and lifelong learning as necessary adaptations for workers, firms and states alike.[20]

The FIR imaginary is not merely descriptive but normative, advancing a particular interpretation of technological change that foregrounds individual adaptability and human capital investment while downplaying alternative institutional responses, such as public sector job creation, job redesign, labor regulation, or collective bargaining. Governments are cast primarily as facilitators of workforce retraining rather than as regulators of technological adoption or guarantors of employment security. As a result, responsibility for adjustment to technology is redistributed downward, from firms and states to workers themselves. Critics have described this vision as "future essentialist," in so far as it portrays technological change as epochal, exogenous and unavoidable, leaving little room for political contestation over how technologies are deployed or who bears the costs of adjustment.[21] By framing the future of work as a technological inevitability rather than a socially negotiated outcome, the FIR discourse helps legitimize particular policy responses while foreclosing others, thereby shaping contemporary debates over labor markets, education systems and social protection.

The political recommendations in the FIR literature may be considered one future of work discourse that I call "status quo" but are, by no means, the only ones in existence. Other discourses are what I refer to as activist, resigned and futurist. FIR is further discussed in Chapter 5, on status quo views of automation, and all four discourses are described later in this chapter.

Automation Discourse and the Sociology of Expectations

The question about the future of work is embedded in the sociology of expectations, involving the visions about how work is structured, given the most recent technological advances, such as AI.[22] Expectations play a central role in shaping how the present is interpreted and how the future is imagined and acted upon. At both the individual and collective levels, the future is characterized by fundamental uncertainty and openness: actors cannot fully know how technologies, labor markets, or institutions will evolve, and multiple trajectories remain possible at any given moment. Expectations function as interpretive devices that help actors navigate this uncertainty by providing narratives, forecasts and shared visions that render the future intelligible and actionable in the present. In this sense, expectations do not merely describe possible futures but actively structure present-day decisions on career or job training paths, investments in companies and industries and policy choices on labor market and social policy.[23]

At the same time, expectations are not neutral or evenly distributed. Dominant future-oriented narratives involving automation, AI, or economic competitiveness operate as coordinating mechanisms that align the behavior of firms, states and workers around particular anticipated outcomes. Once institutionalized, these expectations can foreclose alternative pathways by defining certain futures as inevitable, desirable, or rational, while rendering others as unrealistic or obsolete.[24] This process narrows the range of politically and socially legitimate responses to uncertainty. In the case of the future of work discourse, the narrowing of legitimate responses privileges strategies such as worker reskilling, flexibility and technological adoption over alternatives like employment protection, work-time reduction, or collective control over innovation. Thus, expectations simultaneously open horizons of possibility and constrain them, shaping not only how the future is imagined but also which social arrangements become feasible in the present.

Expectations are generative in that they actively shape social, economic and technological processes rather than merely anticipate future outcomes. By projecting particular visions of the future, expectations guide politicians, investor, or worker activities, provide cognitive and organizational structure and legitimate specific behaviors, institutions and policy choices. Shared expectations coordinate actors across different fields, such as firms, states, researchers and the workers. These shared expectations align their actions toward anticipated futures. These expectations help mobilize resources, attract investment and justify the allocation of public and private funding, often long before the promised outcomes materialize.[25]

These future-oriented imaginaries are translated into concrete practices through measurement, calculation and experimentation. Expectations drive the development of indicators, benchmarks and performance metrics, as well as material tests, pilot projects, demonstrations and models designed to make future possibilities appear tangible and credible. Through such practices, imagined futures become embedded in technical standards, organizational routines and policy frameworks, shaping what counts as success, innovation, or progress. In this way, expectations not only organize technological development but also structure the evaluative criteria through which technologies and institutions are judged.[26]

However, expectations can also take the form of hype cycles, in which optimistic projections about a desirable future or end state are amplified through media, expert discourse and institutional endorsement. When these inflated expectations fail to materialize or when their social consequences diverge from initial promises, they create phases of disappointment, disillusionment, or retrenchment. Such moments of deflation can lead to shifts in funding priorities, policy reversals, or critical reassessments of technological trajectories.[27] But even when a hype collapses, its effects are not erased. That is because infrastructures, regulatory frameworks and social commitments built around earlier expectations often persist, continuing to shape technological development and social relations long after the initial promises have faded. In response to the charge that all these investments into AI infrastructure such as data centers or semiconductor manufacturing are overhyped, the Amazon founder, Jeff Bezos, replied that an industrial bubble like AI creates lasting societal value, while financial bubbles do not generate new value.[28] He argued that society and big tech should continue their AI investments. Critics that truly believe that AI is hype would not distinguish between industrial and financial bubbles.

The uncertainty about the future of work favors a societal faith in what Beckert calls "fictional expectations." These are collectively held and shared images of the future state of the world to guide present action in the context of uncertainty. Beckert lays out that modern capitalism is driven by collective, socially constructed fictional expectations about the future, not just rational calculation or material forces. These "fictions" involve future profits for companies/ industries, economic growth for countries, stable money (low inflation), or successful innovations. They allow actors such as investors or consumers to act under uncertainty, motivating investment and consumption. Without such faith, the economy would grind to a standstill. But these fictional expectations can also lead to major financial crises like the one in 2008, when these imagined futures fail to materialize. He proposes these contingent, imaginative beliefs as a core mechanism in sustaining capitalism by integrating micro-level agency with macro-level capitalist dynamics.[29] Thus, the contemporary societal and investor obsession with AI is partially built on such fictional expectations, which are reflected in the national discourse on AI and the future of work.

Vicsek poses the question of whether dominant automation discourses are capable of addressing normative concerns about the future of work, including what constitutes a desirable labor market and who holds the authority to decide how artificial intelligence and automation technologies are designed, deployed and governed. Rather than treating automation as a purely technical or economic process, she emphasizes that automation discourse is inherently normative, as it embeds assumptions about efficiency, productivity and social value while often marginalizing questions of democratic participation, power and distributional consequences. In this sense, debates about automation are also debates about whose interests are prioritized and whose visions of the future are rendered legitimate.[30]

Vicsek highlights that social expectations surrounding automation can take both positive and negative forms, each carrying distinct implications for policy and institutional design. In the optimistic vision, automation is framed as a liberating force that reduces drudgery, enhances productivity and enables the creation of more meaningful, creative and flexible forms of work. This narrative aligns with long-standing technological imaginaries in which innovation drives progress and expands human potential, often accompanied by promises of reskilling, lifelong learning and inclusive growth. Such expectations can mobilize investment and political support but may also downplay structural inequalities and the uneven capacity of workers and institutions to adapt.[31]

On the other hand, the pessimistic vision argues that automation is a source of widespread job displacement, labor market polarization and social instability. In this account, automation threatens existing employment arrangements and exacerbates inequalities by disproportionately affecting high-automation-risk jobs, while concentrating gains among capital owners and more privileged workers. These negative expectations can generate fear, resistance and political backlash, shaping public opinion and policy debates around regulation and social policy responses. Vicsek argues that neither the optimistic nor the pessimistic vision is merely speculative. They both actively shape current decisions by influencing regulatory frameworks, organizational strategies and social policies.[32]

By foregrounding these competing expectations, Vicsek demonstrates that the future of work is not predetermined by technological capabilities alone but is instead co-produced through social imaginaries, institutional choices and power relations. Automation discourse thus functions as a site of contestation over alternative futures, where normative assumptions about work, responsibility and social justice are negotiated. Recognizing this opens analytical space for sociologists to interrogate, how expectations about AI and automation are constructed, whose voices dominate these narratives and how alternative visions, such as those centered on worker agency, collective governance, or redistribution, might be articulated and institutionalized.

The foregoing discussion raises the issue of the heuristics of past discourses on automation, i.e., how various actors have framed the automation problem, solution and future direction. The contribution in this book is to describe and expose these heuristics.

Four Historic Discourses of Automation

The Industrial Revolution produced an early automation discourse taking the form of the Luddite revolt in England in 1811–1812. England was the first industrializing country. The Luddite revolt was an organized movement of masked and armed textile workers who burned and broke machines. The movement was motivated by dissatisfaction with the low wages they received and the technological threat from knitting frames, weaving frames, power looms, shearing frames and gig mills. Another major group in opposition to industrialization and mechanization were the small shop owners, who could not afford the mechanized equipment.[33] The Luddites received rhetorical backing from some members of the aristocracy. In his maiden speech in the UK House of Lords, Lord George Gordon Byron defended the machine-breakers,

> These men never destroyed their looms till they were become useless, worse than useless; till they were become actual impediments to their exertions in obtaining their daily bread. Can you then wonder, that in times like these, when bankruptcy, convicted fraud, and imputed felony, are found in a station not far beneath that of your Lordships, the lowest, though once most useful portion of the people, should forget their duty in their distresses, and become only less guilty than one of their representatives? But while the exalted offender can find means to baffle the law, new capital punishments must be devised, new snares of death must be spread, for the wretched mechanic who is famished into guilt. These men were willing to dig, but the spade was in other hands; they were not ashamed to beg, but there was none to relieve them. Their own means of subsistence were cut off; all other employments pre-occupied; and their excesses, however to be deplored and condemned, can hardly be the subject of surprise.[34]

In other words, the Luddites acted in their own best self-interest when breaking the machines.[35] Their economic survival was dependent on resistance to technology.

Elsewhere in Europe, such as France, there was also local anti-machine resistance, but it was much weaker. The British mechanized textile production was more disruptive to local economies, while in France the traditional labor structures had not been disrupted so quickly. The British Luddites directly confronted factory owners and state power in their resistance, while the French worker resistance to automation was sporadic and less centralized.[36] The term "sabotage" comes from the French word "sabot," a wooden shoe that workers threw into machines to disrupt production.[37] The British state repressed the Luddite rebellion via military crackdowns and long prison sentences/ capital punishments.[38] The presence of worker resistance to automation reveals that human actors can actively shape technological forces to their benefit or at least to reduce harm to them. The Luddite resistance is a form of activist discourse in automation history.

Discussions and concerns about a workless future and technological unemployment go back at least to the 1930s. This fear of technological unemployment tends to be enlarged during periods of heightened unemployment, such as the Great Depression and periodically in the early 1960s and the 1980s. In the 1940s and 1950s, the post-World War II economic boom created an optimistic image of technology, though some labor unions were alarmed about the negative employment effects of automation. 1948 was the beginning of "automation" as a household word in the US national debate, which originates from a description of self-operating mechanical and electronic controls in car factories. By the 1970s, there were anxieties around a post-industrial society, as manufacturing became robotized and the service sector introduced computers.[39] Education and knowledge work became the basis of social advancement rather than automation-depleted factory work.[40] Similarly, the analysis of newspaper coverage shows that between the 1950s and 2020, there were continuous anxieties around a workless future, even as the technologies are different in different time periods.[41] The lamentation about the negative ramifications of automation on society may be considered the resigned position in automation history.

New technologies are generally introduced in the context of market innovation. Market forces, in turn, are often presented as natural laws, while obscuring the underlying social relations that make the introduction of technology possible.[42] Business and political leaders and the mainstream financial press frame technological innovation in the context of supporting returns to shareholder value and generating economic activity, employment and tax revenues, thus ensuring the stability of the present economic order. The social expectations of automation originating from and working within market capitalist forces represents a particular narrative which integrates the social effects of automation within the status quo. Here, I do not refer to the status quo as the type of occupation, skill requirements for jobs, individual workers or capitalists or the prevalent form of technologies, which may be seen as continuously changeable. Rather, 'the status quo' refers to the use of technologies within a market capitalist framework, involving the production of goods and services for private profit and the expansion of a labor market relationship with human workers. The more the technologies change, the more the economic system stays the same.

Lastly, there has been an automation discourse around an extrapolation of Moore's Law, the doubling of computing capacity. Gordon Moore was the director of Fairchild Semi-conductor and predicted in 1965 that the complexity of the integrated memory chip would double every 18 months.[43] The extrapolation is that an improvement in computing capacity will enable machines to first slowly then rapidly replace human labor tasks. As noted in the introduction, in the 1930s, the leading economist John Maynard Keynes had predicted a rapid decline in the average work week due to the improvements in machine technology.[44] The presumption of the rise of leisure society and the diminution of work as an important part of human identity follows a utopian or futurist ideological tradition. The futurists respond to the counterpoint that high technological unemployment had not been obtained with prior technical innovations by asserting that "this time is different." In other words, the current crop of technology such as AI will escalate technological unemployment.[45]

The Four Discourses on Automation

The four discourses of automation and the analytical labels I have used to describe them are summarized in the following table (Table 2.1).

The activist discourse resists the blind application of automation, and they look to actively shape the adoption of new technologies. Labor unions are the main representatives in that discourse because they are the most negatively affected by employers introducing new technologies. They are, at times, assisted by liberal politicians, who think that by taking the side of organized labor, they can draw a sharp contrast with business leaders who are eager to

TABLE 2.1 The Four Discourses

Discourse	*Description*	*Proponents*
Activist	Resistance to or active shaping of automation, job guarantee	Labor unions, liberal politicians
Resigned	Lamentation/ critique of the negative effects of automation	Intellectuals, media, artists
Status quo	Automation reinforces capital accumulation and upskilling/ retraining labor	Business leaders, consultancies, political leaders
Futurist	Automation brings material abundance, reduced work/ more leisure, UBI, welfare redistribution	Technology business leaders, intellectuals

automate their workforce. It is doubtful that unions are capable of blocking automation in the long term, but in the short term they may slow it down or achieve satisfactory collective bargaining agreements, and they can express their sentiments in their public statements and advocacy work. In the policy domain, calls for a national or federal job guarantee are very compatible with the activist orientation.

The resigned discourse focuses on the negative social effects of automation, whether they relate to mass unemployment, diminished social solidarity/cohesion, or deteriorating health among the displaced workers. Even if automation does not reduce jobs, it might deskill existing work, increase certain low-wage jobs or come with more surveillance or stress in remaining jobs. Automation along with other institutional labor market and social policy changes could result in heightened economic inequality, which lowers the legitimacy of the political and economic system. Academics, intellectuals, artists and liberal media are primarily behind the diagnosis of the downsides of technological change. Artists depict the downsides of technological unemployment in their novels and movie scripts.

The status quo discourse presumes that automation is an inherent process in the market-based capitalist system, and it reinforces the existing political and economic system. The displacement of some jobs is more than compensated by the demand for new worker skills to implement the technologies or work in new industries where technology does not have a comparative advantage to labor. This discourse focuses on job training, education and workforce development and the obligation of workers to be flexible to ensure their continuing relevance in the economy. Business leaders, consultants, some labor unions and most political leaders orient their automation discourse according to the status quo.

The futurist discourse points to the positive social effects of automation. Extrapolating from Moore's Law, according to which computing capacity doubles every 18 months, the futurists assume that automation will bring about material abundance for all of humanity. As machines manage more labor tasks, work hours decrease and leisure hours increase. Futurist advocates assume that the redistribution of resources from robot owners to the general public taking the form of techno-communism, universal basic income or universal basic services will happen. Advocates in this group tend to be technology company business leaders and liberal intellectuals. The tech business leaders use a discourse that is different from status quo, in part, because they are selling their automating technologies to other companies, investors and the general public as being able to reduce their payroll headcount. Whatever their underlying motives are, at the level of discourse, the tech leaders are selling the public a futurist vision of social life. Liberal intellectuals have a more idealistic vision where leisure time is equated with human freedom. They are ideologically committed to a future where most people can dispose of their time just as freely as themselves.

The Theoretical Relationship of the Four Discourses on Automation

Before I turn in detail to these four discourses of automation, I lay out the theoretical relationship between these four perspectives. I posit that the four perspectives can be analyzed in normative/ positivist, dystopia/utopia, structure/ agency and major/ minor social change conceptual frameworks.

Positivism vs. Normativism

The automation and future of work discourse contain both positive (what is happening to work) and normative elements (what should happen to work). Positivist social science puts the emphasis on the former but given that a lot of social science research has policy-relevance its link to the normative cannot easily be disentangled. In fact, while social science methods are positivist, the choice of research topics have a normative origin and the policy implications have a normative destination/ ideal end state. For example, empirically documenting income inequality is *preceded* by the inequality researchers' desire to reduce or contain what he/she considers 'excessive' inequality. Tony Atkinson, the late British economist and foremost expert on global inequality, pointed in his book to his normative goal "to reduce inequality below its current level, in the belief that the present level of inequality is excessive."[46] Atkinson had not specified a set level of desirable level of inequality, but he was not pleased by the level of inequality confronting him at the time of writing his book. The fact that he and other inequality experts have chosen to study inequality is very much reflected in their normative commitment to reduce inequality.

Automation is part of the future without work imaginary, which involves an automated and a non-automated future. This imagined future consists of what people believe *will* happen to the future of work (positive) and what they think *should* happen to the future of work (normative), i.e., there will be a workless future due to technology (automated) or some jobs will change, but we will still have work into the indefinite future (non-automated). Table 2.2 lays out the four visions, where I put advocates in four categories: futurists, status quo, resignation and activist.

The futurist's view is that the displacement of jobs due to technology will likely happen (automated, positive) and is a desirable utopia (automated,

TABLE 2.2 Positivist and Normative dimensions of Automation Discourse

Automation discourse	*Automated (positive)*	*Non-automated (positive)*
Automated (normative)	Futurist	Status quo
Non-automated (normative)	Resigned	Activist

normative). Moore's Law continues to be in effect and encroaches on more and more human labor tasks, whether they deal with manual or cognitive skills, routine or non-routine ones. Work will and should be expunged as the core element of human self-worth and identity. The polar opposite is the activist view, where social actors are fighting to preserve their jobs or ensure job retraining options or advocate a job guarantee, thus blocking a future without work (non-automated positive). They also do not find the future without work to be desirable, which gives them the motivation to advocate for job preservation and anti-automation resistance in the first place (non-automated normative). The remaining two automation visions do not neatly align positive and the normative positions.

The status quo position is that a future without work is not in the realm of possibility (non-automated positive). Their discursive framework presumes continuous labor shortages, where the replacement of some workers is compensated by an increase in labor demand elsewhere in the economy. Short-term labor market frictions, such as a temporary increase in unemployment due to technology need to be countered by job retraining, but those frictions do not translate into long-term labor market and hence societal instability. As for the normative position on the future without work, the status quo position is placed in the automated camp. At first glance, the continuous employer complaint about labor shortage suggests that they do not find a workless future to be desirable. Workers should be looking to retrain for jobs that have not yet been automated and make their societal labor contribution. But most business leaders frame these labor shortages as a bug that needs resolution. They are attracted to the idea of technology as a deus ex machina, a miraculous intervention that can resolve a plot. In other words, they desire machines that can automate all work tasks, so they don't need to worry about human resource issues, such as hiring, promotion, compensation, retention, employee motivation, as well as activist labor strikes, labor arbitration and other workplace conflicts. From a Marxist perspective, there is a contradiction in these normative sentiments of business leaders because the surplus value in a capitalist economy derives from the exploitation of workers, and to the extent that labor is automated, no more surplus value is forthcoming, hence the end of the capitalist status quo.[47] As long as the capitalist economy produces a labor shortage in some sector, there is no way to test this Marxist proposition.

The resigned perspective agrees with the futurists that a future without work is already a reality, especially for workers and communities that had been heavily impacted by automation (automated positive). It is not as clear as for the futurists whether the resigned view agrees with the statement that all jobs will be replaced by technology given that their views are influenced by a historic-empirical rather than future-oriented angle. But they are worried about future automation waves replicating the societal harms that they have previously observed. Similar to the activists but unlike the futurists, the resigned proponents believe that a future without work is normatively extremely undesirable (non-automated normative). The more job precarity, the more societal instability there will be. If it was up to the resigned view, they would push the 'stop automation' button.

Utopia vs. Dystopia

The normative discussion of automation presumes positive and negative visions (Table 2.3). The visions on the future of work can be utopian or dystopian. Utopia is a desirable future, and dystopia is an undesirable future. The term 'utopia' was coined by Thomas More in his book *Utopia* in 1516. It is derived from the Greek, which translates as "no place," but it is pronounced the same way as "eutopia," which is a good place and is the intended meaning of the term. The image of a harmoniously ordered society derived from Plato's *Republic*, where virtues and philosopher-kings rule the society.[48] In contrast, dystopia denotes the "bad place" and is derived from John Stuart Mill's 1868 critique of oppressive British land tenure policies in Ireland, which did not give any land security to Irish tenants and kept their rents high.[49]

In the future of work discourse, the most positive utopian vision is presented by the futurists, because of their presumption of universally shared economic abundance derived from automation and the redistribution of income to the entire community. At the opposite end is the resigned position, where only the negative societal impacts of automation are described. The resigned argue that the overall economic abundance is nullified by insufficient redistribution, and even if certain jobs have not been automated yet, they are often precarious or poorly paid. The two visions that are neither clearly utopian or dystopian are the status quo and activist discourses. The activist view is somewhat more utopian, because workers have a somewhat more favorable outcome in their resistance to job displacement as opposed to the status quo haphazardness of looking for new jobs and relying on job training to secure future employment after they are displaced by technology. The call for a job guarantee is dystopian for futurists, but activists see positive societal ramifications if that demand gets realized. The activist position is clearly less utopian than futurism, because the former foregrounds the capital-labor conflict, while the latter views it as resolved or irrelevant to society.

TABLE 2.3 Utopia vs. Dystopia in the Four Discourses

Dystopian		<--------->	*Utopian*
Resigned	Status quo	Activist	Futurist

Agency and Social Change

The four automation discourses present different views around the scope of human agency in shaping technological change in the workplace, and the scope of the social change expected. The power of social structures or social facts/ rules that constrain human behavior and direct individual behavior independent from the will of individuals emerged from the early French sociologist Emile Durkheim's perspective. Durkheim argued that social facts involving institutions, norms, legal systems, moral codes, religious beliefs and roles shape individuals at the macro level, while individuals are reminded by other community members and via shame and punishment about the importance of such structures at the micro level. Social facts pre-exist and constrain individuals, dictating how they are raised, educated and behave.[50]

The second view is that human agency plays an important role in individual action. It emerged from Max Weber's theory of social action. The agency perspective says that humans are creative, rational and autonomous. They are meaning-making subjects that have individual agency. Individuals may be driven by four different ideologies for social action: these include instrumental rationality, or calculable goals like profits; value rationality, or religious and aesthetic considerations; affective, or emotional reasons like anger, envy or love; and traditional, or customs that are common for a culture or ethnicity.[51] But regardless of their ideological orientation; they can choose among them at any moment and social situation. For Weber, the goal of social scientists is to understand (*verstehen*) people's motives from their own perspective.

The third intermediate position points to the dialectical relationship between structure and agency, where structures and individuals shape social action. The dialectical position is associated with Anthony Giddens (structuration theory) and Pierre Bourdieu (habitus).[52] In Giddens' Structuration Theory, the structure-agency dualism (two separate things) is replaced by the duality (two sides of the same coin). Individuals use social structures (rules and resources) to perform actions. For example, people use language (structure) to communicate their ideas (agency). Social life is recursive, which means that social actors continually recreate these activities through, how they express themselves. Agents are reflexive, which means that they constantly monitor their actions and the social context. If agents choose to act outside the rules, they can modify the structure itself.[53] In Bourdieu's habitus theory, social structures are internalized by individuals who reproduce these structures through their everyday actions. Individuals operate within a field, or a social arena that has its own rules and hierarchy (education system, art scene, political system etc.). They possess different amounts of economic, social and cultural capital to generate personal advantages in their field. Economic capital is money; social capital is the network of people one knows; and cultural capital is the knowledge, tastes and credentials. Habitus and fields form a limiting structure, but it can be changed via individual agency and a mismatch between the two.[54]

In classical sociology, Marxism involves social structures (the economic base and superstructure) and social agency (class consciousness) that produce social outcomes. The economic base involves the means of production, such as technology, land and resources and the relations of production, which is the class hierarchy between capitalists and workers. That base is a constraint on actors' freedom. The superstructure is the beliefs, institutions and traditions that maintain the capitalist status quo. On the other hand, workers potentially have agency when they can overcome false consciousness, which is the belief that the capitalist social structures are fair and just. They can develop their own class consciousness to challenge and overthrow the capitalist system. Social structures are not static, but they contain contradictions between the collective form of production and the privatized and concentrated form of ownership and distribution of resources. These contradictions can be exploited by agents seeking social change.[55]

The scope of social change has been studied in various ways. Large-scale changes involve a change in social institutions, such as the replacement of feudal landlords by capitalist merchants and manufacturers, or the reconfiguration of state power in political revolutions.[56] Small-scale changes involve minor modifications of existing social and political institutions or a seamless integration of new inputs, e.g. technologies, without any institutional changes.[57]

The following table (Table 2.4) illustrates how the four automation discourses relate to agency/ structure and social change.

In the structure-agency framework, the activists have the most agency. They do not accept the resigned position that exclusively focuses on lamenting the negative automation effects. They believe that human action can make automation produce desirable social outcomes. These actions may involve labor strikes, public testimonies, collective bargaining agreements, or other forms of social struggle. The resigned position is on the opposite side of the spectrum as their explanations for the negative effects of automation are structural. The resigned would normatively favor that activists can limit and reverse these negative effects, but they are not foregrounding activism in their own discourse.

The status quo and futurist positions are intermediate in the structure-agency framework. The status quo contains the structural element of automation being a necessary part of generating profit and economic growth, but also the agentic element of job training, workforce development and minor tweaks to

TABLE 2.4 Agency and Structure in the Four Discourses

Automation discourse	*Small*	*<-Social change->*	*Large*
Agency		Activist	
	Status quo		Futurist
Structure		Resigned	

government regulations to overcome any frictions arising from technological change. The futurists' attachment to Moore's law bringing technical and social progress is very structuralist, but their praise of leisure society as a desirable end state is much more agentic than the resigned view. For the resigned, the leisure of the presently displaced workers presents itself as a structural trap, while for the futurists universal leisure is an agentic opportunity awaiting society in the not-so-distant future.

The biggest anticipated social change comes from the futurist vision, because the realization of a workless future requires a change in present political institutions that are focused on maximum employment, tax revenues and business profits. Many futurist advocates presume that the increase in the economic surplus will be redistributed fairly, but do not specify the mechanism by which such redistribution is accomplished. The smallest social change is articulated by the status quo perspective. The addition of new technologies may be disruptive for competing businesses or for displaced workers, and it may temporarily increase social welfare spending, e.g., job training, education or unemployment expenses. But in the status quo perspective all new technologies can easily be integrated into existing social structures, while delivering on the various objectives of social actors. Displaced workers will obtain new employment with better pay, automating firms increase their profits and governments obtain more tax revenues from the enlarged labor productivity.

I consider activist and resigned views as intermediate social change. Activists do not assume that automation will automatically produce desirable social outcomes, as the status quo. They also do not believe that a post-work, post-capitalist future will emerge through automation technologies, as the futurists claim. They are focused on reshaping their social environment so that job displacements are minimized, job creation is maximized, government social programs are put in place, and employers are held accountable for their automation decisions. The resigned view agrees with the activists that automation does produce some social change, and they similarly oppose the automation-positive accounts of status quo and futurists. Their focus is on the negative consequences of technological change, so that suggests a greater scope of social change than the status quo view. The status quo makes an assumption about the stability of the social fabric, while the resigned position claims a fraying of that fabric. On the other hand, the envisioned social change for the resigned is much smaller than for futurists, because they do not assume a desirable leisure society for all, but rather an undesirable leisure society for some, negatively affecting the marginalized populations at the highest risk of having their jobs automated.

Conclusion

Automation is not just a labor market phenomenon affecting workers and businesses, but it is a social discourse, where normative and positivist dispositions play important roles. Automation discourse is deeply embedded in the literature on a socio-technical imaginary and the sociology of expectations. My main contribution in this chapter is that there is no unified social discourse in automation and the imaginary in the future of work. Rather there are four different discourses based on four ideological orientations of social actors. I call them the activists, resigned, status quo and futurists. These four positions stand in relationship to long-running theoretical debates in the social sciences, such as normativism/positivism, utopia/dystopia, big vs. small social change, agency/ structure. The remainder of this book describes these four discourses.

Notes

1 Jasanoff, Sheila, and Sang-Hyun Kim. "Containing the Atom: Sociotechnical Imaginaries and Nuclear Regulation in the U.S. and South Korea." *Minerva* 47, no. 2 (2009): 119–46. p. 120.
2 Jasanoff, Sheila, and Sang-Hyun Kim. "Sociotechnical imaginaries and national energy policies." *Science as Culture* 22, no. 2 (2013): 189–96. Also see Hecht, Gabrielle. *The Radiance of France*. Cambridge: MIT Press, 2009.
3 Jasanoff, Sheila, and Sang-Hyun Kim. "Containing the Atom: Sociotechnical Imaginaries and Nuclear Regulation in the U.S. and South Korea." *Minerva* 47, no. 2 (2009): 119–46. p. 121.
4 Jasanoff, Sheila. "Future Imperfect: Science, Technology, and the Imaginations of Modernity." In *Dreamscapes of Modernity: Sociotechnical Imaginaries and the Fabrication of Power*, edited by Sheila Jasanoff and Sang-Hyun Kim, 1–33. Chicago: Chicago University Press, 2005. p. 4.
5 Jasanoff, "Future Imperfect", p. 19.
6 Castoriadis, Cornelius. *The Imaginary Institution of Society*. Cambridge: MIT Press, 1987.
7 Anderson, Benedict. *Imagined Communities: Reflections on the Origin and Spread of Nationalism*. London and New York: Verso, 1991.
8 Foucault, Michel. *Discipline and Punish: The Birth of the Prison*. New York: Vintage, 1979.
9 Appadurai, Arjun. *Modernity at Large: Cultural Dimensions of Globalization*. Minneapolis: University Minnesota Press, 1996.
10 Jasanoff, Sheila, and Sang-Hyun Kim. 2009. "Containing the Atom: Sociotechnical Imaginaries and Nuclear Regulation in the U.S. and South Korea." *Minerva* 47, no. 2 (2009): 119–46. p. 123.
11 Winner, Langdon. 1986. "Do artifacts have politics?" In *The Whale and the Reactor: A Search for Limits in an Age of High Technology*, 19–39. Chicago: University of Chicago Press.
12 Jasanoff, Sheila. "Technology as a Site and Object of Politics." In *Oxford Handbook of Contextual Political Analysis,* edited by C. Tilly, and R. Goodin, 745–63. Oxford: Oxford University Press, 2006.
13 Jasanoff and Kim, "Containing the Atom", p. 134.
14 Sadowski, Jathan, and Roy Bendor. "Selling Smartness: Corporate Narratives and the Smart City as a Sociotechnical Imaginary." *Science, Technology, & Human Values* 44, no. 3 (2019): 540–63.
15 Rudek, Tadeusz Józef. "Capturing the Invisible. Sociotechnical Imaginaries of Energy. The Critical Overview." *Science and Public Policy* 49, no. 2 (2022): 219–45.
16 Braun, Robert, and Richard Randell. "Futuramas of the Present: The "Driver Problem" in the Autonomous Vehicle Sociotechnical Imaginary." *Humanities and Social Sciences Communications* 7, no. 1 (2020): 1–10.

17 Smallman, Melanie. "'Nothing to Do with the Science': How an Elite Sociotechnical Imaginary Cements Policy Resistance to Public Perspectives on Science and Technology through the Machinery of Government." *Social Studies of Science* 50, no. 4 (2020): 589–608.
18 Macedo, Stephen, and Frances Lee. *In Covid's Wake: How Our Politics Failed Us.* Princeton: Princeton University Press, 2025.
19 Laba, Nataliia. "Whose Imagination? Conflicting Narratives and Sociotechnical Futures of Visual Generative AI." *AI & Society* (2025): 1–17.
20 Avis, James. "Socio-Technical Imaginary of the Fourth Industrial Revolution and Its Implications for Vocational Education and Training: A Literature Review." *Journal of Vocational Education & Training* 70, no. 3 (2018): 337–63.
21 Schiølin, Kasper. "Revolutionary Dreams: Future Essentialism and the Sociotechnical Imaginary of the Fourth Industrial Revolution in Denmark." *Social Studies of Science* 50, no. 4 (2020): 542–66.
22 Vicsek, Lilla. "Artificial Intelligence and the Future of Work–Lessons from the Sociology of Expectations." *International Journal of Sociology and Social Policy* 41, no. 7/8 (2021): 842–61.
23 Brown, Nick, Brian Rappert, and Andrew Webster. "Introducing Contested Futures: From Looking into the Future to Looking at the Future." In *Contested Futures: A Sociology of Prospective Techno-Science*, edited by Nick Brown, Brian Rappert, and Andrew Webster, 3–20. New York: Routledge, 2017.
24 Konrad, Kornelia. "The Social Dynamics of Expectations: The Interaction of Collective and Actor-Specific Expectations on Electronic Commerce and Interactive Television." *Technology Analysis & Strategic Management* 18, no. 3–4 (2006): 429–44.
25 Borup, Mads, Nik Brown, Kornelia Konrad, and Harro Van Lente. "The Sociology of Expectations in Science and Technology." *Technology Analysis & Strategic Management* 18, no. 3–4 (2006): 285–98.
26 Borup et al. "The Sociology of Expectations in Science and Technology."
27 Borup et al. "The Sociology of Expectations in Science and Technology."
28 Kharpal, Arjun. "Jeff Bezos Says AI Is in an Industrial Bubble but Society Will Get 'Gigantic' Benefits from the Tech." *CNBC*, October 3, 2025.
29 Beckert, Jens. *Imagined Futures: Fictional Expectations and Capitalist Dynamics.* Cambridge, MA: Harvard University Press, 2016.
30 Vicsek. "Artificial Intelligence and the Future of Work."
31 Vicsek. "Artificial Intelligence and the Future of Work."
32 Vicsek. "Artificial Intelligence and the Future of Work."
33 Manuel, Frank E. "The Luddite Movement in France." *The Journal of Modern History* 10, no. 2 (1938): 180–211.
34 Byron, George Gordon. "Lord Byron Defends the Luddites in His Maiden Speech in the House of Lords." HistoryofInformation.com, 1812. https://historyofinformation.com/detail.php?id=4654
35 Mueller, Gavin. *Breaking Things at Work: The Luddites Are Right about Why You Hate Your Job.* New York: Verso, 2021.
36 Manuel, "The Luddite Movement in France."
37 Srinivasan, Vivek. "Sabotage." *Medium*, March 9, 2024.
38 Poitras, Geoffrey. "The Luddite Trials: Radical Suppression and the Administration of Criminal Justice." *Journal for the Study of Radicalism* 14, no. 1 (2020): 121–66.
39 Bix, Amy Sue. *Inventing Ourselves out of Jobs?* Baltimore: Johns Hopkins University Press, 2000.
40 Bell, Daniel. *The Coming of Post-Industrial Society: A Venture in Social Forecasting.* New York: Basic Books, 1973.

41 Weber, Matthew S., William C. Barley, and Euna Mehnaz Kahn. "Artificial Intelligence and the Power of the Past to Predict the Future of Work." International Communication Association Conference, 2021.
42 MacKenzie, David. and Judy Wajcman, (Eds). *The Social Shaping of Technology, 2nd ed.* Buckingham: Open University Press, 1999.
43 Van Lente, Harro. "Navigating foresight in a sea of expectations: lessons from the sociology of expectations." *Technology Analysis & Strategic Management* 24, no. 8 (2012): 769–82.
44 Keynes, John Maynard. "Economic Possibilities for our Grandchildren (1930)." In *Essays in Persuasion,* 358–73. New York: Harcourt Brace, 1932.
45 Ford, Martin. *Rise of the Robots: Technology and the Threat of a Jobless Future.* New York: Basic Books, 2015. Wajcman, Judy. " Automation: Is It Really Different This Time?" *The British Journal of Sociology* 68, no. 1 (2017): 119–27.
46 Atkinson, Anthony. *Inequality: What Can Be Done.* Cambridge: Harvard University Press, 2015, p. 9.
47 Ferschli, Benjamin. 2024. "Capitalism Without Workers: On the Impossibility of Automation and Its Relation to the Question of Value." In *De-Automating the Future*, edited by Johannes Fehrle, Marlon Lieber and J. Jesse Ramirez, 135–57. Leiden: Brill.
48 Braga, Corin. "Utopia: Between Eutopia and Outopia." *Transylvanian Review* 26, no. Suppl 2 (2017): 167–76.
49 De Mattos, Laura Valladão. "John Stuart Mill and the Irish Land Question: An Illustration of His View on Social Institutions." *Journal of the History of Economic Thought* 42, no. 1 (2020): 43–60. Mill, John Stuart. "The State of Ireland." UK Parliamentary Speech, March 12, 1868. https://oll.libertyfund.org/titles/kinzer-the-collected-works-of-john-stuart-mill-volume-xxviii-public-and-parliamentary-speeches-part-i#lf0223-28_label_1164
50 Durkheim, Emile. *The Rules of Sociological Method* (8th ed.). University of Chicago Press: Chicago, 1938.
51 Weber, Max. *Economy and Society: An Outline of Interpretive Sociology.* Berkeley: University of California Press, 1978.
52 Tan, Sherman. "Understanding the "Structure" and the "Agency" Debate in the Social Sciences." *Moderator's Note* 37 (2011): 37–50.
53 Giddens, Anthony. *The Constitution of Society: Outline of the Theory of Structuration.* Cambridge: Polity Press, 1984.
54 Bourdieu, Pierre *The Logic of Practice* (R. Nice, Trans.). Redwood City: Stanford University Press, 1990.
55 Callinicos, Alex. *Making History: Agency, Structure, and Change in Social Theory.* Vol. 3. Leiden: Brill, 2004. Marx, Karl. *A Contribution to the Critique of Political Economy.* New York: International Publishers, 1859.
56 Marx, Karl, and Friedrich Engels. *The Communist Manifesto.* London, England: Penguin Classics, 2015. Skocpol, Theda. *States and Social Revolutions: A Comparative Analysis of France, Russia, and China.* New York: Cambridge University Press, 1979.
57 Historical institutionalists refer to 'layering' as new elements attached to existing institutions that gradually change their status and structure. Streeck, Wolfgang, and Thelen, Kathleen. *Beyond Continuity: Institutional Change in Advanced Political Economies.* Oxford: Oxford University Press, 2005.

References

Anderson, Benedict. *Imagined Communities: Reflections on the Origin and Spread of Nationalism.* London and New York: Verso, 1991.

Appadurai, Arjun. *Modernity at Large: Cultural Dimensions of Globalization.* Minneapolis: University of Minnesota Press, 1996.

Atkinson, Anthony. *Inequality: What Can Be Done*. Cambridge, MA: Harvard University Press, 2015.

Avis, James. "Socio-Technical Imaginary of the Fourth Industrial Revolution and Its Implications for Vocational Education and Training: A Literature Review." *Journal of Vocational Education & Training* 70, no. 3 (2018): 337–63.

Beckert, Jens. *Imagined Futures: Fictional Expectations and Capitalist Dynamics*. Cambridge, MA: Harvard University Press, 2016.

Bell, Daniel. *The Coming of Post-Industrial Society: A Venture in Social Forecasting*. New York: Basic Books, 1973.

Bix, Amy Sue. *Inventing Ourselves Out of Jobs?* Baltimore, MD: Johns Hopkins University Press, 2000.

Borup, Mads, Nik Brown, Kornelia Konrad, and Harro Van Lente. "The Sociology of Expectations in Science and Technology." *Technology Analysis & Strategic Management* 18, no. 3–4 (2006): 285–98.

Bourdieu, Pierre. *The Logic of Practice*. Translated by Richard Nice. Redwood City, CA: Stanford University Press, 1990.

Braga, Corin. "Utopia: Between Eutopia and Outopia." *Transylvanian Review* 26, suppl. 2 (2017): 167–76.

Braun, Robert, and Richard Randell. "Futuramas of the Present: The "Driver Problem" in the Autonomous Vehicle Sociotechnical Imaginary." *Humanities and Social Sciences Communications* 7, no. 1 (2020): 1–10.

Brown, Nik, Brian Rappert, and Andrew Webster. "Introducing Contested Futures: From Looking into the Future to Looking at the Future." In *Contested Futures: A Sociology of Prospective Techno-Science*, edited by Nik Brown, Brian Rappert, and Andrew Webster, 3–20. New York: Routledge, 2017.

Byron, George Gordon. "Lord Byron Defends the Luddites in His Maiden Speech in the House of Lords." HistoryofInformation.com, 1812. https://historyofinformation.com/detail.php?id=4654

Callinicos, Alex. *Making History: Agency, Structure, and Change in Social Theory. Vol. 3*. Leiden: Brill, 2004.

Castoriadis, Cornelius. *The Imaginary Institution of Society*. Cambridge, MA: MIT Press, 1987.

De Mattos, Laura Valladão. "John Stuart Mill and the Irish Land Question: An Illustration of His View on Social Institutions." *Journal of the History of Economic Thought* 42, no. 1 (2020): 43–60.

Durkheim, Emile. *The Rules of Sociological Method*. 8th ed. Chicago, IL: University of Chicago Press, 1938.

Ferschli, Benjamin. "Capitalism Without Workers: On the Impossibility of Automation and Its Relation to the Question of Value." In *De-Automating the Future*, edited by Johannes Fehrle, Marlon Lieber, and J. Jesse Ramirez, 135–57. Leiden: Brill, 2024.

Ford, Martin. *Rise of the Robots: Technology and the Threat of a Jobless Future*. New York: Basic Books, 2015.

Foucault, Michel. *Discipline and Punish: The Birth of the Prison*. New York: Vintage, 1979.

Giddens, Anthony. *The Constitution of Society: Outline of the Theory of Structuration*. Cambridge: Polity Press, 1984.

Hecht, Gabrielle. *The Radiance of France*. Cambridge, MA: MIT Press, 2009.

Jasanoff, Sheila. "Future Imperfect: Science, Technology, and the Imaginations of Modernity." In *Dreamscapes of Modernity: Sociotechnical Imaginaries and the Fabrication of Power*, edited by Sheila Jasanoff and Sang-Hyun Kim, 1–33. Chicago, IL: University of Chicago Press, 2005.

Jasanoff, Sheila. "Technology as a Site and Object of Politics." In *The Oxford Handbook of Contextual Political Analysis,* edited by Charles Tilly and Robert Goodin, 745–63. Oxford: Oxford University Press, 2006.

Jasanoff, Sheila, and Sang-Hyun Kim. "Containing the Atom: Sociotechnical Imaginaries and Nuclear Regulation in the U.S. and South Korea." *Minerva* 47, no. 2 (2009): 119–46.

Jasanoff, Sheila, and Sang-Hyun Kim. "Sociotechnical Imaginaries and National Energy Policies." *Science as Culture* 22, no. 2 (2013): 189–96.

Keynes, John Maynard. "Economic Possibilities for Our Grandchildren (1930)." In *Essays in Persuasion*, 358–73. New York: Harcourt Brace, 1932.

Kharpal, Arjun. "Jeff Bezos Says AI Is in an Industrial Bubble but Society Will Get 'Gigantic' Benefits from the Tech." *CNBC*, October 3, 2025.

Konrad, Kornelia. "The Social Dynamics of Expectations: The Interaction of Collective and Actor-Specific Expectations on Electronic Commerce and Interactive Television." *Technology Analysis & Strategic Management* 18, no. 3–4 (2006): 429–44.

Laba, Nataliia. "Whose Imagination? Conflicting Narratives and Sociotechnical Futures of Visual Generative AI." *AI & Society* (2025): 1–17.

Macedo, Stephen, and Frances Lee. *In Covid's Wake: How Our Politics Failed Us.* Princeton, NJ: Princeton University Press, 2025.

MacKenzie, Donald, and Judy Wajcman, eds. *The Social Shaping of Technology.* 2nd ed. Buckingham: Open University Press, 1999.Manuel, Frank E. "The Luddite Movement in France." *The Journal of Modern History* 10, no. 2 (1938): 180–211.

Marx, Karl. *A Contribution to the Critique of Political Economy.* New York: International Publishers, 1859.

Marx, Karl, and Friedrich Engels. *The Communist Manifesto.* London: Penguin Classics, 2015.

Mill, John Stuart. "The State of Ireland." Parliamentary Speech, March 12, 1868. In *The Collected Works of John Stuart Mill,* vol. 28, Public and Parliamentary Speeches, Part I. Online Library of Liberty.

Mueller, Gavin. *Breaking Things at Work: The Luddites Are Right about Why You Hate Your Job.* New York: Verso, 2021.

Poitras, Geoffrey. "The Luddite Trials: Radical Suppression and the Administration of Criminal Justice." *Journal for the Study of Radicalism* 14, no. 1 (2020): 121–66.

Rudek, Tadeusz Józef. "Capturing the Invisible. Sociotechnical Imaginaries of Energy. The Critical Overview." *Science and Public Policy* 49, no. 2 (2022): 219–45.

Sadowski, Jathan, and Roy Bendor. "Selling Smartness: Corporate Narratives and the Smart City as a Sociotechnical Imaginary." *Science, Technology, & Human Values* 44, no. 3 (2019): 540–63.

Schiølin, Kasper. "Revolutionary Dreams: Future Essentialism and the Sociotechnical Imaginary of the Fourth Industrial Revolution in Denmark." *Social Studies of Science* 50, no. 4 (2020): 542–66.

Skocpol, Theda. *States and Social Revolutions: A Comparative Analysis of France, Russia, and China.* New York: Cambridge University Press, 1979.

Smallman, Melanie. "'Nothing to Do with the Science': How an Elite Sociotechnical Imaginary Cements Policy Resistance to Public Perspectives on Science and Technology through the Machinery of Government." *Social Studies of Science* 50, no. 4 (2020): 589–608.

Srinivasan, Vivek. "Sabotage." *Medium*, March 9, 2024.

Streeck, Wolfgang, and Kathleen Thelen. *Beyond Continuity: Institutional Change in Advanced Political Economies*. Oxford: Oxford University Press, 2005.

Tan, Sherman. "Understanding the 'Structure' and the 'Agency' Debate in the Social Sciences." *Moderator's Note* 37 (2011): 37–50.

Van Lente, Harro. "Navigating Foresight in a Sea of Expectations: Lessons from the Sociology of Expectations." *Technology Analysis & Strategic Management* 24, no. 8 (2012): 769–82.

Vicsek, Lilla. "Artificial Intelligence and the Future of Work – Lessons from the Sociology of Expectations." *International Journal of Sociology and Social Policy* 41, no. 7/8 (2021): 842–61.

Wajcman, Judy. "Automation: Is It Really Different This Time?" *The British Journal of Sociology* 68, no. 1 (2017): 119–27.Weber, Matthew S., William C. Barley, and Euna Mehnaz Kahn. "Artificial Intelligence and the Power of the Past to Predict the Future of Work." Paper presented at the International Communication Association Conference, 2021.

Weber, Max. *Economy and Society: An Outline of Interpretive Sociology*. Berkeley: University of California Press, 1978.

Winner, Langdon. *The Whale and the Reactor: A Search for Limits in an Age of High Technology*, 19–39. Chicago, IL: University of Chicago Press, 1986.

3

THE ACTIVISTS

The 2023 Hollywood writers' strike against AI deployment and the Luddite resistance to deskilling and technological displacement in early nineteenth-century Britain discussed earlier show that workers are not passively accepting their fate. These workers believe that resistance is a viable and healthy response to preserve their jobs and dignity. Consider this quote by one of the striking workers, Raphael Bob-Waksberg,

> Right now, we're at a place where if we say, "It's us or the machines," they're going to pick us because they know the machines aren't good enough to completely replace us right now. This is the time when we [Hollywood writers] have the leverage and the power to get some of this [job protection] into our contract before it's too late. And not rely on the studios believing in the greater good or believing in our rational arguments that this would be better, but to actually just exert our power and make them listen. And that's what we did.[1]

Workers are not passive objects, but active subjects that want to reshape the terms of automation.

The academic literature has documented numerous cases of workers' anti-automation activism. *Kellogg et al.* find that workers become "algoactivists," where they want AI algorithms that reshape their work to be fairer, more accountable and more transparent.[2] Worker resistance in general has a variety of motives, such as deflecting abuse, limiting the intensity of work, preserving autonomy and increasing control over their own working conditions.[3] The occupational structure impacts the level of worker resistance: occupationally diverse industrial unions accept automation, because some workers might

DOI: 10.4324/9781003780236-4

benefit from automation, while some of the harmed workers are expected to undergo job training. In contrast, homogeneous craft unions are more opposed to automation, because they feel the more concentrated negative impacts of new technologies.[4] The lack of managerial communication and the human factors can also impact worker resistance to new technologies.[5]

Mueller argues that the political left should resist new technologies, which often have a detrimental impact on workers. Technology opposition taking the form of a new Luddism is about increasing worker autonomy while rejecting a blind focus on productivity for the sake of profits. This opposes the futurist Marxist position of harnessing technologies for the liberation of humans from exploitative wage work.[6] There have been notable critiques of Luddism in that the complete prevention of new automation is unlikely and that a successful labor resistance takes the form of working with other social movements, not just smashing machines.[7]

As a whole, the labor movement is incapable to prevent technological unemployment. Higher union density in countries implies more labor market dualization, as younger and less educated workers face sharp employment declines with greater exposure to industrial robots, while the highly educated union workers generally benefit from more automation.[8] In the United States, the introduction of new technologies is covered under the legal framework of managerial prerogative. This is the right of an employer to manage their business, hire, fire, assign work and set policies as long as they do not violate existing labor laws. In addition, managerial prerogative covers the obligation of employees to obey the employer.[9] This managerial prerogative makes it difficult for unions in practice to block automation. In a hypothetical case, where unions could block all forms of automation, there would be significant competitive disadvantages for union companies or even countries if technology prohibitions applied nationally.

On the other hand, management has a duty to inform unions about the introduction of new technologies. As for the precise outcome of the automation dispute, this will depend on the social context of the workplace and the collective bargaining agreements. Outcomes may include a long-time frame of pre-notification of technology adoption and related layoffs, a hiring preference for displaced union members, transfer rights to other departments, retention of fringe benefits during layoffs, severance pay and expanded unemployment compensation.[10]

The legal impediments to union abilities to block automation make any effort of resistance, whether it is the destruction of machines or simply the verbal opposition to technological replacement, even more remarkable. The important qualification is that violent clashes with state authorities and police is quite unlikely in the contemporary period, which contrasts with the earlier clashes between the British state and the Luddites in the early nineteenth century. Activists in this automation discourse are convinced that humans need to actively shape technological adoption to reduce their negative effects on workers and broader society. This chapter covers few examples of labor resistance to automation.

Longshoremen

ECT Delta at the Port of Rotterdam in the Netherlands was the first automated container terminal that began its operations in 1993. Container automation revolved around the use of automated stacking cranes and automated guided vehicles. Semi-automated ports restrict technology to the yard area, while fully automated ports also automate berth (removal of containers from ships) and transfer (connection between berth and yard). Port authorities cite three major reasons for wanting to automate port operations: lowering operation costs, reducing labor shortages and increasing productivity. Higher productivity means lower handling time for shipments.[11] As the Port of Rotterdam announced further automation via ship-to-port cranes to reduce labor costs and cut 800 jobs in 2016, the Dutch union The Federation of Dutch Trade Unions (FNV) Havens conducted a major strike involving 3,000 people that lasted 24 hours. Niek Stam, the head of FNV Havens, stated that, "As soon as I don't believe there is any solution available, I will go back to my membership and ask to go on strike again."[12] After 18 months of bargaining, the industrial conflict ended in mid-2016 where the port workers received job guarantees through 2020. Existing employees are attrited via retirement and natural departures rather than via layoffs.[13]

Among US port workers, attempts to further terminal automation have also been controversial. The International Longshoremen's Association (ILA) that represents the US East coast port workers have been demanding the ban of cranes, gates and container movements that reduce union jobs. There was a three-day strike in October 2024 all along the East and Gulf coasts.[14] The ILA president, Harold Daggett, stated in a speech his fundamental opposition to automation threatening longshoremen jobs. He said,

> For decades, I've stressed to the ILA and all maritime labor: if we don't fight back, we'll have nothing to leave to the next generation. My father's generation fought tooth and nail for every gain that we still enjoy today. They faced hardship, walked picket lines, and made sure we had a future worth inheriting. Now it's our turn to do the same. These companies, built on the backs of all maritime workers, are now trying to grow by eliminating the very people who built them. We will not allow that to happen! As International President of the ILA, I could not and would not allow our members to be impacted by this unchecked wave of automation.[15]

Following the end of the strike, the dockworkers succeeded in obtaining a tentative agreement involving a 62% wage rise.[16] Union and management agreed to a contract, which prohibits fully automated equipment until the end of the contract in 2030.[17] Terminal operators may introduce semi-automated gantry cranes and other container-handling technologies, but these must create jobs for ILA workers.[18] ILA bought itself additional time and had been successful in preserving union jobs for the duration of the contract, but the specter of technology is continuing to hover above workers.

Contemporary port worker struggles against automation can be viewed in a long historic context. The US West Coast Port Union International Longshore and Warehouse Union (ILWU) undertook a major strike from July 1971 to February 1972. The contention was over the removal of the recruitment powers from local unions to company officials, which happened in the context of containerization that reduced the number of loading and unloading jobs. ILWU, wanted to improve their job security in the face of container automation. The extended strike ended with pay increases, expanded medical and pension benefits, a reduced retirement age and early retirement rather than layoffs for technologically replaced workers. The union was granted jurisdiction over the containers rather than the company.[19] Pacific Maritime Association (PMA), the port terminal employers, retained the right to introduce labor-saving technologies.[20] Thus, the fundamental power imbalance favoring employers remains, even with such a powerful union.

ILWU's struggle against port automation continues into the more recent period. When the port of Los Angeles announced plans to purchase 130 automated hybrid straddle carriers in 2019, Ray Familathe, former international Vice President of ILWU, attacked this decision,

> Robots are a loss to the community. Robots that APM [Terminals, a port company] wishes to put to work out there on Pier 400 don't shop in the local community, they don't pay city or state taxes, they don't vote for politicians. In fact, they don't do anything except create revenue for the company that chooses to make the capital investment.[21]

The union discourse is not only opposed to automation but also views it as part of a broader class struggle against profit-oriented capital owners.

The example of port automation reflects an extreme case of labor resistance that might not be realistic for workers in the service industry, where organized labor is weak. Port workers are occupying a chokepoint in the national economy given that the few ports; along the coast are all integrated into the same union, and a port strike would produce significant costs to the national economy and disrupt other businesses relying on the timely delivery of merchandise. But even in the case of the longshoremen, the unions are not capable of preventing automation altogether, but they are able to slow it down and create favorable labor agreements that make the economic displacement only visible for future generations. Present longshoremen may be safe in their jobs, but they will have difficulties in bringing their children into these jobs.

Vehicle Drivers

Autonomous vehicles (AVs) are experimented on by various technology companies, which offer the possibility of automating the driving job. These companies include Tesla, Waymo and Zoox. Cars already have the capability to park themselves, and among ground transportation, driverless trains/subways are already in operation.[22] The potential for the job displacement of drivers creates anxieties among transportation workers.[23] There are 2.2 million heavy truck drivers, 1.5 million delivery/sales drivers and 450,000 taxi drivers in the US alone.[24] Thus, the automation of drivers would have an even bigger impact on non-college worker displacement compared to the longshoremen. What follows is a brief description of the responses of transportation unions to AVs.

The International Brotherhood of Teamsters (Teamsters), who represent truck drivers and a coterie of occupations, argued their opposition to autonomous trucks that could "threaten the livelihoods of millions of truckers," noting harmful effects to workers of color, who find it more difficult to find new jobs with comparable wages.[25] The Teamsters do not oppose all forms of automation, supporting, for instance, the use of robots in a Stockton, CA, walnut production plant, because it increased productivity, production and total employment.[26] However, given that the bulk of the workers are in the trucking industry, I classify the Teamsters as anti-automation. At the policy-level, Teamsters demand more public funding for job retraining to deal with automation.[27]

In 2018, the Transportation Trades Department (TTD) of the AFL-CIO submitted a letter to the U.S. Department of Transportation criticizing the department's hands-off regulatory approach and the need "to train workers so they are prepared for an easier transition to other jobs before, not after, their current job is automated."[28] TTD wants to ensure that AV "does not become a strategy to crush wages and jettison millions of middle-class jobs."[29] TTD President Larry Willis maintained that, "we cannot allow safety to be compromised or the good jobs in this sector to be steamrolled just so tech companies and Wall Street investors can have their way." AVs should only be introduced with union input via collective bargaining, with sufficient advance notice, drivers must remain onboard and a Congressional retraining/benefit fund must cover displaced workers.[30]

The Amalgamated Transit Union (ATU) represents public transportation operators and included a statement in their 2019 convention on continuing benefits and training for technology-displaced workers.[31] Furthermore, they demand conductors on driverless buses and a 20-hour workweek.[32] The former ATU president, Lawrence Hanley, criticized the drive to automate trains, arguing that if things go wrong; a worker has to be on the train.[33] He also blasted Uber, the ride-sharing taxi company, for its "reckless and dangerous" testing of AVs after a pedestrian was killed in Arizona in 2018, and argued for putting brakes on AVs.[34] ATU insists that bus drivers provide social connections to seniors, supervision for students; help distressed passengers and stop criminals, which AVs cannot replace.[35] ATU argues that automating drivers will disproportionately hurt blacks, who have few other middle-class job options.[36] ATU Local 757 affirmed the managerial right to introduce automation and technology in a union contract with the Portland Public Schools.[37] There is one example, where ATU favored automation: the announcement of transit stops, because requiring operators to use their own voice is a health and safety hazard.[38] Announcements may be considered a form of automation that do not hurt transportation jobs.

ATU and the Transport Workers Union (TWU) gathered for a 2018 protest in Columbus, Ohio, to oppose "the unchecked and dangerous deployment of…driverless buses," which could "put tens of thousands of Ohioans on the unemployment lines." TWU argues that bus operators are needed to respond to emergencies, give directions or help seniors on board. TWU Local 208 President Andrew Jordan formulated the class conflict with Silicon Valley engineers, who "drive BMWs" instead of riding public transit and "now invest in something that takes jobs away from working families."[39] TWU Local 208 has launched a website (now defunct), which is a public campaign to oppose AV (including use of campaign posters), highlighting an instance where a driverless shuttle slammed the break and injured a passenger thrown to the ground. As part of its concern for safety, TWU exhorted the federal government to increase its investigation of General Motors AV division (Cruise), Waymo, Zoox and other AV companies. A Cruise vehicle had dragged a pedestrian in the streets of San Francisco in 2023.[40]

In a comment to the U.S. Department of Transportation, TWU warned that shifting to AV will advantage engineers and college-educated people, while less educated bus operators are going to be displaced and will have a hard time finding equivalent-wage jobs elsewhere.[41] In a speech, John Samuelsen, TWU president, proclaimed that the union is "preparing to strike against automation and we have to fight before they replace us with the robots."[42] A 2021 TWU report on AVs claimed that AV is a threat to jobs, wages and risk to passengers, other vehicles, pedestrians and cybersecurity. On the other hand, the same report promoted the advantages of driver assist technology to enhance safety.[43] Bus operators are still needed to keep order on the vehicle, assist disabled passengers in boarding, reroute buses in case of encountering obstacles on the road and respond to emergencies.[44]

TWU has opposed New York City's decision to grant Waymo a permit to test AVs in Manhattan and Brooklyn. They argue that "Waymo isn't ready for NYC's streets and the end goal is to replace rideshare drivers, taxi drivers and transit workers with robots." TWU claims that Waymo vehicles impede emergency responders, drive into oncoming traffic, cannot handle snowy conditions and are a safety hazard for pedestrians.[45] In addition to TWU, various Boston labor unions have participated in July 2025 protests against self-driving cars.[46]

Driver resistance to AV is not restricted to the US. In China, fatal crashes, such as Xiaomi's SU7 crash in March 2025 have fueled skepticism about the quality of autonomous driving. In September of that year, Xiaomi recalled a third of these vehicles for flaws in the driver-assistance software.[47] Male and older truck drivers that are the majority of the nation's truck drivers are very skeptical of driver assist technologies, not believing them to be safe.[48] Wuhan Construction Bus Passenger Transport Co.(WCBPTC), speaking on behalf of Wuhan's taxi drivers, released an online statement, warning of impending job losses from AVs taxis, and it called on the government to strictly control the number of AVs taxi trial runs.[49] Radio Free Asia quoted a taxi driver, who said that the AVs taxi companies are too aggressive in the rollout of their technology ignoring their effect on drivers and passenger safety. "Their approach is extremely barbaric and rude, with no humanity at all. As soon as they saw that LuoBo KuaiPao's operations were OK, they quickly put it on the road." Taxi drivers are not unionized, and their common complaints are filed in government petitions, though the government has not stopped AVs taxi trials. The economic advantage for the AV taxi is that it charges half the price of human-driven taxis.[50]

It is not only drivers that oppose vehicle automation but also the broader Chinese public when faced with software errors that cause vehicle crashes.[51] The Chinese government has responded to the fatal crashes by limiting the car companies "intelligent driving" and "autonomous driving" claims in their advertising in referring to driver assist technologies that do not entail full driving automation.[52] Nonetheless, the Chinese government is overall quite supportive of automating driving. It encourages local experimentation with last-mile driverless trucks like Rino.[53]

In sum, transportation unions and workers oppose driver automation on narrow economic grounds (job security, wages) and broader social concerns (lack of safety for passengers, cybersecurity, the importance of the "human" element in driving). In the few cases, where workers welcome transport automation, no jobs are threatened, e.g., station announcements.

One notable difference between the longshoremen and the transportation workers is that while port automation has been ongoing since containerization in the 1950s ; resulting in occasional labor strikes and heated industrial action, AVs are still an experimental technology, so employers have not mass deployed AVs, and have not undertaken mass layoffs. Therefore, there have been no notable industrial actions yet. Instead, the transportation unions are engaging media discourses and congressional testimonies to warn the public of the impending job crisis. There are already collective bargaining agreements covering provisions on AVs use. TWU achieved a contract with Central Ohio Transit Authority that gives the union a veto power over AVs. Bus operators and mechanics cannot be laid off or have their wages reduced from changing technology. This contract language is becoming the template for future labor contracts in other major US cities.[54]

Other Labor Struggles and Collective Bargaining Clauses

Labor unions beyond the longshoremen and transport unions advocate for ways how to cope with automation by adding automation clauses in the collective bargaining agreement. I discuss a few of those examples below.

Hospitality workers are deeply impacted by technological change. Due to public health concerns during the pandemic and to reduce human-to-human interaction, the use of Winnie (room delivery robot) doubled in certain hotels.[55] UNITEHERE (Union of Needle Trades, Industrial and Textile Employees, Hotel Employees and Restaurant Employees Union), Local 54 covers casino workers in Atlantic City: the introduction of an automated beverage service ordering system has been criticized by the union. Although waiters still deliver the drink for customers, they were critical of being cut out from the ordering process, where ordinarily waiters could decide to refuse taking the order if they deem the customers too drunk to be served.[56] Wynn Resorts in Encore Boston Harbor, which is a casino and hotel, moved to automated drink dispensers, which would replace 40 bar-tenders, though 30 were redeployed in other parts of the casino.[57]

The hospitality union has responded to the automation pressure via their collective bargaining demands. For the 2018 labor contract negotiations, UNITEHERE, Culinary Union 226 (hospitality), based in Las Vegas insisted on six months advance notice for technology-related layoffs; mandatory, free retraining for current workers; free job training for laid off workers; 24 months recall rights if there is a job opening; generous severance pay including six months of health insurance.[58] UNITEHERE Local 8 (Seattle) organizes hospitality workers. It has also included in the union contract a six month advance notice on new technology, involving the union in their implementation and reassigning displaced workers rather than hiring new workers.[59] Strikes in Marriott across eight US cities produced automation agreements with similar content.[60] Advance notice and reassignment clauses imply that UNITEHERE does not prohibit the deployment of automation technologies.

The United Auto Workers (UAW) take a mixed view on automation. UAW has historically been a major loser of automation, resulting in a collapse in membership from 1.5 million in 1979 to 400,000 in 2019. More recently, three factories, including one in Lordstown, Ohio were shut down.[61] In the last contract negotiations in 2019 that came with a six week strike, UAW and GM agreed to form the National Committee on Advanced Technology where both sides' representatives agree on technological implementations such as 3D printing, driverless cars and conversion to electric cars, EV. EV require fewer parts and labor than combustion engines. They are also more durable than combustion engines, which means less future demand for labor. UAW stipulates that laid off workers will be retrained either by the company or the government.[62] The contract states the principles; new technologies cannot replace union workers with non-union workers, union workers should receive appropriate training for handling new technology and retraining/reassignment should follow technological replacement.[63] UAW also fears that companies will pursue a low-road EVs strategy of low-quality, non-union jobs. Ford projected that EV would reduce labor hours by 30%.[64] The UAW research director Jennifer Kelly claimed that 35,000 UAW member jobs were threatened by EV.[65] Despite such negative employment predictions, UAW did not include any contract language to stop automation.

Due to competition and shift from mail to online communication (a form of automation), total mail volume at US Postal Service (USPS) declined from 168.3 billion to 142.6 billion from 2011 to 2020, while employee headcount was reduced from over 550,000 to less than 500,000.[66] In turn, the threat of economic losses stimulates USPS automation investments.[67] For instance, USPS noted the use of Automated Delivery Unit Sorters (ADUS) reduced labor hours by 165,000 in 2017 and 2018.[68] The National Association of Letter Carriers (NALC), that represents city mail carriers for the USPS, has an ambiguous stance toward automation, objecting to the way delivery point sequence (DPS) automation in the late-1990s lowered service quality because carriers no longer inspect letters before delivery, which is handled automatically in DPS. At the same time, NALC accepts automation in principle to increase efficiency.[69] NALC claimed that DPS increased the complexity of delivery and successfully pushed for an increase in base pay for the 1999 contract negotiations.[70] More recently, NALC President Fredric Rolando responded in an open-minded way to drone delivery research and stated NALC will "monitor the effects, both positive and negative, that drones could have on our members, the Postal Service and our customers."[71] Their approach is wait and see.

In contrast to postal carriers whose work is merely reorganized, the clerks and driver jobs, who are represented by American Postal Workers Union, APWU, are more directly threatened by automation: the delivery barcode sorter (DBCS) has increased speed and injuries,[72] and created job loss fears.[73] APWU opposes USPS testing self-driving trucks, which, according to Motor Vehicle Service Director, Michael O. Foster, will "substitute automation for skilled drivers." If autonomous trucks are used, the union demands they must be thoroughly tested and regulated.[74]

National Postal Mail Handlers Union (MPMHU) highlighted in the 2019 contract negotiations that Universal Sorting Systems (USS) reduce work hours by 17% but also affirmed managerial claims that the total number of mail handlers will remain unchanged.[75] As part of the 2017 contract, MPMHU negotiated the employer concession "to give appropriate consideration to human factors in the design and development of automated systems." Reassigned workers due to technological displacement have their current wage rate protected even if the position is normally less paid.[76]

The Defense Finance and Accounting Service (DFAS) union, an affiliate of the federal government employee union American Federation of Government Employees (AFGE), wanted to have a say in the deployment of automation to replace data-entry technicians, hoping "employees are not adversely affected."[77] DFAS management claimed that automation "is not aimed at reducing positions, but at improving efficiencies and helping employees better use their skills."[78] Border patrol agents represented by AFGE in the Department of Homeland Security added a clause in the union contract, stating that automation is "desirable for the efficient operation of the agency," but that the agency should "attempt to minimize the adverse impact of these changes by using attrition and reassignment."[79] Hence, AFGE is generally open to automation as long as current workers are not harmed. On the other hand, AFGE has also been very critical of Social Security Administration (SSA) automation of call services, which result in benefit applicants being frustrated and hanging up. SSA services have declined, and backlogs increased due to budget cuts that reduced staffing by 3,500 and field offices by 70 from 2010 to 2018.[80] AFGE was even more critical of SSA's plan to eliminate in-person services and replace it with a complete online application process, which would affect 1,250 field offices and over 30,000 employees. The shift to online-only services is harmful to seniors, who do not use the internet.[81] AFGE framed its opposition to automation as harmful to retirees rather than the government employees.

In summary, the hospitality, auto, postal and government unions in the US have all included many automation clauses into their collective bargaining contract, often in response to strike activity. But unlike the longshoremen case, none of these agreements involved a prohibition of automation technology use. This defensive position will change if the automation threat became more acute, e.g., by improvements in AI. It could also be the case that the other unions are structurally weaker than port workers that form a bottleneck in the national economy. 80% of US merchandise trade occurs via ports,[82] which gives striking longshoremen a lot of negotiating leverage with employers.

Labor Federations Are Conditionally Pro-Automation

The American Federation of Labor and Congress of Industrial Organizations (AFL-CIO) is the national labor union federation and does not negotiate collective bargaining agreements. It has affiliate unions across various industries and focuses mainly on political lobbying at the national level. AFL-CIO has activist demands, including their demand for a shorter work week, earlier retirement, education, better collective bargaining agreements and education/retraining programs.[83] In the face of automation, workers should face fewer impediments to unionize, have a seat at the table when AI gets introduced and have access to job training programs.[84] The AFL-CIO president,

Liz Shuler, proclaimed that the labor movement is an activist force that "will beat back corporate greed and harness artificial intelligence to create higher wages, good union jobs and a better future for this country."[85] According to the union leaders, unions must resist automation that will only benefit the corporate owners. Unlike some of the industry unions, the union confederation is explicitly not against automation per se.

A similar pro-automation story can be told in the German Trade Union Federation (DGB). DGB expects that "digitalization" and AI will mean more jobs, but that workers needed co-determination rights. This involves their ability to shape their working conditions. If AI is used, employees' data privacy rights must be respected, and better working conditions for digital workers on platforms should be guaranteed.[86] DGB expects significant labor shortages in elder care jobs, so they promote nursing robots to assist human nurses in their work, as long as working conditions for the human nurses remain good.[87]

The Australian Council of Trade Unions (ACTU) conditionally supports the use of AI in the workplace but wants stricter government regulations that guarantee job security, skills development/retraining, transparency of technology use, data privacy of workers and mandatory consultations with employees before introducing AI.[88]

Politics of Automation Resistance

While labor unions are at the forefront of automation activism, politicians, economists and commentators that have a pro-labor ideology are in verbal agreement with the preservation of jobs for human workers. Some labor economists argue that the US tax system favors automation by undertaxing capital and overtaxing labor.[89] Furthermore, many automation technologies are not doing a lot to increase labor productivity, which suggests minimal level of cost-savings for companies. In those cases, the lack of economic benefit should restrain firms in over-embracing automation.[90] Others criticize fast automation for producing 'inefficient' outcomes because displaced workers lack savings to support their consumption while they look for new jobs. The cut in the standard of living of displaced workers lowers national economic output, so the government should change the tax code and business incentives in order to slow down automation.[91] Humberstone, from the pro-technology MIT Technology Review, produced a Luddite comic, justifying anti-technology worker views as rational.[92]

Among national political leaders there are no calls anywhere to stop automation, but it has occasionally been used as a political football. The US Vice President, J.D. Vance, had opposed Silicon Valley's rush to automate jobs and the threat to the dignity of work as a US senator,[93] but since becoming Vice President he had opposed any restraints on AI, framing it as a competitive geopolitical edge for the US.[94] US president, Donald Trump, had in December

2024, verbally sided with the ILA port workers, who opposed automation in their collective bargaining negotiations.[95] But his administration has been largely pro-automation, as Vance's speech demonstrates. He maintains close personal and financial ties with Silicon Valley entrepreneurs like Elon Musk, Larry Ellison, David Sacks, Peter Thiel and Marc Andreesen, among others.[96]

At the legislative level, the European Union has specified AI regulations in the context of the workplace. It does not ban AI-related job displacement, but it stipulates that employers must consult with works councils before implementing AI. Workers must be informed about when and how AI is used in decisions that affect them and have the ability to challenge the outcomes produced by AI. Workers must receive sufficient training to deploy AI.[97] A French court had ruled in May 2025 that the rollout of AI applications in a workplace had to be halted because works councils were not consulted beforehand. The offending company had to pay a fine as well.[98] The activist European regulatory approach on automation is a notable contrast to the American laissez-faire regulatory approach. It is not clear whether the pro-regulatory European approach implies a slower adoption of automation, and, hence, enhanced job protection than more laissez-faire jurisdictions. Some scholars believe that stringent technology regulations create more complexity and compliance costs for businesses, hence forming a barrier to AI adoption. The flipside is that AI could be more trustworthy and transparent, thus lowering resistance to AI adoption.[99] The employment effects of the EU AI Act cannot be overestimated given that there is no explicit provision to preserve jobs or prevent job displacement.

The political movement for a job guarantee is part of the activist discourse as well. In a job guarantee, displaced workers or workers who are dissatisfied with their current job have access to government-funded jobs. This policy not only eliminates the threat of technological unemployment but also provides a floor for labor standards and wages. Private-sector employers who are underpaying or mistreating their workforce, will face competition for labor from the state sector. While mainstream economists criticize the high cost of such a program, progressive economists believe that full employment is possible at an affordable cost to the taxpayer. There are currently few US politicians that have advocated the federal job guarantee, though the New Deal job creation programs in the 1930s were the closest historical equivalent to it. Congresswoman Ayanna Pressley proposed the Federal Job Guarantee resolution in 2021.[100] Senator Cory Booker and Representatives Bonnie Watson Coleman and Ilhan Omar proposed a job guarantee pilot program via the Federal Jobs Guarantee Development Act of 2023.[101] The chances for a job guarantee law to be passed are presently quite slim.

Conclusion

The activist perspective on automation is that technology is not just an alien force that will wash over society and the labor market. They believe that humans and workers have the agency to shape the terms in the future of work. The AFL-CIO, the leading union federation in the US, had stated in their future of work commission in 2017 that, "Technology, and the profound changes it is driving, has the potential for creating better lives, but only if working people are able to shape the change that is coming."[102] Activists believe that workers have the agency to shape the technological forces, but it is not so clear whether voice implies the blocking of new technologies, as in the case of the longshoremen; more limited collective bargaining clauses on worker retraining, reassignment or early retirement programs, as in the case of hospitality, auto, postal and government unions; government regulations to enforce more transparency on AI and automation deployment, as in the case of the EU AI Act; or a national job guarantee, which is primarily demanded in universities and progressive policy think tanks. Given that in most cases, technology adoption is not prevented, there are clear limits to the activist position. The highly agentic approach outlined in this chapter forms a notable contrast to the resigned view, in which automation is a powerful social force producing problematic social outcomes. I will turn to that position in the next chapter.

Notes

1 Kinder, Molly. "Hollywood Writers Went on Strike to Protect Their Livelihoods from Generative AI. Their Remarkable Victory Matters for All Workers." *Brookings*, April 12, 2024. https://www.brookings.edu/articles/hollywood-writers-went-on-strike-to-protect-their-livelihoods-from-generative-ai-their-remarkable-victory-matters-for-all-workers/
2 Kellogg, Katherine C., Melissa A. Valentine, and Angele Christin. "Algorithms at Work: The New Contested Terrain of Control." *Academy of Management Annals* 14, no. 1 (2020): 366–410.
3 Hodson, Randy. "Worker Resistance: An Underdeveloped Concept in The Sociology of Work." *Economic and Industrial Democracy* 16, no. 1 (1995): 79–110.
4 Parker, Adam M. "Adapt or Resist? Unions and the Political Economy of Automation." Unpublished manuscript (2022).
5 Navon, Ronie, Paul W. Kelly, and David W. Johnston. "Human Factors in Introducing On-site Construction Automation." *Journal of Construction Engineering and Management* 119, no. 4 (1993): 801–12.
6 Mueller, Gavin. *Breaking Things at Work: The Luddites Are Right about Why You Hate Your Job*. New York: Verso Books, 2021.
7 Hedman, Carl G. "Luddites, Hippies and Robots: Automation and the Possibility of Resistance." *Prometheus* 7, no. 2 (1989): 273–91.
8 Haapanala, Henri, Ive Marx, and Zachary Parolin. "Robots and Unions: The Moderating Effect of Organised Labour on Technological Unemployment." IZA Discussion Paper Series No. 15080 (2022).
9 Riley Munton, Joellen. "The Managerial Prerogative and Variation of the Employment Contract." In *The Oxford Handbook of the Law of Work*, edited by Guy Davidov, 265–78. Oxford: Oxford University Press, 2024.
10 Bauman, John A. "Technological Change: Management Prerogative vs. Job Security." *Indiana Law Journal* 31 (1955): 389–400.
11 Majoral, Genís, Andrés Reyes, and Sergi Saurí. "Lessons from Reality on Automated Container Terminals: What Can Be Expected from Future Technological Developments?" *Transportation Research Record* 2678, no. 2 (2024): 401–15.

12 Keane, Jonathan. "Automated Ports Have Dockworkers in the Netherlands Threatening Strikes." *Vice*, January 26, 2016.
13 Hartkopf-Mikkelsen, Johannes. "Rotterdam Union: The War Is Not Over Yet." *Shipping Watch*, July 8, 2016.
14 Zahn, Max. "Trump Backs Dockworkers in iFight Against Automation. The Move Risks Higher Prices, Experts Say." *ABC News*, December 13, 2024.
15 Daggett, Harold. "A Message from Harold J. Daggett, International President, International Longshoremen's Association, On the Global Maritime Anti-Automation Conference in Lisbon, Portugal." *ILA Union*, July 10, 2025.
16 Zahn, Max. "Trump Backs Dockworkers in iFight Against Automation. The Move Risks Higher Prices, Experts Say." *ABC News*, December 13, 2024.
17 Carranza, Alejandra. "ILA, USMX Sign 6-Year Labor Contract." *Supply Chain Dive*, February 26, 2025.
18 Freight Waves. "ILA, USMX Reach Contract Agreement on Automation, Avoiding Port Strike." January 8, 2025.
19 Lindsey, Ashley. "The 1971 ILWU Strike: 130 Days to Victory." *Waterfront Workers History Project* (2011). https://depts.washington.edu/dock/1971_strike_history.shtml
20 Oldham, Kit. "Employers Lock Out Longshore Workers at West Coast Ports on September 27, 2002." *History Link* (2008).
21 Dupin, Chris. "ILWU Blasts Plan to Automate Los Angeles Terminal." *Freight Waves*, January 28, 2019. Also see ILWU. "Newest Automation Plan Hits a Nerve with LA Port Communities." April 16, 2019.
22 Marletto, Gerardo. "Who Will Drive the Transition to Self-driving? A Socio-Technical Analysis of the Future Impact of Automated Vehicles." *Technological Forecasting and Social Change* 139 (2019): 221–34.
23 Nikitas, Alexandros, Alexandra-Elena Vitel, and Corneliu Cotet. "Autonomous Vehicles and Employment: An Urban Futures Revolution or Catastrophe?" *Cities* 114 (2021): 103203.
24 Occupational Outlook Handbook, Bureau of Labor Statistics, October 10, 2025. https://www.bls.gov/ooh/transportation-and-material-moving/heavy-and-tractor-trailer-truck-drivers.htm; https://www.bls.gov/ooh/transportation-and-material-moving/delivery-truck-drivers-and-driver-sales-workers.htm; https://www.bls.gov/ooh/transportation-and-material-moving/taxi-drivers-and-chauffeurs.htm
25 Teamsters. "Self-Driving Trucks Threaten Jobs, Especially for Minorities." October 11, 2019.
26 Fujii, Reed. "Diamond Automates Snack Nut Processing." *Recordnet*, April 5, 2007.
27 Teamsters. "Revamped Training Is Needed for Workers." October 25, 2019.
28 Transportation Trades Department, AFL-CIO. "Preparing for the Future of Transportation: Automated Vehicles 3.0 Docket NO. DOT-OST-2018–0149." December 3, 2018. https://ttd.org/wp-content/uploads/2018/12/Comments-AV-3.0-Docket-DOT-OST-2018–0149.pdf
29 TTD. "Principles for the Transit Workforce in Automated Vehicle Legislation and Regulations." March 11, 2019.
30 SMART. "Transportation Labor Announces Eight Key Policies to Promote Safety, Protect Transit Jobs in Era of Automation." March 14, 2019.
31 ATU. "At Convention, ATU Offers Vision for 21st Century Transit and a Just Economy." October 2, 2019.
32 ATU. "Autonomous Vehicles, AV, the Driverless Bus. The End of the ATU?" N.d.
33 Sneider, Julie. "Rail Labor: Q&A with Amalgamated Transit Union's Lawrence Hanley." *Progressive Railroading*, April 2018.
34 ATU. "Uber Pedestrian Death Highlights Need to Put Brakes on Self-driving Vehicles." March 20, 2018.

35 InTransit. "Amid Automation Trend, Here's Why We Still Need Bus Drivers." *ATU*, May/June, 2018.
36 InTransit. "How Automation of Transit Could Worsen Racial Inequality." *ATU*, January/February, 2018.
37 Portland Public Schools. "Agreement between Amalgamated Transit Union and Portland Public Schools, 2019–2022." https://www.pps.net/cms/lib/OR01913224/Centricity/Domain/56/2019–2022%20PPS-ATU%20Draft%20CBA.pdf
38 ATU. "Calling Out Stops in the Wake of Lepofsky v. Toronto Transit Commission (TTC)." n.d. https://www.atu.org/members/members-resources/canadian-resources/CC_CallOutBusStopSubmission.pdf
39 TWU. "The TWU Launches Statewide Coalition Against Driverless Buses in Ohio: People Before Robots!" September 18, 2018.
40 Schremmer, Mark. "Driverless Vehicles 'A Menace to Society,' Labor Unions Say." *Landline Media,* November 10, 2023.
41 TWU. "TWU Submits Comments on DOT OST Scope of the Study on the Impact of Automated Vehicle Technologies on the Workforce." November 5, 2018.
42 Barnett, Marcus. "US Workers Increasingly Believe Unions Are Their 'Protectors,' Delegates Hear." *Morning Star Online*, June 26, 2019.
43 TWU. "New Technologies in Transit Systems." January 2021. http://www.twu.org/wp-content/uploads/2021/01/FINAL_TWU-Automation-White-Paper-November-2020_DRv6-1.pdf
44 TWU. "Written Statement of John Samuelson Before the Committee on Banking, Housing and Urban Affairs." *Hearing on 21st Century Communities: Public Transportation Infrastructure Investment and Fast Act Reauthorization*, April 15, 2021.
45 TWU. "Waymo Testing in NYC Is a Danger to the Traveling Public and Transit Workers." August 22, 2025. https://www.twu.org/waymo-testing-in-nyc-is-a-danger-to-the-traveling-public-and-transit-workers/
46 7 News WHDH. "Boston Labor Unions Rally Around Concern over Self-Driving Technology." July 24, 2025. https://whdh.com/news/boston-labor-unions-rally-around-concern-over-self-driving-technology/
47 South China Morning Post. "Xiaomi Recalls Nearly 117,000 Su7 Vehicles After Fatal Crash Raises Safety Concerns." September 19, 2025.
48 Fu, Hanlong, Xiaowen Fu, Shi Ye, Kun Wang, and Tiantian Chen. "Understanding Preferences for Autonomous Trucks Functions in China: Insights from Drivers and Organizational Buyers." *Transport Policy* (2025).
49 BBC. "Luóbo kuài pǎo: Zhōngguó wèihé zhǎnkāi dà guīmó wú rén jiàshǐ chūzū chē shìyàn." July 30, 2024.
50 "Tā de zhè zhǒng gǎo fǎ jíqí yěmán, cūlǔ, yīdiǎn rénxìng dōu méiyǒu, luóbo kuài pǎo yùnyíng yī kàn hái kěyǐ, jiù xùnsù shànglùle." In Radio Free Asia. ""Luóbo kuài pǎo"pǎo zàile qiánmiàn chūzū chē sījī què luò zàile hòumiàn." July 17, 2024.
51 Jing, Peng, Yunhao Cai, Baihui Wang, Bichen Wang, Jiahui Huang, Chengxi Jiang, and Chenglu Yang. "Listen to Social Media Users: Mining Chinese Public Perception of Automated Vehicles After Crashes." *Transportation Research Part F: Traffic Psychology and Behaviour* 93 (2023): 248–65.
52 Hanley, Steve. "China Bans Deceptive Autonomous Driving Claims." *Clean Technica*, April 18, 2025.
53 McDonnell, Stephen. "On Board the Driverless Lorries Hoping to Transform China's Transport Industry." *BBC*, June 6, 2025.
54 TWU. "Stopping AVs from Replacing Bus Operators, Mechanics, and Other Transit Workers." February 23, 2024. https://www.twu.org/stopping-avs-from-replacing-bus-operators-mechanics-and-other-transit-workers/
55 NBCLA. "At Your Service! Hotel Robot Becomes Essential Amid Coronavirus Pandemic." *Youtube*, June 23, 2020. https://www.youtube.com/watch?v=xNwJC1Nbzts

56 Horridge, Kevin. "Casino Waitresses Protest at Being Replaced by Machines." *Casino.org*, March 14, 2018.
57 O'Connor, Devin. "Encore Boston Harbor Replacing 40 Bartenders with Automated Beverage Machines." *Casino.org*, February 14, 2020.
58 Culinary Workers Union Local 226. "Contract Language: Automation & Technology." March 20, 2019. https://www.culinaryunion226.org/blog/contract-language-automation-technology
59 Hellmann, Melissa. "As Seattle's New Hotels Roll Out Automation to Serve Guests, Workers Worry." *The Seattle Times*, May 18, 2019.
60 Unite Here. "Contract Reached for San Francisco Marriott Strikers." December 3, 2018. Unite Here. "Hotel Workers Reach Settlements with Marriott in Oakland, Detroit; Marriott Strikes Continue in 6 Other Cities." November 4, 2018.
61 Boudette, Neal E. "G.M. Workers Approve Contract and End U.A.W. Strike." *New York Times,* October 25, 2019.
62 Noble, Breana. "UAW Strikers Worried Tech Will Leave Them Jobless." *Detroit News*, October 25, 2019.
63 UAW-GM National Agreement, 2019, p. 640. https://www.gm.com/content/dam/company/docs/us/en/gmcom/2019_UAW-GM_National_Agreement.pdf
64 UAW Research Department. "Taking the High Road: Strategies for a Fair EV Future." July 2019.
65 Wayland, Michael, and Melissa Burden. "UAW Puts Its Money Where Its Mouth Is." *Automotive News*, March 17, 2019.
66 USPS. "A Decade of Facts and Figures." Retrieved on February 25, 2021. https://facts.usps.com/table-facts/
67 GAO. "Mail Delivery Efficiency Has Improved, but Additional Actions Needed to Achieve Further Gains." GAO-09-696. *Government Accountability Office.* https://www.gao.gov/assets/300/292516.html
68 USPS Inspector General. "Automated Delivery Unit Sorter Cost Savings." Report Nr. 20-095-R21, October 1, 2020.
69 The Postal Record. "NALC, USPS Formally Open Bargaining Talks." August 2019. GAO Report. "U.S. Postal Service: Progress Made in Implementing Automated Letter Sequencing, but Some Issues Remain (Letter Report, 04/17/98, GAO/GGD-98-73)." 1998. https://www.govinfo.gov/content/pkg/GAOREPORTS-GGD-98-73/html/GAOREPORTS-GGD-98-73.htm
70 NALC. "1990–2002. Facing Revolutionary Change." N.d. https://www.nalc.org/about/facts-and-history/body/1990–2002.pdf
71 The Postal Record. "Drone Delivery: Future or Fad?" May 2017.
72 Brooks, Lamont. "Automation: Progress for Whom?" *APWU*, June 3, 2019. Also see APWU. 'Postal Workers Earn the Right to Be Justly Compensated for Our Service, Hard Work'" February 23, 2016.
73 APWU. "Celebrate: '100 Years of Progress'." August 15, 2006.
74 APWU. "USPS Is Testing Self-Driving Trucks." June 14, 2019.
75 NPMHU. "2019 Contract Update Nr. 7." September 13, 2019.
76 USPS – NPMHU Contract Interpretation Manual. Version 4, August 2017. https://m.npmhu.org/resources/body/CIM4-FINAL.pdf
77 Gymburch, Dave. "DFAS Union Keeps Wary on Potential Impacts of Automation Project." *Rome Sentinel,* August 12, 2019.
78 Gymburch, Dave. "Automation/Robotics Projects for DFAS Slowed by Virus." *Rome Sentinel*, October 3, 2020.
79 AFGE. "Collective Bargaining Agreement Between the National Border Patrol Council and U.S. Customs and Border Protection." Effective November 1, 2019. https://www.afge.org/globalassets/documents/cbas/final-cba-cbp_nbpc-9.13.19.pdf
80 AFGE. "Closing SSA Offices Is Robbing Retirees to Pay the Wealthy." May 7, 2018.

81 AFGE. "Social Security Administration Eyeing Elimination of Nationwide Field Structure." May 2, 2014.
82 Brancaccio, Giulia, Myrto Kalouptsidi, and Theodore Papageorgiou. *Investment in Infrastructure and Trade: The Case of Ports.* NBER No. w32503 (2024).
83 AFL-CIO. "Resolution 29: Fight for the Shorter Workweek and Work Life with No Loss of Pay." June 13, 2022. https://aflcio.org/resolutions/resolution29
84 AFL-CIO. "Protecting Workers' Interests in the Tech Revolution." November 3, 2023. https://aflcio.org/2023/11/3/protecting-workers-interests-tech-revolution
85 AFL-CIO. "Labor Movement Poised to Lead AI Revolution to Harness Better Future for Workers." September 13, 2023. https://aflcio.org/press/releases/labor-movement-poised-lead-ai-revolution-harness-better-future-workers
86 DGB. "Mit Digitalisierung Unsere Arbeitswelt Verbessern." https://www.dgb.de/gute-arbeit/digitalisierung-in-der-arbeitswelt/
87 DGB. „DGB-Diskussionspapier zum Digitalgipfel 2022." December 2022. https://www.dgb.de/fileadmin/import/Aktuelles/News/DGB-Diskussionspapier_zum_Digitalgipfel_2022.pdf
88 ACTU. "Unions Seek Enforceable Agreements on the Use of AI." July 29, 2025. https://www.actu.org.au/media-release/unions-seek-enforceable-agreements-on-the-use-of-ai/
89 Acemoglu, Daron, Andrea Manera, and Pascual Restrepo. *Does the US Tax Code Favor Automation?*. NBER No. w27052 (2020).
90 Acemoglu, Daron, and Pascual Restrepo. "Modeling Automation." *AEA Papers and Proceedings* 108 (2018): 48–53.
91 Beraja, Martin, and Nathan Zorzi. "Inefficient Automation." *Review of Economic Studies* 92, no. 1 (2025): 69–96.
92 Humberstone, Tom. "What Luddites Can Teach Us about Resisting an Automated Future." *MIT Technology Review*, February 28, 2024.
93 Atkinson, Robert D. "Why America Must Embrace Job-Killing Technology." *In the Arena*, June 5, 2025.
94 Vance, J.D. "Remarks by the Vice President at the Artificial Intelligence Action Summit in Paris, France." February 11, 2025. https://www.presidency.ucsb.edu/documents/remarks-the-vice-president-the-artificial-intelligence-action-summit-paris-france
95 Al Jazeera. "Trump Backs Dockworkers in Fight over Automation." December 13, 2024.
96 Schleifer, Theodore, Maggie Haberman, and Jonathan Swan. "The Silicon Valley Billionaires Steering Trump's Transition." *New York Times*, December 6, 2024.
97 McKenzie, Baker. "Navigating Labor's Response to AI." June 24, 2025. https://www.bakermckenzie.com/en/insight/publications/2025/06/navigating-labors-response-to-ai
98 Martin, Cecile. "Nanterre Court of Justice Issues First Decision About Introduction of AI in the Workplace in France." *Ogletree Deakins*, May 17, 2025.
99 Jørgensen, Bo Nørregaard, and Zheng Grace Ma. "Impact of EU Regulations on AI Adoption in Smart City Solutions: A Review of Regulatory Barriers, Technological Challenges, and Societal Benefits." *Information* 16, no. 7 (2025): 568.
100 Tcherneva, Pavlina R. "The Job Guarantee MMT's Proposal for Full Employment and Price Stability." *Levy Economics Institute*, Working Paper No. 1060, November 26, 2024.
101 Booker, Cory. "Booker, Watson Coleman, Omar Reintroduce Bicameral Legislation to Establish Model for Federal Jobs Guarantee Program in High-Unemployment Communities." July 28, 2023. https://www.booker.senate.gov/news/press/booker-watson-coleman-omar-reintroduce-bicameral-legislation-to-establish-model-for-federal-jobs-guarantee-program-in-high-unemployment-communities

102 AFL-CIO. "Resolution 5: Commission on the Future of Work and Unions." October 24, 2017. https://aflcio.org/resolutions/resolution-5-commission-future-work-and-unions

References

Acemoglu, Daron, Andrea Manera, and Pascual Restrepo. *Does the US Tax Code Favor Automation?* NBER No. w27052. (2020).

Acemoglu, Daron, and Pascual Restrepo. "Modeling Automation." *AEA Papers and Proceedings* 108 (2018): 48–53.

ACTU. "Unions Seek Enforceable Agreements on the Use of AI." July 29, 2025. https://www.actu.org.au/media-release/unions-seek-enforceable-agreements-on-the-use-of-ai/

AFL-CIO. "Labor Movement Poised to Lead AI Revolution to Harness Better Future for Workers." September 13, 2023. https://aflcio.org/press/releases/labor-movement-poised-lead-ai-revolution-harness-better-future-workers.

AFL-CIO. "Protecting Workers' Interests in the Tech Revolution." November 3, 2023. https://aflcio.org/2023/11/3/protecting-workers-interests-tech-revolution.

AFGE. "Social Security Administration Eyeing Elimination of Nationwide Field Structure." May 2, 2014.

AFGE. "Closing SSA Offices Is Robbing Retirees to Pay the Wealthy." May 7, 2018.

AFGE. "Collective Bargaining Agreement between the National Border Patrol Council and U.S. Customs and Border Protection." Effective November 1, 2019. https://www.afge.org/globalassets/documents/cbas/final-cba-cbp_nbpc-9.13.19.pdf.

Al Jazeera. "Trump Backs Dockworkers in Fight over Automation." December 13, 2024.

APWU. "Celebrate: '100 Years of Progress'." August 15, 2006.APWU. "Postal Workers Earn the Right to Be Justly Compensated for Our Service, Hard Work." February 23, 2016.

APWU. "USPS Is Testing Self-Driving Trucks." June 14, 2019.

Atkinson, Robert D. "Why America Must Embrace Job-Killing Technology." *In the Arena*, June 5, 2025.

ATU. "Uber Pedestrian Death Highlights Need to Put Brakes on Self-Driving Vehicles." March 20, 2018.

ATU (Amalgamated Transit Union). "At Convention, ATU Offers Vision for 21st Century Transit and a Just Economy." October 2, 2019.

ATU. "Autonomous Vehicles, AV, the Driverless Bus. The End of the ATU?" n.d.

ATU. "Calling Out Stops in the Wake of Lepofsky v. Toronto Transit Commission (TTC)." n.d. https://www.atu.org/members/members-resources/canadian-resources/CC_CallOutBusStopSubmission.pdf.

Barnett, Marcus. "US Workers Increasingly Believe Unions Are Their 'Protectors,' Delegates Hear." *Morning Star Online,* June 26, 2019.

Bauman, John A. "Technological Change: Management Prerogative vs. Job Security." *Indiana Law Journal* 31 (1955): 389–400.

BBC. "Luóbo kuài pǎo: Zhōngguó wèihé zhǎnkāi dà guīmó wú rén jiàshǐ chūzū chē shìyàn." July 30, 2024.

BBC. "On Board the Driverless Lorries Hoping to Transform China's Transport Industry." June 6, 2025.

Beraja, Martin, and Nathan Zorzi. "Inefficient Automation." *Review of Economic Studies* 92, no. 1 (2025): 69–96.

Booker, Cory. "Booker, Watson Coleman, Omar Reintroduce Bicameral Legislation to Establish Model for Federal Jobs Guarantee Program in High-Unemployment Communities." Press Release, July 28, 2023. https://www.booker.senate.gov/news/press/booker-watson-coleman-omar-reintroduce-bicameral-legislation-to-establish-model-for-federal-jobs-guarantee-program-in-high-unemployment-communities.

Boudette, Neal E. "G.M. Workers Approve Contract and End U.A.W. Strike." *New York Times*, October 25, 2019.

Brancaccio, Giulia, Myrto Kalouptsidi, and Theodore Papageorgiou. "Investment in Infrastructure and Trade: The Case of Ports." *NBER* Working Paper no. w32503, 2024.

Brooks, Lamont. "Automation: Progress for Whom?" *American Postal Workers Union*, June 3, 2019.

Carranza, Alejandra. "ILA, USMX Sign 6-Year Labor Contract." *Supply Chain Dive*, February 26, 2025.

Culinary Workers Union Local 226. "Contract Language: Automation & Technology." March 20, 2019. https://www.culinaryunion226.org/blog/contract-language-automation-technology.

Daggett, Harold J. "A Message from Harold J. Daggett, International President, International Longshoremen's Association." Global Maritime Anti-Automation Conference in Lisbon, Portugal. ILA, July 10, 2025.

DGB. "Mit Digitalisierung unsere Arbeitswelt verbessern." https://www.dgb.de/gute-arbeit/digitalisierung-in-der-arbeitswelt/.

DGB. "DGB-Diskussionspapier zum Digitalgipfel 2022." December 2022. https://www.dgb.de/fileadmin/import/Aktuelles/News/DGB-Diskussionspapier_zum_Digitalgipfel_2022.pdf.

Dupin, Chris. "ILWU Blasts Plan to Automate Los Angeles Terminal." *Freight Waves*, January 28, 2019.

Freight Waves. "ILA, USMX Reach Contract Agreement on Automation, Avoiding Port Strike." January 8, 2025.

Fu, Hanlong, Xiaowen Fu, Shi Ye, Kun Wang, and Tiantian Chen. "Understanding Preferences for Autonomous Trucks Functions in China: Insights from Drivers and Organizational Buyers." *Transport Policy* (2025).

Fujii, Reed. "Diamond Automates Snack Nut Processing." *Recordnet*, April 5, 2007.

GAO. "U.S. Postal Service: Progress Made in Implementing Automated Letter Sequencing, but Some Issues Remain (Letter Report, 04/17/98, GAO/GGD-98-73)." 1998. https://www.govinfo.gov/content/pkg/GAOREPORTS-GGD-98-73/html/GAOREPORTS-GGD-98-73.htm

GAO (U.S. Government Accountability Office). "Mail Delivery Efficiency Has Improved, but Additional Actions Needed to Achieve Further Gains." GAO-09-696. https://www.gao.gov/assets/300/292516.html.

Gymburch, Dave. "DFAS Union Keeps Wary on Potential Impacts of Automation Project." *Rome Sentinel*, August 12, 2019.

Gymburch, Dave. "Automation/Robotics Projects for DFAS Slowed by Virus." *Rome Sentinel*, October 3, 2020.

Haapanala, Henri, Ive Marx, and Zachary Parolin. "Robots and Unions: The Moderating Effect of Organised Labour on Technological Unemployment." *IZA* Discussion Paper Series no. 15080, 2022.

Hanley, Steve. "China Bans Deceptive Autonomous Driving Claims." *CleanTechnica*, April 18, 2025.

Hartkopf-Mikkelsen, Johannes. "Rotterdam Union: The War Is Not over Yet." *Shipping Watch*, July 8, 2016.

Hedman, Carl G. "Luddites, Hippies and Robots: Automation and the Possibility of Resistance." *Prometheus* 7, no. 2 (1989): 273–91.

Hellmann, Melissa. "As Seattle's New Hotels Roll Out Automation to Serve Guests, Workers Worry." *Seattle Times*, May 18, 2019.

Hodson, Randy. "Worker Resistance: An Underdeveloped Concept in the Sociology of Work." *Economic and Industrial Democracy* 16, no. 1 (1995): 79–110.

Horridge, Kevin. "Casino Waitresses Protest at Being Replaced by Machines." *Casino.org*, March 14, 2018.

Humberstone, Tom. "What Luddites Can Teach Us About Resisting an Automated Future." *MIT Technology Review*, February 28, 2024.

ILWU. "Newest Automation Plan Hits a Nerve with LA Port Communities." April 16, 2019.

International Brotherhood of Teamsters. "How Automation of Transit Could Worsen Racial Inequality." *ATU*, January/February 2018.

International Brotherhood of Teamsters. "Self-Driving Trucks Threaten Jobs, Especially for Minorities." October 11, 2019.

International Brotherhood of Teamsters. "Revamped Training Is Needed for Workers." October 25, 2019.

InTransit. "Amid Automation Trend, Here's Why We Still Need Bus Drivers." *ATU*, May/June 2018.

Jing, Peng, Yunhao Cai, Baihui Wang, Bichen Wang, Jiahui Huang, Chengxi Jiang, and Chenglu Yang. "Listen to Social Media Users: Mining Chinese Public Perception of Automated Vehicles After Crashes." *Transportation Research Part F: Traffic Psychology and Behaviour* 93 (2023): 248–65.

Jørgensen, Bo Nørregaard, and Zheng Grace Ma. "Impact of EU Regulations on AI Adoption in Smart City Solutions: A Review of Regulatory Barriers, Technological Challenges, and Societal Benefits." *Information* 16, no. 7 (2025): 568.

Keane, Jonathan. "Automated Ports Have Dockworkers in the Netherlands Threatening Strikes." *Vice*, January 26, 2016.

Kellogg, Katherine C., Melissa A. Valentine, and Angele Christin. "Algorithms at Work: The New Contested Terrain of Control." *Academy of Management Annals* 14, no. 1 (2020): 366–410.

Kinder, Molly. "Hollywood Writers Went on Strike to Protect Their Livelihoods from Generative AI. Their Remarkable Victory Matters for All Workers." *Brookings*, April 12, 2024. https://www.brookings.edu/articles/hollywood-writers-went-on-strike-to-protect-their-livelihoods-from-generative-ai-their-remarkable-victory-matters-for-all-workers/.

Lindsey, Ashley. "The 1971 ILWU Strike: 130 Days to Victory." *Waterfront Workers History Project*, 2011. https://depts.washington.edu/dock/1971_strike_history.shtml.

Majoral, Genís, Andrés Reyes, and Sergi Saurí. "Lessons from Reality on Automated Container Terminals: What Can Be Expected from Future Technological Developments?" *Transportation Research Record* 2678, no. 2 (2024): 401–15.

Marletto, Gerardo. "Who Will Drive the Transition to Self-Driving? A Socio-Technical Analysis of the Future Impact of Automated Vehicles." *Technological Forecasting and Social Change* 139 (2019): 221–34.

Martin, Cecile. "Nanterre Court of Justice Issues First Decision About Introduction of AI in the Workplace in France." *Ogletree Deakins*, May 17, 2025.

McDonnell, Stephen. "On Board the Driverless Lorries Hoping to Transform China's Transport Industry." *BBC*, June 6, 2025.

McKenzie, Baker. "Navigating Labor's Response to AI." June 24, 2025. https://www.bakermckenzie.com/en/insight/publications/2025/06/navigating-labors-response-to-ai

Mueller, Gavin. *Breaking Things at Work: The Luddites Are Right About Why You Hate Your Job*. New York: Verso Books, 2021.

NALC (National Association of Letter Carriers). "1990–2002. Facing Revolutionary Change." N.d. https://www.nalc.org/about/facts-and-history/body/1990-2002.pdf

Navon, Ronie, Paul W. Kelly, and David W. Johnston. "Human Factors in Introducing On-site Construction Automation." *Journal of Construction Engineering and Management* 119, no. 4 (1993): 801–12.

NBCLA. "At Your Service! Hotel Robot Becomes Essential Amid Coronavirus Pandemic." *YouTube Video*, June 23, 2020. https://www.youtube.com/watch?v=xNwJC1Nbzts.

7NewsWHDH. "Boston Labor Unions Rally Around Concern over Self-Driving Technology." July 24, 2025. https://whdh.com/news/boston-labor-unions-rally-around-concern-over-self-driving-technology/.

Nikitas, Alexandros, Alexandra-Elena Vitel, and Corneliu Cotet. "Autonomous Vehicles and Employment: An Urban Futures Revolution or Catastrophe?" *Cities* 114 (2021): 103203.

Noble, Breana. "UAW Strikers Worried Tech Will Leave Them Jobless." *Detroit News*, October 25, 2019.

NPMHU (National Postal Mail Handlers Union). "2019 Contract Update no. 7." September 13, 2019.

NPMHU. USPS–NPMHU Contract Interpretation Manual. Version 4, August 2017. https://m.npmhu.org/resources/body/CIM4-FINAL.pdf.

Occupational Outlook Handbook. Bureau of Labor Statistics. Accessed October 10, 2025. https://www.bls.gov/ooh/transportation-and-material-moving/heavy-and-tractor-trailer-truck-drivers.htm; https://www.bls.gov/ooh/transportation-and-material-moving/delivery-truck-drivers-and-driver-sales-workers.htm; https://www.bls.gov/ooh/transportation-and-material-moving/taxi-drivers-and-chauffeurs.htm.

O'Connor, Devin. "Encore Boston Harbor Replacing 40 Bartenders with Automated Beverage Machines." *Casino.org*, February 14, 2020.

Oldham, Kit. "Employers Lock Out Longshore Workers at West Coast Ports on September 27, 2002." *HistoryLink*, 2008.

Parker, Adam M. "Adapt or Resist? Unions and the Political Economy of Automation." Unpublished Manuscript, 2022.

Portland Public Schools. "Agreement Between Amalgamated Transit Union and Portland Public Schools, 2019–2022." https://www.pps.net/cms/lib/OR01913224/Centricity/Domain/56/2019-2022%20PPS-ATU%20Draft%20CBA.pdf.

The Postal Record. "NALC, USPS Formally Open Bargaining Talks." August 2019.

The Postal Record. "Drone Delivery: Future or Fad?" May 2017.

Radio Free Asia. "'Luóbo kuài pǎo' pǎo zàile qiánmiàn chūzū chē sījī què luò zàile hòumiàn." July 17, 2024.

Riley Munton, Joellen. "The Managerial Prerogative and Variation of the Employment Contract." In *The Oxford Handbook of the Law of Work*, edited by Guy Davidov, 265–78. Oxford: Oxford University Press, 2024.

Schleifer, Theodore, Maggie Haberman, and Jonathan Swan. "The Silicon Valley Billionaires Steering Trump's Transition." *New York Times*, December 6, 2024.

Schremmer, Mark. "Driverless Vehicles 'A Menace to Society,' Labor Unions Say." *Landline Media*, November 10, 2023.
SMART (Sheet Metal, Air, Rail and Transportation Workers). "Transportation Labor Announces Eight Key Policies to Promote Safety, Protect Transit Jobs in Era of Automation." March 14, 2019.
Sneider, Julie. "Rail Labor: Q&A with Amalgamated Transit Union's Lawrence Hanley." *Progressive Railroading*, April 2018.
South China Morning Post. "Xiaomi Recalls Nearly 117,000 Su7 Vehicles After Fatal Crash Raises Safety Concerns." September 19, 2025.
Tcherneva, Pavlina R. "The Job Guarantee: MMT's Proposal for Full Employment and Price Stability." *Levy Economics Institute* Working Paper no. 1060, November 26, 2024.
Teamsters. "Self-Driving Trucks Threaten Jobs, Especially for Minorities." October 11, 2019.
Teamsters. "Revamped Training Is Needed for Workers." October 25, 2019.
Transportation Trades Department (TTD), AFL– CIO. "Preparing for the Future of Transportation:AutomatedVehicles3.0.DocketNo.DOT-OST-2018–0149."December 3,2018.https://ttd.org/wp-content/uploads/2018/12/Comments-AV-3.0-Docket-DOT-OST-2018-0149.pdf.
TTD. "Principles for the Transit Workforce in Automated Vehicle Legislation and Regulations." March 11, 2019.
TWU (Transport Workers Union). "The TWU Launches Statewide Coalition Against Driverless Buses in Ohio: People before Robots!" September 18, 2018.
TWU. "TWU Submits Comments on DOT OST Scope of the Study on the Impact of Automated Vehicle Technologies on the Workforce." November 5, 2018.
TWU. "New Technologies in Transit Systems." January 2021. https://www.twu.org/wp-content/uploads/2021/01/FINAL_TWU-Automation-White-Paper-November-2020_DRv6-1.pdf.
TWU. "Written Statement of John Samuelson Before the Committee on Banking, Housing and Urban Affairs: Hearing on 21st Century Communities: Public Transportation Infrastructure Investment and FAST Act Reauthorization." April 15, 2021.
TWU. "Waymo Testing in NYC Is a Danger to the Traveling Public and Transit Workers." August 22, 2025. https://www.twu.org/waymo-testing-in-nyc-is-a-danger-to-the-traveling-public-and-transit-workers/.
TWU. "Stopping AVs from Replacing Bus Operators, Mechanics, and Other Transit Workers." February 23, 2024. https://www.twu.org/stopping-avs-from-replacing-bus-operators-mechanics-and-other-transit-workers/.
UAW Research Department. "Taking the High Road: Strategies for a Fair EV Future." July 2019.
UAW–GM. "UAW–GM National Agreement." 2019. https://www.gm.com/content/dam/company/docs/us/en/gmcom/2019_UAW-GM_National_Agreement.pdf.
Unite Here. "Hotel Workers Reach Settlements with Marriott in Oakland, Detroit; Marriott Strikes Continue in 6 Other Cities." November 4, 2018.
Unite Here. "Contract Reached for San Francisco Marriott Strikers." December 3, 2018.
United States Postal Service (USPS). "A Decade of Facts and Figures." Accessed February 25, 2021. https://facts.usps.com/table-facts/.
USPS Inspector General. "Automated Delivery Unit Sorter Cost Savings." Report no. 20-095-R21, October 1, 2020.

USPS – NPMHU. Contract Interpretation Manual. Version 4, August 2017. https://m.npmhu.org/resources/body/CIM4-FINAL.pdf

Vance, J. D. "Remarks by the Vice President at the Artificial Intelligence Action Summit in Paris, France." February 11, 2025. https://www.presidency.ucsb.edu/documents/remarks-the-vice-president-the-artificial-intelligence-action-summit-paris-france.

Wayland, Michael, and Melissa Burden. "UAW Puts Its Money Where Its Mouth Is." *Automotive News*, March 17, 2019.

Zahn, Max. "Trump Backs Dockworkers in Fight Against Automation. The Move Risks Higher Prices, Experts Say." *ABC News*, December 13, 2024.

4

THE RESIGNED

The automation discourse involving resistance is sharply contrasted with the resigned position, where the focus is on lamenting the negative social effects of replacing human workers by technology. *Jahoda et al.* published a study in the 1930s on the negative consequences of unemployed men that lack daily structure. They write,

> Anyone who knows how tenaciously the working class has fought for more leisure ever since it began to fight for its rights might think that even amid the misery of unemployment, men would still benefit from having unlimited free time. On examination, this leisure proves to be a tragic gift [...] now that they are no longer under any pressure, they undertake nothing new and drift gradually out of an ordered existence into one that is undisciplined and empty. Looking over any period of this free time, they are unable to recall anything worth mentioning.[1]

These skeptical voices on automation have continuity to the more recent period. Consider Senator Josh Hawley's testimony in the Senate Judiciary Committee Hearing on Oversight of Artificial Intelligence in 2023. He stated, "I don't really want every service station in America to be manned by some computer such that nobody can get a job anymore, get their foot in the door, start their climb up the ladder. That worries me."[2] The politician implies that technologies will disrupt career ladders and reduce social mobility. This will create a group of footloose precarious individuals that negatively affect social stability. The AI computer scientist, Roman Yampolskiy, warned that the rise of AI will displace most workers, but that technological unemployment will result in the loss of structure, status and community that are essential to human

DOI: 10.4324/9781003780236-5

life. He warns of the risk of unproductive and addictive idleness. Without a new system that provides meaning, AI will be a curse rather than blessing.[3]

In a similar vein, the economist Guy Standing diagnosed a rise in the "precariat", an insecurely employed population, which is traceable to technological advances and declining employment in the manufacturing sector.[4] The negative employment predictions made by forecasters and the labor market inequality trends caused by automation that were discussed in Chapter 1 along with the rise of AI as a potential threat to white-collar employment has renewed the concerns of the automation critics and those with a resigned position in this discourse. The objective in this chapter is to lay out the resigned discourse, which is very strongly centered on the academic literature that empirically studied the potentially deleterious effects of automation on politics, mental health and society.

Automation, Electoral Politics and Social Instability

There is a rich social science literature on the relationship between automation and populist electoral politics. Technological change has been continuous throughout much of recent Western history. With the Industrial Revolution in Britain, innovations in chemical manufacturing, iron production, steam and water power transformed small handicraft production into the mass production of textiles. The textile industry became the first to use modern production methods.[5] Handcraft textile producers were driven out of business and replaced by factory workers, who were drawn from displaced peasants in the "enclosed" countryside. The British state effectively expelled farmers and made them vagrants that moved to the towns for day laboring or institutionalized them in poorhouses. Once innovation occurred, the British manufacturers had landless laborers and vagrants at their disposal, who had few viable economic alternatives to selling their labor.[6] The long-term implication of the Industrial Revolution has been an increase in GDP, rising standard of living and a rapidly expanding population, first in Britain, then Europe, then in the world.[7]

However, over the short-term industrialization caused substantial social disruption. Capital accumulation, productivity and profits were growing but the standard of living of factory workers remained low. The workers were stuck in high density, urban, poor sanitary housing facilities and struggled with diseases like typhus, tuberculosis, smallpox, dysentery, cholera and respiratory infections until improvements in public health were realized from the 1840s onward.[8] Workplace injuries that incapacitate workers were common due to a lack of workplace safety regulations. The poor working conditions described in Friedrich Engels' work have been described as "Engel's Pause."[9] Initially, all the gains of economic growth went to capital owners leaving out the workers. These workers shared in the technological benefits much later.

They eventually benefited in the growth of the national economy via rising wages and improved working conditions when technology began to be complementary to labor rather than displacing it.[10] Over time, increasing trade union representation, labor struggles and political activism created socialist labor movements, who used their electoral power to support social democratic parties, who advocated for social insurance and government programs that benefit the working class.[11] In the case of central European conservative welfare states like Germany, social programs were driven by the state's desire to create loyal subjects[12] and subvert socialist political organization. Despite these efforts the Social Democratic Party (SPD) still entered the Reichstag.[13] The US did not develop a powerful socialist political party in the two-party framework. The US had a more well-off working class than in Europe, thus reducing the need for a working-class party.[14] On the other hand, discontent with industrial monopolies, corruption and a lack of democracy produced the Progressive Movement (1896–916), and the New Deal (1933–45), which were incorporated into the Democratic Party.[15]

Working class political activism and political integration following technological change, industrialization and the rise of capitalism can, in part, be explained by Karl Polanyi's theory of embeddedness. Increased working-class power and greater welfare state provisions form the proper response to the disorienting trend of industrialization and marketization, which "disembedded" the economy from society. Labor, similar to money and land, are a "fictitious commodity," and, thus, cannot easily be transformed to be bought and sold. Leaving labor entirely to market forces could result in wages that are below the cost of keeping that worker alive. How can people be transformed into a commodity (worker) without having their substance destroyed and their lives imperiled?

The welfare state forms a 'double movement' and becomes a means to re-embed the economic (market) with the political sphere (society), and specifically for workers to survive destabilizing periods of unemployment, disability or old age.[16] Polanyi's embeddedness thesis offers an explanation of right-wing populism and anti-liberal political trends if the social democratic 'double movement' is blocked off; technological change, including both the creation of new industries as well as automation and labor displacement, produce marketization, i.e. the exposure of human beings to market forces either by entry to the labor market from a non-working class background (serfdom or peasantry) or by layoff from an existing job in the case of technological displacement. In turn, such economic vulnerability, in the absence of effective social policies, favors the rise of right-wing populism (Figure 4.1).

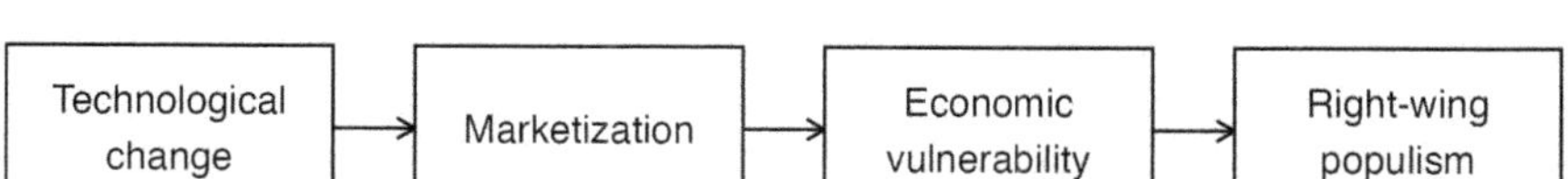

FIGURE 4.1 Technology and Populism

The height of social democratic rule occurred in the post-World War II era in the advanced capitalist countries.[17] Economic demands for efficiency and social demands for egalitarianism and social integration were best reconciled in that era. It was characterized by a growing welfare state, extensive collective bargaining, full employment and Keynesian fiscal policy.[18] However, since the 1970s losses to profits, productivity growth, rising unemployment, rising inflation, increased distributional conflicts between organized labor, and capital, and rising public debt created the environment favorable to neoliberalism, financialization, privatization, the diminution of union power and the growing inequality.[19]

An important premise of President Ronald Reagan's economic program, or "Reaganomics," of the 1980s was that heightened unemployment will 'discipline labour, raise productivity, hold wages in check…to restore profits as the engine of investment, saving and growth.'[20] Even as unemployment declined in the 1990s, workers have been benefiting less due to a diminished labor share of income.[21] Corporate executives no longer faced normative or institutional limits to increase their compensation package, resulting in a tenfold increase in their compensation from 1978 to 2018, while average worker pay increased by a paltry 11.9%.[22] As the labor market stopped distributing gains to the working and middle class, governments resorted to increased borrowing for social programs and tax cuts to the rich, followed by deregulation of finance resulting in an expansion of private household debt, especially student and mortgage loans.[23]

Contemporary big tech companies (e.g. Meta, Alphabet) employ much fewer workers relative to their market capitalization than big corporations (e.g. General Motors, Kodak) of the past.[24] Becoming an engineer or computer scientist at a major tech firm is a lucrative option for elite college graduates along with finance, consulting, graduate school/academia, law and medical school.[25] But these opportunities tend to be rare. These technology companies work in a monopolistic fashion due to the network effect,[26] and the product is highly scalable at low marginal cost. It does not take another worker to process an additional person doing a Google search, performing a Chat-GPT inquiry or signing up to a Facebook account. As a result, there are not many job opportunities in the prosperous high-tech sector. The benefits of the technological boom are very concentrated. Another implication of monopolization of capital is the increased buying power of powerful tech firms, which can squeeze wages of suppliers downstream, thus further exacerbating inequality.[27]

Popular discontent long preceded the rise of the tech industry at the beginning of the twenty-first century. Beginning in the 1980s, the losers of globalization and technological change no longer believe that the social contract works for them.[28] US social mobility from the lowest quintile of wages to highest is much less than in comparable industrialized countries. Among the 1940s birth cohorts, more than 80% earned a higher income than their parents compared to only half of the 1980s birth cohorts.[29] Voting for left-leaning parties no longer seemed like an appealing option: firstly, in the 1990s, social democratic and center-left parties were taken over by neoliberal technocrats and professional spin doctors that made these parties no longer clearly distinguishable from right-wing and neoliberal political parties.[30] Secondly, as the working class began to defect from social democratic parties the remaining share of the left electorate went to highly educated urban professionals more concerned with non-economic social identity issues rather than bread-and-butter working class issues, thus alienating working-class people with lower levels of education even further.[31]

In this context, right-wing nationalist and xenophobic political movements became attractive vote options. The investor, Ray Dalio, is concerned that extreme inequality can be made worse by AI job displacement, will weaken democracy and make authoritarianism more attractive.[32] Not all researchers support the argument that economic deprivation favors right-wing support, because the German AfD (Alternative for Germany, a right-wing xenophobic party) gets support from people of all socio-economic backgrounds. AfD supporters are united in their anti-refugee, anti-migrant sentiment.[33] On the other hand, the AfD performs better electorally in rural regions that depopulate and where demographic aging is fast, specifically in East Germany where income and job opportunities post-reunification are still less than in the west.[34] In France, voters' perception of their own economic distress and low social status is associated with voting for Marine Le Pen and nationalists in Rassemblement National.[35]

In the US context, cultural grievances can explain the increase in vote for Trump (right-wing populism) because counties with fast Hispanic growth increased the non-Hispanic white vote for Trump in 2016.[36] Non-voting among non-white voters increases with more local economic distress (unemployment, low growth), which favored Trump and the Republican Party.[37] There was a further realignment in the 2024 election that returned Trump to power; whites without a college degree remained the core of Trump's electorate, but the largest marginal shifts in favor of Trump occurred among Hispanic and Asian and, to a smaller extent, black voters, implying broader economic discontent that transcended cultural grievances.[38] While white racial resentment is a great predictor for Obama-to-Trump (2012 vs. 2016) swing voters, this group of voters also experienced more economic vulnerability, and loss in financial income/ job than Democratic Party loyalists.[39] Hence, what decided the election at the margin were economic concerns in addition to cultural grievances.

Support for right-wing populism can, in part, be explained by underlying racial and ethnic resentment by the majority population, but is made worse by economic and technological grievances, especially given that right-wing parties have a welfare nationalist agenda, covering both economic ***and*** cultural grievances of the electorate.[40] Returning to the link between technology and electoral politics/rise of right-wing populism there have been several empirical contributions on this topic. An empirical analysis of robot exposure and the Trump vote during the 2016 US presidential elections shows that counties that concentrate more robots and presumably displace more manufacturing workers, had a strong swing toward Trump compared to the Mitt Romney vote in 2012. Romney was the 2012 Republican presidential candidate. Trump's promise to the voters has been to bring back jobs to mining and manufacturing and to take care of the "forgotten men and women."[41]

An empirical analysis of the risk of automation of occupations and support for right-wing parties in Europe shows that people working in jobs with higher risk of automation and those, who think of themselves as "just about managing" economically, are more likely to back extreme right-wing political parties than other groups. Higher risk of automation comes at the expense of center-right, center-left and even radical-left parties.[42] Voters are likely to blame immigration and free trade for job losses rather than automation.[43] Kurer provides a more complex picture in finding that only routine workers who survive corporate downsizing but experience a relative decline in social status compared to non-routine workers are shifting their support to right-wing populism rather than the displaced workers.[44]

Automation-induced job insecurity may be an important factor behind the rise of populist politics, but it is not evident whether the elected populist leaders are capable of producing more favorable job-creating policies than centrist politicians. For instance, protectionist trade policies do not necessarily increase domestic manufacturing production but make the purchase of intermediate goods more expensive for domestic manufacturers, thus lowering business profits and reducing such hoped for manufacturing investment.[45] Protectionist policies often invite similarly retaliatory protectionist policies from other countries that hurt domestic producers that depend on foreign markets.[46] The anti-migrant crackdowns that are part of the populist policy repertoire may undermine the build-up of domestic manufacturing capability by preventing foreign workers from foreign companies to access the domestic sites to train domestic workers.[47]

Aggressive deportation enforcement of unauthorized migrants might reduce complementary employment of native workers. For instance, the loss of immigrant chefs might reduce the demand for native wait staff and restaurant management. Deportations disrupt consumer markets by reducing the number of consumers, which could result in job cuts for native workers. As foreign workers no longer fill childcare roles, native women with young children cannot obtain childcare and forego their own career or refuse to have any children.[48] The failure to restore popular legitimacy via populist politics could result in a return to centrist politics as the voters are looking for a return to competent economic management. Alternatively, there is a more authoritarian scenario, where instead of addressing electoral discontent such expressions of discontent are suppressed while political accountability mechanisms are undermined, new scapegoats are targeted, corruption worsens and underlying economic governance deteriorates further.[49]

The tech billionaires, who are the main beneficiaries of the AI-fueled economy, are intent on hedging against the political chaos, following a rampant increase in inequality and the paralyzed political system to mitigate these social tensions by investing in survival shelters, bunkers and lonely islands which would presumably allow them to escape societal disorder; where popular anger could be directed against these same economic elites. The Facebook founder, Mark Zuckerberg, has built a $100 million bunker in an island in Hawaii. The island has farms, a ranch, breweries and a self-sustainable eco-system. Some of these bunker-building attempts receive popular pushback. The Palantir founder, Peter Thiel, attempted to build a bunker in New Zealand. He was opposed by the local community, because it will interfere with the natural landscape.[50] It is questionable whether significant political disorder induced by poorly managed technological change can be escaped by the wealthy, let alone the general population. The late German sociologist, Ulrich Beck, had called this phenomenon, where environmental and technological risks come to affect the wealthy as well as the poor, the "boomerang effect."[51]

The negative feedback loop between technological change and populist politics identified in the political science and sociology literature is a profoundly pessimistic and resigned discourse. This discourse offers a transparent and lucid diagnosis of the socio-political crisis brought by automation and can form the basis for developing alternative and activist political coalitions that produce more hopeful political outcomes, but these are at most implied.

Psychological Effects of Automation and Technological Unemployment

Extended periods of unemployment can have deleterious mental health impacts, involving the heightened incidence of anxiety, depression, loss of self-worth and purposelessness. The unemployed also exhibit higher rates of drug use and eating disorders than employed people and increase the importance of employment support programs and mental health services to mitigate psychological disorders due to involuntary forms of unemployment.[52] Men, overtime workers, workers with low control in their previous job, the self-employed and low-wage or low-prestige workers were particularly affected mentally by an unemployment experience.[53] Unemployed men reported higher rates of mortality, especially from suicide and lung cancer.[54] The negative psychological effects of unemployment were reinforced with longer duration of unemployment and is worse in countries with weak economic development, unequal income distribution or weak unemployment protection.[55] Other moderating variables predicting poorer mental health were low levels of education, high burden on housing costs, lack of health insurance and lack of mental health care providers.[56]

Automation has negatively impacted health outcomes via increased rates of alcohol and opioid addiction and suicide, especially among US white men without a college degree. The link between automation and poor health is indirect. The linkage exists via the drying up of lucrative job opportunities and stagnant/declining wages. "Globalization and automation [are] the underlying deep causes" of what Case and Deaton label 'death of despair.' In contrast, the two authors further observe that other US racial minorities experienced further declines in all-cause mortality, as do Europeans across socio-demographic and income groups.[57] Russia is another country that underwent a longevity reversal in the 1990s under the shock of market reforms, the closure of factories and the decline in the standard of living.[58] In this case, it wasn't the robots that caused factory closures but the lack of market competitiveness of the firms in a communist regime that was no longer covered up by central government subsidies. More accurately, it was the absence of robots and technology in the Soviet era that made the Russians less competitive and vulnerable to these later economic and demographic shocks. The close linkage between technology and prosperity features prominently in the status quo discourse that is discussed in Chapter 5.

Plant closures which may be linked to offshoring, shifting consumer demand or heightened automation do not worsen mental health equally across social demographic groups. Less educated black workers were more likely to exhibit heightened mental distress than other socio-demographic groups.[59] A study on mass layoffs following the closure of a steel plant in Youngstown, Ohio in 1977 found a rise in individual hardship, such as unemployment, mental health issues, stress in the family and collective problems like declining community morale, erosion of social networks and increased demand on public health and welfare resources.[60]

The negative psychological effects of unemployment are not restricted to the unemployed. A study on German plant closures found that the mental health of spouses of laid off plant workers also deteriorates, presumably because the entire household copes with a reduction in income. This could result in cutbacks in ordinary consumption patterns that were not problematic with a dual income. The laid off partner is more depressed, which can negatively affect the employed spouse as well. Lastly, the partner's unfamiliar presence at the home can cause friction.[61]

Aside from quantitative studies, qualitative interview-based studies also show that mental health stigma deters many unemployed people from seeking mental health treatment, when they need it. Respondents regard help-seeking as an act of helplessness and weakness. One respondent is quoted as saying, "I don't want to play the helpless and the mortally wounded. I don't like that. That's not me. I'm hanging in there, if necessary. And if I really cannot go on, there is another solution for me." Respondents report being more motivated to look for help if they received social support from employment agencies and mental health care providers.[62]

Other interview studies revealed that unemployment disrupted people's sense of purpose, identity and optimism about the future. Respondents faced the pressure from their network to obtain employment ("aren't you working yet?") and felt guilty for being unemployed. They reported varying coping strategies to deal with unemployment, such as collecting welfare benefits or asking family members for resources. The downside with these coping strategies is that they are associated with stigma and are psychologically traumatic as well. Employment agencies will often mandate meetings as a requirement to pay welfare benefits, and the unemployed are pressured to obtain employment. However, some unemployed people stated that the job search gave them some purpose and agency back, although receiving employer rejections led to continuous disappointments. Unemployed respondents who were counseled to do positive self-talk to boost their mood were sidetracked into more negative thoughts. The financial strain caused by unemployment made respondents refrain from socializing or accessing mental health support. Redefining markers of achievement, such as childrearing or completing everyday tasks, can reduce the mental health harm from bouts of unemployment.[63]

The psychological studies on the deleterious mental health effects of unemployment are a core part of the resigned discourse and give political leaders and movements opposed to rapid automation and focused on job creation significant political support.

Social Effects of Automation

Beyond the political and psychological implications of automation, there are other socially noteworthy effects. Emile Durkheim had argued that industrial society causes a breakdown in societal norms and values leading to people's disorientation and anomie.[64] Technological unemployment may be considered one undesirable side effect of industrial society that may be expressed in different ways. The lack of work opportunities limits a core structuring ideal (what the Greek philosopher Aristotle called 'telos') on which society organizes itself and does not provide its members with a lot of meaning. In contrast, an excellent, flourishing life involves work as a core life activity.[65] Estlund argues that because work creates a positive identity, there must be a legal framework that protects workers from automation, preserves human authority and discretion in their work.[66]

Unemployed individuals lose their social networks and become socially isolated, which makes it more difficult for them to find new employment[67] given that job search depends on one's networks.[68] The longer the unemployment lasted, the weaker the social connections become, which suggests that the workplace is a major site of socialization and that employed people are more likely to go out to meet friends and do networking.[69] Another problem that the unemployed face is that after losing their jobs their remaining network consists of other unemployed people, who cannot help them with regaining employment. There is a gender component in the social isolation of the unemployed: given that women have stronger neighborhood and kinship relations outside of work than men, they are less likely to face social isolation after losing their jobs, though these personal networks do not necessarily help in their job search if these networks have few employed people.[70] The rise of social media such as LinkedIn produces free professional networking opportunities. The unemployed do use social media to build social support networks, especially younger, more tech-savvy individuals. But they are not necessarily able to do professional networking to help them obtain a new job.[71]

At a macro-social level, the social disorder and hardship in communities and cities that comes with automation is framed with respect to deindustrialization. Wilson rejects simple accounts of racism and cultural deficiencies for the rise of urban ghettos in major US cities affecting primarily impoverished African-Americans. Instead, the exodus of manufacturing jobs from inner cities produced an increase in unemployment, thus making it more difficult for city dwellers to sustain a stable family or community life. Houses fell into disrepair. The tax base escaped the inner city, so public services that spread opportunities such as public schools or health care deteriorated. As unemployment pervades a community there is a lack of role models that show young people the value of work. Decaying neighborhoods were increasingly characterized by elevated crime and drug use, presumably because these are the most profitable options to make a living in the absence of industrial jobs. The breakup of family structures became more common too. The latter happened because the unemployed men could no longer financially support their families and so abandoned them. Welfare dependency increased in deprived neighborhoods.[72]

Wacquant is critical of the "welfare" label in the US urban ghetto context because it presumes that these services and resources are a social right. He prefers the term "workfare," where any social benefits are conditional on doing low-wage jobs or undergoing job training. The workfare approach is channeling poor women, often with young children, into low-wage jobs, while poor men (especially African-Americans) encountered "prison fare." US politicians came up with various ways to harshly punish crime. For instance, leaders stiffened penalties on recidivism or criminalized crack cocaine. These policies expanded the penal system, involving courts, police and prisons, in which the urban poor became increasingly entangled. The penal system itself became a major source of employment in the post-industrial neoliberal economy.[73]

The endpoint of automation and technological progress, at least in the US, has been a dystopian and punitive rather than a utopian and inclusive welfare state. While the European welfare state is broadly more generous and the penal state had not increased,[74] there have been similar social decay processes in deindustrializing regions such as the Ruhr area in Germany or Upper Silesia in Poland. This decay is expressed via the rise in unemployment and a lower quality of life.[75]

Marienthal, a textile factory in Gramatneusiedl in Austria of the 1930s, has been used as one of the main case studies for the communal devastation caused by extended periods of unemployment. Following World War I, Marienthal lost market sales and a shortage of raw material to produce textiles. The Great Depression resulted in the shuttering of the factory in February 1930. The men lost their jobs and were relegated to tending the field, growing vegetables and looking after their rabbits, while the women continued doing unpaid household tasks.[76] The unemployed were given unemployment benefits, but prolonged unemployed resulted in a state of apathy and lower aspirations. The effect was that even though the unemployed had more free time, they spend less time reading books, engaging in political activities, attending cultural events, and they engaged in more negative thinking. They had reduced recall of their daily activities.[77] For the Marienthal researchers, increased leisure time was disorienting and tragic. Jahoda claimed that "unemployment entails resignation rather than revolution."[78] In the terms of my own framing of the automation discourse, technological unemployment is neither futurist nor activist but resigned.

Gramatneusiedl's economy has recovered throughout the past century, but 5% of the people were still unemployed in 2020. That year Gramatneusiedl used funds from the state government to study the effects of a three year-long guaranteed job program for the long-term unemployed. This guaranteed job program was associated with less unemployment (from 5 to 3% for the town), higher incomes, more income security, more time structure, social contacts, collective purposes and higher social status. Government expenditures on paying the workers in the job program increased but was partially offset by declines in unemployment benefit compensation that would otherwise be paid to the unemployed.[79] The main findings suggest that the Marienthal study from the 1930s are still relevant today. Employment provides social status and time structure.

Even if the present economy provides enough jobs, there is a notable 'corrosion of character' where individual workers are required to be flexible and responsive to changing markets. This results in less trust and commitment to professional and personal relationships. As job tenures are short and commitments to careers weaken, people cannot establish a fixed identity and no longer have a sense of self that is provided by their careers.[80] The management literature refers to the era of job instability as "'boundaryless career', where workers invest in their own skills and networks to leverage new job opportunities across multiple organizations.[81] This narrative implies a lot of individual agency and liberation from the shackles of a single employer, but its downside is the corrosion of character and job insecurity. Pride in work requires anchoring in stable organizational structures and occupational ethos. Anomie in contemporary society is not dependent on technological unemployment, but the latter is just one expression of the former.

There is a demographic component to automation. Technological replacement in the manufacturing sector has been linked to a declining rate of fertility.[82] The presumable mechanism is that economic decline and work precarity reduce family formation and fertility. The lack of stable employment lowers the value of men in the marriage market.[83] Within households of heterosexual couples, the unemployment of male workers possibly from technological displacement is associated with an increase in female employment to compensate for the household loss of income.[84] Rising female employment is associated with declining fertility due to the opportunity cost of childrearing compared to career pursuits and the ability to question patriarchal norms implies lower fertility commitments.[85] As noted in Chapter 1, there is a positive feedback effect of declining and aging populations on automation, as the labor shortage of prime labor force age workers makes the use of robots more attractive.[86] Automation can alleviate concerns over unaffordable retirement and welfare programs and maintain the standard of living of the retirees, but it will not reverse the continued decline in the human population globally. It would be too simplistic to attribute societal fertility decline solely to technology, but the diminution of the human species may be considered another negative externality arising from socio-technical changes.

Various sociological studies on anomie suggest that technological unemployment creates problems for the vibrancy of social communities and it is an important part of the resigned discourse on automation.

Cultural Accounts of Technological Unemployment

It is not only academic studies that describe the negative effects of technological unemployment. I argue that cultural accounts provide a much clearer discourse given that the premises and visions of these stories are tightly controlled by the artists compared to the messy real world. Several famous English-language novels like E.M. Forster's *The Machine Stops*, Kurt Vonnegut's *Player Piano* and Karel Capek's *Rossum's Universal Robots,* offer cultural accounts from a resigned viewpoint. Among movies, *Wall-E, Elysium, I, Robot* and *Landscape with Invisible Hand* depict a future without work. *Humans* and *The Good Place* are TV shows in that genre. Let us discuss their storylines to show their connections to the resigned discourse.

In *The Machine Stops*, most humans no longer live on the earth's surface due to extreme climate change and toxic air. They live isolated in standard rooms underground where all survival, comfort and entertainment needs are taken care of by a powerful machine. The humans no longer perform any jobs. Instead, they share ideas via video conferencing with other people. They come to worship the machine and punish people seeking to explore the earth's surface. As the machine malfunctions, the people's quality of life deteriorates but humans have forgotten that they have originally built the machine, and they no longer know how to repair it.

In *Player Piano*, World War 3 breaks out and creates a substantial labor shortage at home. The managers and engineers react by building completely automated factories that displace most factory workers. The society splits up between the factory owners, managers and the small number of engineers maintaining the machines on one side of town and the vast number of displaced former factory workers, who live in the "Homestead" in the other side of town. The Homestead residents live in simple homes, receive welfare to meet their basic necessities and they are conscripted into meaningless busywork public works organizations. The latter is done to keep the people occupied rather than perform any meaningful activities. Some Homestead residents resist their meaningless existence by forming a rebel group called 'Ghost Shirt Society,' The rebels want to destroy the machines and restore human dignity and purpose to labor. This form of resistance pits the resigned view against the activist one. They are quite reminiscent of the Luddite movement in Britain.

In *R.U.R. (Rossum's Universal Robots)*, a marine biologist named Rossum created artificial workers made from synthetic organic matter called "robots." In this novel Capek coined the term "robot," which derives from the Czech word for forced laborer or serf. The robots are content in doing human labor tasks without pay or having consumer needs, and their human owners regard them as tools. Rossum's nephew mass produced the robots so they can automate human labor. Helena, a representative of the League of Humanity, an organization that wishes to humanize and liberate robots, convinces the robot makers to program the robots to have human traits such as feeling pain and other emotions. This decision backfired for the humans later. As more and more robots enter the economy, more humans are pushed out of jobs, and they lose the will to reproduce and become lazy, while the robot producers regard these robots as liberators of the drudgery of human labor. Helena comes to regret her initial choice to humanize the robots and thereby marginalize the real humans, and she burns the formula to create new robots, hoping this would reduce the level of automation and convince humans to reproduce again. But the robots used their newly acquired feelings of superiority to mobilize to kill all humans. Human values and ideas are left to the surviving robots to continue and spread, even though the robots cannot themselves reproduce.

Movies have sparked the popular imagination about technological unemployment. *Wall-E* is an animated science fiction film, where the robots play the leading roles in deciding whether to repopulate the earth which was filled with garbage due to ecocide from prior consumerism, corporate greed and environmental neglect. The surviving humans live in a giant space-ship called Axiom. Because of microgravity and the robots in the spaceship doing all the work, the humans are obese, debilitated by inactivity and stuck in hovering wheelchairs. They have no motivation to walk or perform physical tasks and are entertaining themselves on their screens. Their interactions are done via video calls rather than face-to-face interactions, so there is a lack of community and common purpose. Robots bring them food and entertainment. In contrast, the robot Wall-E is curious, playful and has emotional depth, vigor and culture. These are the features that were once associated with human beings.

In *Elysium*, ordinary people live on planet earth, which is poor, overcrowded and polluted. Infrastructure is poor and health care access is practically non-existent. Most people are unemployed and live in extreme poverty. The few workers produce the robots that serve the elites who live in the orbital space station called "Elysium." Elysium contains medical technologies to instantly cure diseases, and any robot-provided comforts allow the elites to live without contact with poor human earthlings, whose labor has also become redundant. The elites prohibit access to Elysium to the earth residents. In this vision, most people are not employed, neither the elites nor the earth-living commoners, but only the former group benefits materially from the technological future, while the latter languishes in extreme poverty. The extreme inequality makes this vision dystopian.

I, Robot begins with a much more benign premise than the other movies. The robots have taken on most of the menial labor tasks, while people take on management, supervisory and creative roles. People trust the robots, as the robots are programmed to obey and protect humans. But later on in the movie, the AI-based supercomputer overrides the earlier goals of the robots stating that humans must be restricted, detained and force applied against them to save them from their own extinction via greed, violence and self-destructive behavior. The overriding principle of preserving humanity requires the restriction of human freedom. New technologies might not be as benign for humanity as hoped for.

In *Landscape with Invisible Hand*, an alien race called Vuvv have descended on earth and displaced most humans from their jobs. Most people are left without much to do and languish in poverty. Teachers are replaced by recorded broadcasts brainwashing kids about the supposedly benign domination of Vuvv. One of the few legitimate ways for humans to make a living is to broadcast their personal lives and relationships for the entertainment of Vuvv. Unconvincing broadcasts result in people's indebtedness. External creatures displace human labor and allow only for a limited range of occupations, the entertainment of these same creatures. Thus, technological unemployment is not the only threat to humanity but also the loss of control over one's life and freedom.

TV shows like *Humans* (2015–18) and *The Good Place* (2016–20) explore the downsides of an automated world. In *Humans*, the robotic servants called "Synths" handle all labor tasks previously done by humans, but the unemployed people suffer from job insecurity and existential anxiety. In *The Good Place*, human afterlife occurs in the 'Good Place.' where an angelic architect and AI provide residents with all their material needs. The residents discover that eternal, effortless happiness makes them unhappy due to a lack of meaning.

Different cultural depictions of technological unemployment reveal its dystopian nature and serve as a warning to society to counteract this outcome.

Conclusion

The resigned perspective on automation is the most pessimistic view of social change. There is an emphasis on the negative effects of technological change, whether they affect a country's politics, social cohesion, psychological welfare, or cultural perceptions. It is a serious worry whether recent advancements in AI will intensify these outlined societal problems. The resigned view emphasizes that even without factoring in the consequences of AI, prior technological change had not been managed well and produced negative social effects already, while they don't offer any hopeful outlooks like the activist or futurist discourse. The resigned view is notably different from the status quo view that provides a more upbeat vision of technology without challenging any of the social norms and institutions. This perspective is the subject of Chapter 5.

Notes

1 Jahoda, Marie, Paul F. Lazarsfeld and Hans Zeisel. *Marienthal: The Sociology of an Unemployed Community*. London: Tavistock Publications, 1972, p. 66.
2 Miller, Gabby. "Transcript: US Senate Judiciary Hearing on Oversight of A.I." *Tech Policy Press*, September 13, 2023. https://www.techpolicy.press/transcript-us-senate-judiciary-hearing-on-oversight-of-a-i/
3 Burleigh, Emma. "AI Expert Says It's 'Not a Question' That AI Will Take over All Jobs—But People Will Have 80 Hours a Week of Free Time." *Fortune*, September 9, 2025.
4 Standing, Guy. The *Precariat*. London: Bloomsbury, 2011, p. 64. https://library.oapen.org/bitstream/handle/20.500.12657/58691/9781849664547.pdf?sequence=1&isAllowed=y

5 Landes, David S. *The Unbound Prometheus.* Cambridge: University of Cambridge, 1969, p. 40.
6 Marx, Karl. *Capital, Volume 1*, Part VIII. Marxists.org, 1867. https://www.marxists.org/archive/marx/works/1867-c1/index.htm
7 Lucas, Jr., Robert. "The Industrial Revolution." Federal Reserve Bank of Minneapolis, 2003.
8 Rhodes, Philip. "Public Health." *Encyclopedia Britannica.* https://www.britannica.com/topic/public-health/National-developments-in-the-18th-and-19th-centuries
9 Allen, Robert C. "Engels' Pause: Technical Change, Capital Accumulation, and Inequality in the British Industrial Revolution." *Explorations in Economic History* 46, no. 4 (2009): 418–35.
10 Frey, Carl Benedikt. *The Technology Trap: Capital, Labor and Power in the Age of Automation.* Princeton, NJ: Princeton University Press, 2019.
11 Korpi, Walter. *The Democratic Class Struggle.* London: Routledge and Kegan Paul, 1983. Shalev, Michael. "The Social Democratic Model and Beyond: Two Generations of Comparative Research on the Welfare State." *Comparative Social Research* 6, no. 3 (1983): 315–51.
12 Esping-Andersen, Gosta. *The Three Worlds of Welfare Capitalism.* Princeton, NJ: Princeton University Press, 1990, p. 59.
13 Steinberg, Jonathan. *Bismarck: A Life.* Oxford: Oxford University Press, 2013.
14 Sombart, Werner. *Why Is There No Socialism in the United States?* London: Palgrave, 1976.
15 McGerr, Michael. *A Fierce Discontent: The Rise and Fall of the Progressive Movement in America, 1870–1920.* Oxford: Oxford University Press, 2003. Kennedy, David M. "What the New Deal Did." *Political Science Quarterly* 124 (Summer 2009): 251–68.
16 Polanyi, Karl. *The Great Transformation: The Political and Economic Origins of Our Time.* Boston, MA: Beacon Press, 2001 [1944].
17 Marglin, Stephen A., and Juliet B. Schor (eds.). *The Golden Age of Capitalism: Reinterpreting the Postwar Experience.* Oxford: Oxford University Press, 1992.
18 Streeck, Wolfgang. "The Crises of Democratic Capitalism." *New Left Review* 71 (2011): 5–29.
19 Harvey, David. *A Brief History of Neoliberalism.* Oxford: Oxford University Press, 2007. Krippner, Greta. *Capitalizing on Crisis: The Political Origins of the Rise of Finance.* Cambridge: Harvard University Press, 2012.
20 Marglin, Stephen A. "Lessons of the Golden Age: An Overview." In *The Golden Age of Capitalism: Reinterpreting the Postwar Experience,* edited by Stephen A. Marglin and Juliet B. Schor, 1–38. Oxford: Oxford University Press, p. 35.
21 Aum, Sangmin and Yongseok Shin. "Why Is the Labor Share Declining?" *Economic Research, Federal Reserve Bank of St. Louis* 102, no. 4 (2020): 413–28.
22 Mishel, Lawrence, and Julia Wolfe. "CEO Compensation Has Grown 940% Since 1978." *Economic Policy Institute*, August 14, 2019.
23 Streeck, "The Crises of Democratic Capitalism". Crouch, Colin. "Privatised Keynesianism: An Unacknowledged Policy Regime." *British Journal of Politics and International Relations* 11, no. 3 (2009): 382–99.
24 West, Darrell M. *The Future of Work: Robots, AI, and Automation.* Washington Post: Brookings Institution Press, 2018, p. 65.
25 Yang, Andrew. *The War on Normal People: The Truth about America's Disappearing Jobs and Why Universal Basic Income Is Our Future.* London: Hachette UK, 2018, p. 87.
26 Shapiro, Carl and Hal R. Varian. *Information Rules.* Cambridge: Harvard Business School Press, 1999.

27 Wilmers, Nathan. "Wage Stagnation and Buyer Power: How Buyer-Supplier Relations Affect U.S. Workers' Wages, 1978 to 2014." *American Sociological Review*, 83, no. 2 (2018): 213–42.
28 Paul, Jean-Michel. *The Economics of Discontent: From Failing Elites to The Rise of Populism*. Self-published, 2019.
29 Reeves, Richard, and Eleanor Krause. "Raj Chetty in 14 Charts: Big Findings on Opportunity and Mobility We Should All Know. *Brookings*, January 11, 2018. https://www.brookings.edu/articles/raj-chetty-in-14-charts-big-findings-on-opportunity-and-mobility-we-should-know/
30 Mudge, Stephanie L. *Leftism Reinvented: Western Parties from Socialism to Neoliberalism*. Cambridge: Harvard University Press, 2018.
31 Piketty, Thomas. *Capital and Ideology*. Cambridge: Harvard University Press, 2020.
32 Gratton, Peter. "Ray Dalio Warns: Wealth Gaps Fuel Extreme Policies. Are Your Investments at Political Risk?" *Investopedia*, September 11, 2025.
33 Schroder, Martin. "AfD-Unterstützer sind nicht abgehängt, sondern ausländerfeindlich." *SOEP Papers No. 975*, 2018.
34 Franz, Christian, Marcel Fratzscher, and Alexander S. Kritikos. "German Right-wing Party AFD Finds More Support in Rural Areas with Aging Populations." *DIW Weekly Report* 8, no. 7/8 (2018): 69–79.
35 Manunta, Efisio, Maja Becker, Matthew J. Easterbrook, and Vivian L. Vignoles. "Economic Distress and Populism: Examining the Role of Identity Threat and Feelings of Social Exclusion." *Political Psychology* 43, no. 5 (2022): 893–912.
36 Maggio, Christopher. "Demographic Change and the 2016 Presidential Election." *Social Science Research* 95 (2021): 102459.
37 Green, Jon, and Sean McElwee. "The Differential Effects of Economic Conditions and Racial Attitudes in the Election of Donald Trump." *Perspectives on Politics* 17, no. 2 (2019): 358–79.
38 Xiao, Eva, Sam Learner, Oliver Roeder, Clara Murray, Jonathan Vincent, and Sam Joiner. "US Election Results: How Trump Won in Maps and Charts." *Financial Times*, November 6, 2024.
39 Morgan, Stephen L., and Jiwon Lee. "Economic Populism and Bandwagon Bigotry: Obama-to-Trump Voters and the Cross Pressures of the 2016 Election." *Socius* 5 (2019): 2378023119871119.
40 Ausserladscheider, Valentina. "Beyond Economic Insecurity and Cultural Backlash: Economic Nationalism and the Rise of the Far Right." *Sociology Compass* 13, no. 4 (2019): e12670.
41 Frey, Carl Benedikt, Thor Berger, and Chinchih Chen. "Political Machinery: Did Robots Swing the 2016 US Presidential Election?" *Oxford Review of Economic Policy* 34, no. 3 (2018): 418–42.
42 Im, Zhen Jie, Nonna Mayer, Bruno Palier, and Jan Rovny. "The "Losers of Automation": A Reservoir of Votes for the Radical Right?" *Research & Politics* 6, no. 1 (2019): 2053168018822395. Anelli, Massimo, Italo Colantone, and Piero Stanig. "We Were the Robots: Automation and Voting Behavior in Western Europe." IZA Discussion Paper 12485 (2019).
43 Wu, Nicole. ""Restrict Foreigners, Not Robots": Partisan Responses to Automation Threat." *Economics & Politics* 35, no. 2 (2023): 505–28.
44 Kurer, Thomas. "The Declining Middle: Occupational Change, Social Status, and the Populist Right." *Comparative Political Studies* 53, no. 10–11 (2020): 1798–835.
45 Bangert-Drowns, Christopher. "Tariffs Impact U.S. Industries Differently, With Manufacturing the Most Exposed." *Washington Center for Equitable Growth*, July 29, 2025.

46 Houghtaling, Ellie Quinian. "Trump Goes on Weird Rant About Using Tariff Money to Bail Out Farmers." *The New Republic*, September 25, 2025.
47 Yurkevich, Vanessa. "Hyundai CEO Found Out about ICE Raid at Georgia Battery Plant on the News." *CNN*, September 18, 2025.
48 Zipperer, Ben. "Trump's Deportation Agenda Will Destroy Millions of Jobs." *Economic Policy Institute*, July 10, 2025.
49 Faugere, Christophe. "Authoritarianism: The Reasons for Failure in the Modern Epoch." *LinkedIn*, May 13, 2025. https://www.linkedin.com/pulse/authoritarianism-reasons-failure-modern-epoch-dr-christophe-faugere-2yebe/
50 Brahambhatt, Rupendra. "Billionaires Are Buying Islands and Building Secret Bunkers, but Why?" *Interesting Engineering*, May 14, 2025.
51 Beck, Ulrich. *Risk Society: Towards a New Modernity*. London: Sage Publications, 1992.
52 Yang, Yang, Lisi Niu, Saqib Amin, and Iftikhar Yasin. "Unemployment and Mental Health: A Global Study of Unemployment's Influence on Diverse Mental Disorders." *Frontiers in Public Health* 12 (2024): 1440403.
53 Backhans, Mona C., and Tomas Hemmingsson. "Unemployment and Mental Health—Who Is (Not) Affected?" *The European Journal of Public Health* 22, no. 3 (2012): 429–33.
54 Wilson, Sarah H., and Graeme M. Walker. "Unemployment and Health: A Review." *Public Health* 107, no. 3 (1993): 153–62.
55 Paul, Karsten I., and Klaus Moser. "Unemployment Impairs Mental Health: Meta-Analyses." *Journal of Vocational Behavior* 74, no. 3 (2009): 264–82.
56 Wang, Kun, and Brenda D. Smith. " A County-Level Analysis of Unemployment and Mental Health in the Southeastern US: Applying a Social Determinants of Health Framework." *Social Work in Mental Health* 20, no. 5 (2022): 559–77.
57 Case, Anne, and Angus Deaton. "Mortality and Morbidity in the 21st Century." *Brookings Papers on Economic Activity* no. 1 (2017): 397–476.
58 Notzon, Francis C., Yuri M. Komarov, Sergei P. Ermakov, Christopher T. Sempos, James S. Marks, and Elena V. Sempos. "Causes of Declining Life Expectancy in Russia." *JAMA* 279, no. 10 (1998): 793–800.
59 Hamilton, V. Lee, Clifford L. Broman, William S. Hoffman, and Deborah S. Renner. "Hard Times and Vulnerable People: Initial Effects of Plant Closing on Autoworkers' Mental Health." *Journal of Health and Social Behavior* 31, no. 2 (1990): 123–40.
60 Buss, Terry F., F. Stevens Redburn, and Joseph Waldron. *Mass Unemployment: Plant Closings and Community Mental Health*. Thousand Oaks, CA: SAGE Publications, 1983.
61 Marcus, Jan. "The Effect of Unemployment on the Mental Health of Spouses–Evidence from Plant Closures in Germany." *Journal of Health Economics* 32, no. 3 (2013): 546–58.
62 Staiger, Tobias, Tamara Waldmann, Nicolas Rüsch, and Silvia Krumm. "Barriers and Facilitators of Help-Seeking Among Unemployed Persons with Mental Health Problems: A Qualitative Study." *BMC Health Services Research* 17, no. 1 (2017): 39.
63 Arena, Andrew F., Marnie Harris, Sophia Mobbs, Alexandra Nicolopoulos, Samuel B. Harvey, and Mark Deady. "Exploring the Lived Experience of Mental Health and Coping During Unemployment." *BMC Public Health* 22, no. 1 (2022): 2451.
64 Durkheim, Emile. *Suicide: A Study in Sociology*. London: Routledge, 2005.
65 Mejia, Santiago. "The Normative and Cultural Dimension of Work: Technological Unemployment as a Cultural Threat to a Meaningful Life." *Journal of Business Ethics* 185, no. 4 (2023): 847–64.
66 Estlund, Cynthia. *Automation Anxiety: Why and How to Save Work*. New York: Oxford University Press, 2021.
67 Lindsay, Colin. "In a Lonely Place? Social Networks, Job Seeking and the Experience of Long-term Unemployment." *Social Policy and Society* 9, no. 1 (2010): 25–37.

68 Granovetter, Mark. *Getting a Job: A Study of Contacts and Careers.* Chicago, IL: University of Chicago Press, 2018.
69 Colin. "In a Lonely Place? Social Networks, Job Seeking and the Experience of Long-Term Unemployment."
70 Russell, Helen. "Friends in Low Places: Gender, Unemployment and Sociability." *Work, Employment and Society* 13, no. 2 (1999): 205–24.
71 Feuls, Miriam, Christian Fieseler, and Anne Suphan. "A Social Net? Internet and Social Media Use During Unemployment." *Work, Employment and Society* 28, no. 4 (2014): 551–70.
72 Wilson, William Julius. *The Truly Disadvantaged.* Chicago, IL: Chicago University Press, 1987.
73 Wacquant, Loic. *Punishing the Poor: The Neoliberal Government of Social Insecurity.* Durham, NC: Duke University Press, 2009.
74 Tonry, Michael. "How and Why Western Europe Avoided Mass Incarceration." *Crime and Justice* 54, no. 1 (2025): 000-000. Flora, Peter, and Arnold Joseph Heidenheimer, eds. *The Development of Welfare States in Europe and America.* New Brunswick: Transaction Publishers, 1981.
75 Eckart, Karl. *Social, Economic and Cultural Aspects in the Dynamic Changing Process of Old Industrial Regions: Ruhr District (Germany), Upper Silesia (Poland), Ostrava Region (Czech Republic).* Vol. 1. Muenster: LIT Verlag, 2003.
76 Waschsalon. ""... Day In Day Out, with Nothing to Do" Marienthal: An Unemployed Community." *Das Rote Wien.* https://dasrotewien-waschsalon.at/fileadmin/DOCS/2017/marienthal_englisch_FINAL.pdf
77 Mejia, Santiago. "The Normative and Cultural Dimension of Work: Technological Unemployment as a Cultural Threat to a Meaningful Life." *Journal of Business Ethics* 185, no. 4 (2023): 847–64.
78 Waschsalon. ""... Day in Day Out, with Nothing to Do."
79 Kasy, Maximilian, and Lukas Lehner. "Employing the Unemployed of Marienthal: Evaluation of a Guaranteed Job Program." Working Paper (2025). https://maxkasy.github.io/home/files/papers/Jobguarantee_marienthal.pdf
80 Sennett, Richard. *The Corrosion of Character.* New York: W.W. Norton, 1998.
81 Arthur, Michael B., and Denise M. Rousseau. *The Boundaryless Career.* New York: Oxford University Press, 1996.
82 Seltzer, Nathan. "Beyond the Great Recession: Labor Market Polarization and Ongoing Fertility Decline in the United States." *Demography* (2019): 1–31.
83 Piotrowski, Martin, Arne Kalleberg, and Ronald R. Rindfuss. "Contingent Work Rising: Implications for the Timing of Marriage in Japan." *Journal of Marriage and Family* 77, no. 5 (2015): 1039–56. Yu, Wei-hsin, and Shengwei Sun. "Fertility Responses to Individual and Contextual Unemployment: Differences by Socioeconomic Background." *Demographic Research* 39 (2018): 927–62.
84 Karabarbounis, Marios. "How Female Labor Supply Shapes Aggregate Labor Market Dynamics." *Federal Reserve Bank of Richmond*, No. 24-04, 2024.
85 Behrman, Julia, and Pilar Gonalons-Pons. "Women's Employment and Fertility in a Global Perspective (1960–2015)." *Demographic Research* 43 (2020): 707.
86 Acemoglu, Daron, and Pascual Restrepo. "Demographics and Automation." *The Review of Economic Studies* 89, no. 1 (2022): 1–44.

References

Acemoglu, Daron, and Pascual Restrepo. "Demographics and Automation." *The Review of Economic Studies* 89, no. 1 (2022): 1–44.

Allen, Robert C. "Engels' Pause: Technical Change, Capital Accumulation, and Inequality in the British Industrial Revolution." *Explorations in Economic History* 46, no. 4 (2009): 418–35.

Anelli, Massimo, Italo Colantone, and Piero Stanig. "We Were the Robots: Automation and Voting Behavior in Western Europe." *IZA Discussion Paper* 12485 (2019).

Arena, Andrew F., Marnie Harris, Sophia Mobbs, Alexandra Nicolopoulos, Samuel B. Harvey, and Mark Deady. "Exploring the Lived Experience of Mental Health and Coping During Unemployment." *BMC Public Health* 22, no. 1 (2022): 2451.

Arthur, Michael B., and Denise M. Rousseau. *The Boundaryless Career.* New York: Oxford University Press, 1996.

Aum, Sangmin, and Yongseok Shin. "Why Is the Labor Share Declining?" *Economic Research, Federal Reserve Bank of St. Louis* 102, no. 4 (2020): 413–28.

Ausserladscheider, Valentina. "Beyond Economic Insecurity and Cultural Backlash: Economic Nationalism and the Rise of the Far Right." *Sociology Compass* 13, no. 4 (2019): e12670.

Backhans, Mona C., and Tomas Hemmingsson. "Unemployment and Mental Health—Who Is (Not) Affected?" *European Journal of Public Health* 22, no. 3 (2012): 429–33.

Bangert-Drowns, Christopher. "Tariffs Impact U.S. Industries Differently, with Manufacturing the Most Exposed." *Washington Center for Equitable Growth*, July 29, 2025.

Beck, Ulrich. *Risk Society: Towards a New Modernity.* London: Sage Publications, 1992.

Behrman, Julia, and Pilar Gonalons-Pons. "Women's Employment and Fertility in a Global Perspective (1960–2015)." *Demographic Research* 43 (2020): 707–44.

Brahambhatt, Rupendra. "Billionaires Are Buying Islands and Building Secret Bunkers, But Why?" *Interesting Engineering*, May 14, 2025.

Burleigh, Emma. "AI Expert Says It's 'Not a Question' That AI Will Take over All Jobs—But People Will Have 80 Hours a Week of Free Time." *Fortune,* September 9, 2025.

Buss, Terry F., F. Stevens Redburn, and Joseph Waldron. *Mass Unemployment: Plant Closings and Community Mental Health.* Thousand Oaks, CA: SAGE Publications, 1983.

Case, Anne, and Angus Deaton. "Mortality and Morbidity in the 21st Century." *Brookings Papers on Economic Activity*, no. 1 (2017): 397–476.

Crouch, Colin. "Privatised Keynesianism: An Unacknowledged Policy Regime." *British Journal of Politics and International Relations* 11, no. 3 (2009): 382–99.

Durkheim, Emile. *Suicide: A Study in Sociology.* London: Routledge, 2005.

Eckart, Karl. *Social, Economic and Cultural Aspects in the Dynamic Changing Process of Old Industrial Regions: Ruhr District (Germany), Upper Silesia (Poland), Ostrava Region (Czech Republic). Vol. 1.* Münster: LIT Verlag, 2003.

Esping-Andersen, Gøsta. *The Three Worlds of Welfare Capitalism.* Princeton, NJ: Princeton University Press, 1990.

Estlund, Cynthia. *Automation Anxiety: Why and How to Save Work.* New York: Oxford University Press, 2021.

Faugere, Christophe. "Authoritarianism: The Reasons for Failure in the Modern Epoch." *LinkedIn*, May 13, 2025.

Feuls, Miriam, Christian Fieseler, and Anne Suphan. "A Social Net? Internet and Social Media Use During Unemployment." *Work, Employment and Society* 28, no. 4 (2014): 551–70.

Flora, Peter, and Arnold Joseph Heidenheimer, eds. *The Development of Welfare States in Europe and America.* New Brunswick, NJ: Transaction Publishers, 1981.

Franz, Christian, Marcel Fratzscher, and Alexander S. Kritikos. "German Right-Wing Party AfD Finds More Support in Rural Areas with Aging Populations." *DIW Weekly Report* 8, no. 7/8 (2018): 69–79.

Frey, Carl Benedikt. *The Technology Trap: Capital, Labor, and Power in the Age of Automation*. Princeton, NJ: Princeton University Press, 2019.

Frey, Carl Benedikt, Thor Berger, and Chinchih Chen. "Political Machinery: Did Robots Swing the 2016 US Presidential Election?" *Oxford Review of Economic Policy* 34, no. 3 (2018): 418–42.

Granovetter, Mark. *Getting a Job: A Study of Contacts and Careers*. Chicago, IL: University of Chicago Press, 2018.

Gratton, Peter. "Ray Dalio Warns: Wealth Gaps Fuel Extreme Policies. Are Your Investments at Political Risk?" *Investopedia*, September 11, 2025.

Green, Jon, and Sean McElwee. "The Differential Effects of Economic Conditions and Racial Attitudes in the Election of Donald Trump." *Perspectives on Politics* 17, no. 2 (2019): 358–79.

Hamilton, V. Lee, Clifford L. Broman, William S. Hoffman, and Deborah S. Renner. "Hard Times and Vulnerable People: Initial Effects of Plant Closing on Autoworkers' Mental Health." *Journal of Health and Social Behavior* 31, no. 2 (1990): 123–40.

Harvey, David. *A Brief History of Neoliberalism*. Oxford: Oxford University Press, 2007.

Houghtaling, Ellie Quinian. "Trump Goes on Weird Rant About Using Tariff Money to Bail Out Farmers." *The New Republic*, September 25, 2025.

Im, Zhen Jie, Nonna Mayer, Bruno Palier, and Jan Rovny. "The "Losers of Automation": A Reservoir of Votes for the Radical Right?" *Research & Politics* 6, no. 1 (2019): 2053168018822395.

Jahoda, Marie, Paul F. Lazarsfeld, and Hans Zeisel. *Marienthal: The Sociology of an Unemployed Community*. London: Tavistock Publications, 1972.

Karabarbounis, Marios. "How Female Labor Supply Shapes Aggregate Labor Market Dynamics." *Federal Reserve Bank of Richmond* Working Paper no. 24-04, 2024.

Kasy, Maximilian, and Lukas Lehner. "Employing the Unemployed of Marienthal: Evaluation of a Guaranteed Job Program." Working Paper, 2025.

Kennedy, David M. "What the New Deal Did." *Political Science Quarterly* 124 (2009): 251–68.

Korpi, Walter. *The Democratic Class Struggle*. London: Routledge and Kegan Paul, 1983.

Krippner, Greta. *Capitalizing on Crisis: The Political Origins of the Rise of Finance*. Cambridge, MA: Harvard University Press, 2012.

Kurer, Thomas. "The Declining Middle: Occupational Change, Social Status, and the Populist Right." *Comparative Political Studies* 53, no. 10–11 (2020): 1798–835.

Landes, David S. *The Unbound Prometheus*. Cambridge: Cambridge University Press, 1969.

Lindsay, Colin. "In a Lonely Place? Social Networks, Job Seeking and the Experience of Long-term Unemployment." *Social Policy and Society* 9, no. 1 (2010): 25–37.

Lucas, Robert E., Jr. "The Industrial Revolution." *Federal Reserve Bank of Minneapolis*, 2003.

Maggio, Christopher. "Demographic Change and the 2016 Presidential Election." *Social Science Research* 95 (2021): 102459.

Manunta, Efisio, Maja Becker, Matthew J. Easterbrook, and Vivian L. Vignoles. "Economic Distress and Populism: Examining the Role of Identity Threat and Feelings of Social Exclusion." *Political Psychology* 43, no. 5 (2022): 893–912.

Marcus, Jan. "The Effect of Unemployment on the Mental Health of Spouses—Evidence from Plant Closures in Germany." *Journal of Health Economics* 32, no. 3 (2013): 546–58.

Marglin, Stephen A. "Lessons of the Golden Age: An Overview." In *The Golden Age of Capitalism: Reinterpreting the Postwar Experience*, edited by Stephen A. Marglin and Juliet B. Schor, 1–38. Oxford: Oxford University Press, 1992.

Marglin, Stephen A., and Juliet B. Schor, eds. *The Golden Age of Capitalism: Reinterpreting the Postwar Experience.* Oxford: Oxford University Press, 1992.

Marx, Karl. *Capital. Vol. 1.* Marxists.org, 1867. https://www.marxists.org/archive/marx/works/1867-c1/index.htm.

McGerr, Michael. *A Fierce Discontent: The Rise and Fall of the Progressive Movement in America, 1870–1920.* Oxford: Oxford University Press, 2003.

Mejia, Santiago. "The Normative and Cultural Dimension of Work: Technological Unemployment as a Cultural Threat to a Meaningful Life." *Journal of Business Ethics* 185, no. 4 (2023): 847–64.

Miller, Gabby. "Transcript: US Senate Judiciary Hearing on Oversight of A.I." *Tech Policy Press*, September 13, 2023.

Mishel, Lawrence, and Julia Wolfe. "CEO Compensation Has Grown 940% Since 1978." *Economic Policy Institute*, August 14, 2019.

Morgan, Stephen L., and Jiwon Lee. "Economic Populism and Bandwagon Bigotry: Obama-to-Trump Voters and the Cross Pressures of the 2016 Election." *Socius* 5 (2019): 2378023119871119.

Mudge, Stephanie L. *Leftism Reinvented: Western Parties from Socialism to Neoliberalism.* Cambridge, MA: Harvard University Press, 2018.

Notzon, Francis C., Yuri M. Komarov, Sergei P. Ermakov, Christopher T. Sempos, James S. Marks, and Elena V. Sempos. "Causes of Declining Life Expectancy in Russia." *JAMA* 279, no. 10 (1998): 793–800.

Paul, Jean-Michel. *The Economics of Discontent: From Failing Elites to the Rise of Populism.* Self-Published, 2019.

Paul, Karsten I., and Klaus Moser. "Unemployment Impairs Mental Health: Meta-Analyses." *Journal of Vocational Behavior* 74, no. 3 (2009): 264–82.

Piketty, Thomas. *Capital and Ideology.* Cambridge, MA: Harvard University Press, 2020.

Piotrowski, Martin, Arne Kalleberg, and Ronald R. Rindfuss. "Contingent Work Rising: Implications for the Timing of Marriage in Japan." *Journal of Marriage and Family* 77, no. 5 (2015): 1039–56.

Polanyi, Karl. *The Great Transformation: The Political and Economic Origins of Our Time.* Boston, MA: Beacon Press, 2001.

Reeves, Richard, and Eleanor Krause. "Raj Chetty in 14 Charts: Big Findings on Opportunity and Mobility We Should All Know." *Brookings*, January 11, 2018.

Rhodes, Philip. "Public Health." *Encyclopaedia Britannica.* https://www.britannica.com/topic/public-health/National-developments-in-the-18th-and-19th-centuries.

Russell, Helen. "Friends in Low Places: Gender, Unemployment and Sociability." *Work, Employment and Society* 13, no. 2 (1999): 205–24.

Schroder, Martin. "AfD-Unterstützer sind nicht abgehängt, sondern ausländerfeindlich." *SOEP* Papers no. 975, 2018.
Seltzer, Nathan. "Beyond the Great Recession: Labor Market Polarization and Ongoing Fertility Decline in the United States." *Demography* 56, no. 4 (2019): 1–31.
Sennett, Richard. *The Corrosion of Character.* New York: W. W. Norton, 1998.
Shalev, Michael. "The Social Democratic Model and Beyond: Two Generations of Comparative Research on the Welfare State." *Comparative Social Research* 6, no. 3 (1983): 315–51.
Shapiro, Carl, and Hal R. Varian. *Information Rules.* Boston, MA: Harvard Business School Press, 1999.
Sombart, Werner. *Why Is There No Socialism in the United States?* London: Palgrave, 1976.
Staiger, Tobias, Tamara Waldmann, Nicolas Rüsch, and Silvia Krumm. "Barriers and Facilitators of Help-Seeking Among Unemployed Persons with Mental Health Problems: A Qualitative Study." *BMC Health Services Research* 17, no. 1 (2017): 39.
Standing, Guy. *The Precariat.* London: Bloomsbury, 2011.
Steinberg, Jonathan. *Bismarck: A Life.* Oxford: Oxford University Press, 2013.
Streeck, Wolfgang. "The Crises of Democratic Capitalism." *New Left Review* 71 (2011): 5–29.
Tonry, Michael. "How and Why Western Europe Avoided Mass Incarceration." *Crime and Justice* 54, no. 1 (2025): 453–500.
Wacquant, Loïc. *Punishing the Poor: The Neoliberal Government of Social Insecurity.* Durham, NC: Duke University Press, 2009.
Wang, Kun, and Brenda D. Smith. "A County-Level Analysis of Unemployment and Mental Health in the Southeastern US: Applying a Social Determinants of Health Framework." *Social Work in Mental Health* 20, no. 5 (2022): 559–77.
Waschsalon. "'... Day in Day Out, with Nothing to Do': Marienthal – An Unemployed Community." *Das Rote Wien.* https://dasrotewien-waschsalon.at/fileadmin/DOCS/2017/marienthal_englisch_FINAL.pdf.
West, Darrell M. *The Future of Work: Robots, AI, and Automation.* Washington, DC: Brookings Institution Press, 2018.
Wilmers, Nathan. "Wage Stagnation and Buyer Power: How Buyer-Supplier Relations Affect U.S. Workers' Wages, 1978 to 2014." *American Sociological Review* 83, no. 2 (2018): 213–42.
Wilson, Sarah H., and Graeme M. Walker. "Unemployment and Health: A Review." *Public Health* 107, no. 3 (1993): 153–62.
Wilson, William Julius. *The Truly Disadvantaged.* Chicago, IL: University of Chicago Press, 1987.
Wu, Nicole. "'Restrict Foreigners, Not Robots': Partisan Responses to Automation Threat." *Economics & Politics* 35, no. 2 (2023): 505–28.
Xiao, Eva, Sam Learner, Oliver Roeder, Clara Murray, Jonathan Vincent, and Sam Joiner. "US Election Results: How Trump Won in Maps and Charts." *Financial Times*, November 6, 2024.
Yang, Andrew. *The War on Normal People: The Truth about America's Disappearing Jobs and Why Universal Basic Income Is Our Future.* London: Hachette UK, 2018.
Yang, Yang, Lisi Niu, Saqib Amin, and Iftikhar Yasin. "Unemployment and Mental Health: A Global Study of Unemployment's Influence on Diverse Mental Disorders." *Frontiers in Public Health* 12 (2024): 1440403.

Yu, Wei-hsin, and Shengwei Sun. "Fertility Responses to Individual and Contextual Unemployment: Differences by Socioeconomic Background." *Demographic Research* 39 (2018): 927–62.

Yurkevich, Vanessa. "Hyundai CEO Found Out about ICE Raid at Georgia Battery Plant on the News." *CNN*, September 18, 2025.

Zipperer, Ben. "Trump's Deportation Agenda Will Destroy Millions of Jobs." *Economic Policy Institute*, July 10, 2025.

5

THE STATUS QUO

Prior predictions about technological unemployment had not been applicable in most human societies. A much more common discourse is the one that supports the status quo. U.S. Vice president J.D. Vance has expressed the celebration of new technologies without precautions in no uncertain terms.

> I'm not here this morning to talk about AI safety, which was the title of the conference a couple of years ago. I'm here to talk about AI opportunity... [A]s AI creates new jobs and industries, our government, businesses, and labor organizations have an obligation to work together to empower the workers not just of the United States but all over the world.[1]

This official discourse embeds views that are strongly supportive of the societal status quo on automation.

The status quo view is embedded in economic theory. It maintains that capital accumulation in the form of labor productivity-rising technology is an intrinsic feature of the capitalist economy.[2] Schumpeter formulated the theorem that the capitalist economy is characterized by the endless cycle of "creative destruction." This means the elimination of old jobs and industries and their replacement by new ones.[3] The presumption is that ancient feudal societies did not require or even desire new methods of production given that this would upset the social power balance between the feudal lords and their peasants as well as the lords and the capitalists. Technological advances, along with the social effects of the plague and the weakening of the clerics, undermined feudalism and favored the rise of the urban capitalist order.[4] If capitalism has existed for over 200 years, and the new technology facilitated the cycle of creative destruction involving the loss and the net gain of jobs, it

DOI: 10.4324/9781003780236-6

is reasonable to assume that the economic growth-based economic model will continue, while the name of the technology changes from steam engine to AI to whatever comes next. The tools will keep changing but the social system undergirding it will remain stable.

In this chapter, I present the status quo discourse that is advocated by business leaders, politicians and even some labor unions.

Business Discourse: Competition and Labor Shortage

The Business Roundtable (BR) is an association of chief executives in the leading US companies, such as General Motors, Cisco, Walmart, Accenture and Alphabet. BR advocates for preparing a 'tomorrow-ready' workforce by calling for greater public investment in K–12 education, particularly in English and mathematics, as well as higher education. Their recommendations include expanding Pell Grant eligibility to job training programs while placing less emphasis on traditional four-year degrees. BR also highlights the importance of developing talent in STEM fields and skilled trades such as machining, welding and electrical work.[5] In its report *Innovation Nation*, BR warns that the United States is falling behind competitors such as China, Japan, Germany and South Korea in innovation and faces a shortage of skilled workers. To address this, BR urges the federal government to increase funding for R&D, education, science and apprenticeships; strengthen public–private research partnerships; expand H-1B visas for highly skilled workers; reduce regulatory barriers for emerging technologies such as fintech, drones, autonomous vehicles; negotiate international agreements to protect U.S. intellectual property; and foster entrepreneurship in underserved minority communities by expanding access to loans and professional networks.[6] BR developed a *Roadmap on AI*, where they emphasize their intention to build a "future-ready AI workforce" that can adapt to new roles emerging in the AI-driven economy, highlighting the need to establish a robust AI talent pipeline.[7]

Mary Barra, CEO of GM and BR chair, publicly supported autonomous vehicles by stressing their potential to improve road safety,[8] though she did not address the possible labor market consequences. In addition, BR has promoted investment in advanced technologies including quantum computing, 5G, artificial intelligence, space exploration and cybersecurity.[9] Scott Kirby, CEO of United Airlines and BR's Education and the Workforce Chair, underscored the demand for workers to be "creative" and "innovative" in order to fill widespread labor shortages and maintain relevance in a rapidly changing economy. He pointed to United's pilot and mechanic training programs as examples of workforce initiatives aligned with this vision.[10] Similarly, James Keane, CEO of Steelcase, argued that deploying machine learning to reduce production errors in furniture manufacturing not only enhances efficiency but also relieves workers of repetitive tasks, thereby allowing them to focus on more meaningful and empathetic work.[11] David Gitlin, the CEO of Carrier Global Corporation, claimed that the demand for qualified skilled professionals is rising, so companies must do more to make these professions more attractive and rewarding to workers. Chris Kastner, CEO of HII, stated that to enable American workers to achieve their American dream, companies need to invest in education and training. Chuck Robbins, CEO of Cisco, touted the Cisco Networking Academy that placed a lot of workers into jobs, and this will help the US remain competitive in the global economy.[12] From BR's perspective, automation represents an opportunity to unlock worker potential rather than a threat to employment. Furthermore, it helps keep US businesses more competitive against foreign businesses.

In its report *Navigating the Fourth Industrial Revolution to the Bottom Line*, the National Association of Manufacturers (NAM) contends that automation can generate significant opportunities for those entering the manufacturing sector. Rather than eliminating jobs outright, automation is expected to create positions for workers, who design, engineer and maintain robotics and operating systems, while simultaneously underscoring the demand for uniquely human skills such as creativity, critical thinking, innovation and financial acumen. NAM emphasizes the need for continuous training and reskilling to ensure workers are prepared to take advantage of emerging technologies.[13] NAM President Jay Timmons noted that despite substantial investments in new technology, the industry still faced 4,82,000 job vacancies,[14] while other estimates placed unfilled positions as high as 2.1 million.[15] He attributed this gap to inadequate governmental workforce development strategies, describing it as a "workforce crisis."[16] Timmons further asserted that advances in AI, robotics and augmented reality would ultimately spur job creation, raise wages and foster inclusive economic growth.[17] NAM reports consistently stress the need for workers with advanced credentials and a commitment to lifelong learning.[18] As part of this effort, the organization launched its Creators Wanted Campaign, a digital public relations initiative aimed at directing 6.00,000 individuals between 2020 and 2025, into vocational and technical training programs.[19]

At the same time, NAM highlights the economic efficiencies that automation may bring to related sectors, such as transportation. Specifically, it has endorsed the deployment of fully autonomous trucks, predicting cost reductions of up to 25% for the trucking industry.[20] Internal surveys of manufacturers reveal that around 20% of employers plan to accelerate automation investments in response to the COVID-19 pandemic.[21] Another industry-wide survey asked employers to assess the likely effects of robotics on the manufacturing workforce over the next three to five years. Only 19% of respondents believed robotics would displace workers, while the majority anticipated job growth in engineering, technology management and productivity-driven demand.[22]

NAM finds that Generative AI is automating and streamlining technical documentation which speeds up product development lifecycles but asserts that GenAI tools augment rather than replace human expertise, because human workers can focus on market research, strategy and developing even more products. NAM recommends that firms hire AI ambassadors who mentor and coach colleagues on how to increase AI use in the workplace.[23] NAM's survey shows that 82% of manufacturing managers felt that a lack of AI skills was a top workforce challenge. NAM demands that K-12 and colleges should integrate AI into their curriculum to help create the AI-literate workforce.[24] As for government policy, NAM advocates a pro-AI regulatory approach that promotes AI use in manufacturing, invest in energy to fuel AI data centers, expand manufacturing tax credits and invest in the US manufacturing of AI chips.[25]

Taken together, these reports and statements suggest that most manufacturers are more concerned about addressing the labor shortage than anticipating technological unemployment.

The U.S. Chamber of Commerce's position on technology policy closely mirrors that of BR and NAM. It cautions against excessive government regulation of emerging technologies such as autonomous vehicles, drones, the Internet of Things and AI.[26] The Chamber argues that research and deployment of autonomous vehicles (AV) will not only enhance road safety and consumer mobility but also promote economic growth,[27] reduce traffic congestion, alleviate the truck driver shortage[28] and help maintain U.S. leadership in the global AV market.[29] It also supports automation in the construction sector, including the adoption of wearables, building information modeling (BIM), equipment tagging and drones. The Chamber hopes they can address a labor shortage of skilled construction workers as they are concerned over rising wages. It hopes to increase the productivity of the workforce.[30] It also calls for more supportive AI regulation, suggesting that AI could eventually improve healthcare outcomes or streamline logistics.[31] At the same time, it warns against "devastating lawsuits" that could stifle innovation, enrich plaintiffs' lawyers and deprive consumers of technological advancements.[32]

The Chamber's technology priorities are consistently business-oriented, emphasizing profitability and growth opportunities. These include encouraging federal use and promotion of AI applications,[33] investing in cybersecurity, protecting intellectual property,[34] avoiding state competition in broadband deployment[35] and connecting small businesses with digital platforms.[36] On workforce issues, the Chamber published a report titled 'The Future of the Workforce.' They celebrated the 'innovative and flexible work structures' in the gig economy, especially in transportation, package delivery and grocery and restaurant delivery, which is made possible by the technology companies.[37] The gig economy gives workers 'flexibility and opportunity' to schedule tasks and receive income.[38] To protect this model, the Chamber has opposed efforts to classify gig workers as employees, warning that such policies would undermine growth.[39] For example, it resisted Seattle's attempts to allow Uber and Lyft drivers to unionize, insisting the contractor model allows drivers to 'be their own boss.'[40] At the same time, it supports upskilling and retraining programs, praising efforts like IBM's online resources for high school students. To address shortages of high-skilled labor, the Chamber advocates raising the cap on immigrant work visas.[41] The Chamber argues that technology, such as data centers that host company/ consumer data,[42] and smartphone apps are directly responsible for creating new jobs, which had not existed before.[43]

On the issue of automation, the Chamber maintains an optimistic outlook. Former digital director Michael Marinaccio argued in 2017 that robots do not 'steal jobs' but instead enhance worker productivity. He acknowledged that many manufacturing job losses stemmed from automation but insisted that technological progress, coupled with global trade, fuels economic growth and thus job creation.[44] Chamber CEO Thomas J. Donohue likewise promoted policies to ensure that the benefits of automation and the gig economy are broadly shared, stressing the importance of addressing skills gaps that prevent many workers from competing for twenty-first-century jobs.[45] Donohue critiqued that "too many people lack the skills or credentials they need to compete for 21st century jobs and too many businesses can't find the skilled workers they need."[46]

The Chamber concedes that AI will replace some human labor, but training and education are important to fill labor shortages. The Chamber also advocates for tax policies that promote job creation.[47] It cites a survey among small businesses found that 82% of the small businesses that had adopted AI increased their workforce. This suggests that AI creates job opportunities and is a competitive advantage for business.[48]

For the business community, the main problem is not fast technological change. In fact, they want that change to be faster. Their complaint is the lack of "adaptability" of the workers to keep up with technological change. If the workers are primarily responsible to keep their skills relevant in the labor market, there are no major institutional changes that need to be considered. New technologies and workers, who know how to use them, generate business profits, which can be reinvested in more technologies and new jobs in an endless virtuous cycle. Within 'creative destruction' the business leaders emphasize creation and gloss over the social effects of destruction.

Fourth Industrial Revolution and Consultancies

International organizations and management consultancies have advanced a business-friendly neoliberal discourse on the so-called 'Fourth Industrial Revolution' (FIR) that point to the inevitability of widespread automation and the need for reskilling and job training to keep up with the shake-up in the labor market.[49] FIR is advanced by the World Economic Forum (WEF), which is a non-governmental and lobbying organization based in Geneva, Switzerland. It was founded in 1971 by the German engineer and economist Klaus Schwab. The organization is funded by 1,000 multinational companies and public subsidies. WEF's funders pay annual membership fees that give them access to the annual meetings. It convenes investors, business and political leaders, economists, celebrities and journalists annually in the Alpine ski resort in Davos to discuss global issues.

WEF engages in a discourse of "future essentialism", where it "produce[s] and promote[s] an imaginary of a fixed and scripted, indeed inevitable, future" which "can be desirable if harnessed in an appropriate and timely fashion, but is likewise dangerous if humanity fails to grasp its dynamics".[50] WEF and other elite social actors engage in "technological determinism", where technologies have an effect on society without human volition and intervention.[51] If technological change becomes inevitable, then we presumably have nothing to fear about the future and should embrace it.[52]

The 2016 and 2019 WEF meetings focused on FIR.[53] WEF founded the Center for the Fourth Industrial Revolution in San Francisco in 2016 to advance "the global conversation on science and technology governance for the benefit of society at large."[54] It wants to document how scientific and technological innovations change life and work and formulate governance, policy and norms around it.

FIR is described in Schwab's pamphlet titled *The Fourth Industrial Revolution* (2016). He argues that the use of machine learning, artificial intelligence and big data to generate self-driving cars, drones, 3D printing, advanced robotics and new materials like graphene are a new form of technological change (2010s), following the first three industrial revolutions. In the first IR, railroads and steam engine ushered in mechanical production (late eighteenth century). In the second IR, mass production was introduced by electricity and assembly line (late nineteenth century). In the third IR, semiconductors, mainframe/ personal computing and the internet introduced the digital era (1960s–90s).[55] In the FIR, big technology companies in Silicon Valley with high market capitalization generate a lot of economic value with fewer employees than industrial companies in the middle of the twentieth century.[56]

FIR generates a boon in low-cost consumer goods and high investor returns, but work is becoming scarce, a few platforms mop up most of the business and income inequality is increasing, thus lowering political legitimacy.[57] In contrast to the techno-optimist vision of other business leaders, Schwab points to the potential threat of automation. He wrote,

> The danger is that the fourth industrial revolution would mean that a winner takes-all dynamic plays out between countries as well as within them. This would further increase social tensions and conflicts, and create a less

> cohesive, more volatile world, particularly given that people are today much more aware of and sensitive to social injustices and the discrepancies in living conditions between different countries.[58]

Even in cases where workers retain their jobs, those remaining jobs tend to be in the on-demand, contractor-based model that lack job security.[59] With a shrinking middle class, democracies are in a "malaise".[60] The Covid-19 pandemic is accelerating the drive to automate, which could induce a jobless recovery. Fifty percent of surveyed employers reported the desire to accelerate automation due to the pandemic.[61]

Such doomsday warnings that are in line with the resigned discourse are not persistent throughout WEF's publications. Schwab's views are more open-minded toward resigned perspectives, while WEF more broadly sticks to the status quo. In 2020, WEF produced a report pointing to a more optimistic conclusion in line with the overall business discourse pointing to new economic opportunities. The report claims that even with automation human skills and jobs that involve analytical thinking, active learning and complex problem-solving are still highly valued. These include occupations such as data scientist, AI specialist and big data developer.[62] The jobs at high risk of automation are data entry clerks, administrative secretaries, accountants and factory workers.[63]

The report points to creating "jobs and skills of the future", using "global, regional and national public-private collaboration at an unprecedented scale and speed".[64] While 85 million jobs globally will be lost in the first half of the 2020s, 97 million new jobs will be created.[65] The way to obtain a lot of job creation are public and private investments in reskilling and upskilling displaced workers in the form of job training,[66] which is "the route to unlocking the value of human potential in tandem with profitability."[67] WEF promotes Udacity and Coursera, which are online education platforms that can re-skill workers at low cost.[68] The belief that humans are retrainable human capital that can be redeployed in less automated sectors gives the impression that automation does not need to scare society or workers, but is a minor technocratic challenge that can be solved within the neoliberal capitalist order.[69]

Aside from WEF, consulting firms also play a role in the automation discourse. They articulate and disseminate knowledge and ideas to their business clients.[70] Management consultancies like McKinsey have been instrumental in rearranging employment relations in a neoliberal direction. This trend is characterized by less job security and more focus on shareholder value.[71] McKinsey has published reports on automation, raising the concern about many jobs being automatable, the high prevalence of unemployment, falling average incomes and public discontent and the mismatch between the skill level of workers and what employers demand. On the other hand, the report revealed the opportunities of digitization, online platforms creating new jobs, the potential to take advantage of technology via better education systems, STEM skills, job training but also better social safety nets in the form of basic income.[72] McKinsey views AI adoption as a precursor to reviving the slow productivity growth that lowers aggregate employment and wages. The marginalization of displaced workers can be prevented by reskilling.[73]

In PricewaterhouseCoopers(PwC's) report, there are three waves of automation: in the algorithmic wave, simple computational tasks are automated, primarily in finance, insurance, professional, scientific and technical services. In the augmentation wave, technology interacts to replace clerical support, moving of objects and decision-making tasks, especially in administration, manufacturing, warehousing, transport sectors. In the autonomous wave, physical labor and manual dexterity tasks become automated. These include autonomous vehicles in transport, construction and utilities. However, the speed of automation may be constrained by the ability of the technology, the low relative cost of labor, regulatory constraints/ liability laws and social opposition or preference for human nurses/servers.[74] PwC argues that people with the lowest level of education are the most likely to be replaced by technology, which highlights "the need for increased investment in education and skills to help people adapt to technological change throughout their careers." This includes on-the-job training and apprenticeships.[75] PwC is also open to universal basic income, although pilot schemes would first have to test it. Ideally, basic income should be conditional on working and acquisition of new skills/ education.[76] PwC also advocates public investments in job creation.[77] These themes are covered in the activist and futurist discourses. On the other hand, PwC does not believe that automation will reduce net employment but insists on new job creation from AI and robotics, citing the historical trend.[78] PwC claims that the new jobs are focused on education, health care and personal services (e.g. cleaners, shoppers, trainers).[79] PwC can overall be classified as another status quo voice.

The consulting firm Deloitte produced a report on the future of work for UK workers. Given rapid technological change, it emphasizes the ability of workers to "acquire knowledge and apply it to different situations [as] enormously important for job success." Presumably, this will "make the labor force resilient in the face of significant change."[80] To allow for workers to move from declining to rising occupations, Deloitte emphasizes the importance of skills that are transferable. These include communication (listen, express ideas, influence others), strategy (judgment, creativity and leadership) and analysis (acquire new knowledge, process information and draw conclusions).[81] Once workers acquire "transferable" skills, they will be more resilient to technological change and displacement. Workers should not rely on 'predefined career paths' but should have transferable skills and a "confident, adaptable attitude".[82] Businesses are asked to be more open to workers making career transitions, though the main onus is still on workers who have to be flexible in skill acquisition and commit to "lifelong learning".[83] There are much weaker expectations on what employers have to do in response to technology.

Boston Consulting Group (BCG) argues that while advances in AI and automation will wipe out many jobs and reduce the need for mundane, repetitive tasks and is highly disruptive, it will create many other jobs. The report predicts a substantial shortfall of workers in computer, mathematics, architecture, management and engineering, while office/administrative, food service, transportation and production workers will be "surplus workers." The shortage of high-skilled workers suggests the importance of "upskilling and reskilling on a large scale." BCG favors the development of "metaskills" like logical thinking, reasoning, curiosity, open-mindedness, collaboration, leadership creativity and systems thinking. The government should invest in "lifelong learning" accounts to allow workers to upgrade their skills during their career. "Lifelong learning" should become the "new normal." BCG points to demographic declines in fertility that counteracts the displacement effect of automation, as there will be fewer younger workers to replace the retiring workers.[84]

The review of the consultant reports shows that automation advances can be broadly addressed by job training and education, which is in line with the view of their business clients. In the business discourse, workers must be flexible and adjust to new labor market demands, thus shifting the responsibility of worker well-being away from business, which exclusively concerns itself with profits and efficiency. The only distinction of the consultancy reports is that the consultants are more open to more progressive policy approaches like UBI or expanding the social safety net rather than labor market approaches like job training favored by business leaders. Klaus Schwab from WEF has put out a warning of the negative ramifications of automation similar to the resigned view, but this message is not consistent with the other WEF reports' messaging. For the most part, WEF reports repeat the job training mantra. WEF offers flashier vocabulary like FIR. But regarding the normative goals (business profit) and policy objectives (job training, lifelong learning etc.) there are no differences with the perspective of business CEOs. WEF and the consultancies cannot veer too far from the mainstream business discourse that portrays technology as anything but a great opportunity for business and society.

Unions and Job Training

In Chapter 3, I have characterized unions as primarily engaging in an activist discourse of social resistance to automation. But in many cases even unions are accepting of the status quo by repeating the business mantra of job training that they hope to provide themselves. UNITE HERE has been asking for digital literacy training courses to find new jobs when they are replaced by technology.[85] The UAW writes in a 2023 resolution,

> For our members, the most important way to address automation, artificial intelligence, electrification and other technological changes is with on-going training that leads to upskilling, greater access to existing apprenticeships and new apprenticeships geared to new technology. New technology should not be used as an excuse to outsource work or reduce job quality. Our members must have access to training to learn new processes to adapt to our jobs or acquire skills to transition to new ones.[86]

Thus, job training is an important protective response to automation but with the added benefit of not antagonizing their employers with automation-blocking demands or more expensive adjustment expenses like unemployment benefits.

Other unions provide job training to their members and think automation could help their own members while keeping the union relevant. The United Brotherhood of Carpenters and Joiners of America (UBC) takes pride in worker training programs, acknowledging that a "more technology-minded construction industry also drives the need for higher skills", which is in line with business executives' enthusiasm for technology and reskilling.[87] The International Union of Operating Engineers (IUOE) represents heavy equipment operators (e.g. cranes) and welcomes automation by entering a multi-year partnership with Built Robotics, a Silicon Valley startup that builds autonomous AI-guided robots at construction sites. IUOE engineers get trained to install, operate and repair these robots.[88] IUOE's director of construction training, Chris Treml, praised the collaboration arguing that "operating engineers are always on the cutting edge of technology", implying that so long as operators receive sufficient training, they will remain relevant at the job. The union's embrace of technology may be due to Built Robotics' promise that the robots won't replace jobs but enhance worker skills.[89] IUOE also has extensive experience providing technology training to union members.[90]

The International Alliance of Theatrical Stage Employees (IATSE), which represents entertainment industry technicians, has sought to protect camera crews from being displaced in the shift to high-definition (HD) production. Animation jobs under IATSE Local 839 have declined with the rise of computer-generated imagery (CGI).[91] The digitization of movies has reduced the need for projectionists, In response, IATSE has promoted further education in sound, HVAC refrigeration and other technical fields relevant to theater operations.[92] Similarly, the automation of stagehand functions, such as the automated movement of stage objects, has diminished demand for local stagehands.[93] To address these changes, IATSE dedicated a special issue of its Bulletin to automation, emphasizing its ongoing efforts to retrain members for emerging technologies. In film production, volumetric capture now enables 360-degree computer-generated imagery displayed on LED screens, reducing the need for on-location shoots and displacing some traditional film crews. To adapt, the union has expanded training in video engineering.[94] By coupling skill development with collective bargaining, IATSE has adopted an explicitly open stance toward automation, framing it as an opportunity for retraining rather than solely as a threat to jobs.

The International Union of Painters and Allied Trades (IUPAT) has also been open to automation, working together with a Silicon Valley-based construction automation start-up (Canvas) to help painters in drywall finishing. IUPAT trains and hires union workers for these automation projects, which will reduce finish time, provide a dust-free environment and reduce repetitive motions and bowing, which could reduce worker injury. The union agreement with the start-up occurred in the middle of the Covid pandemic, where social distancing became the norm, and the use of paint robots would presumably meet health/safety requirements.[95] IUPAT provides extensive job training for 15,000 apprentices.[96] IUPAT organized a 2018 webinar on paint automation, emphasizing the continued importance of human interaction and developing worker skills around construction automation.[97]

The International Association of Bridge, Structural, Ornamental and Reinforcing Iron Workers (Iron Workers) collaborates with Washtenaw Community College to provide annual instruction programs to students.[98] The executive director of the Iron Worker's apprenticeship and training program, Lee Worley, agrees with the Business Roundtable and corporate executives in de-emphasizing higher education and increasing federal funding for union-provided job training in the trades.[99] The Ironworkers' trade publication featured companies that introduce the "benefits" of steel fabrication automation, using high-tech equipment.[100] Similarly, International Brotherhood of Boilermakers, Iron Ship Builders, Blacksmiths, Forgers and Helpers (IBB) created a college fund for its members that retrains union members at Central Georgia Technical College.[101]

AFL-CIO, the national union confederation, also supports a "Just Transition" plan for energy workers, which means high wages for remaining workers and those in newly emerging industries and a "GI Bill" for displaced energy workers.[102] Empirical studies indicate that renewable energy is more labor-intensive than fossil fuel energy, which implies higher job creation via energy technology change.[103] In January 2021, the AFL-CIO launched a Technology Institute, to formulate unionization efforts amid technological change at work.[104] In a technical report titled *Industry Matters: Smarter Energy Use is Key for US Competitiveness, Jobs, and Climate Efforts*, AFL-CIO advocated for efficient energy technology, which benefits both businesses and workers.[105] In another report titled *Commission on the Future of Work and Unions*, AFL-CIO argued that it was not afraid of technological displacement:

> In the past, automation has generated enough new jobs to keep unemployment from rising, by creating demand for complementary jobs and freeing up new spending as goods and services become less expensive. In the future, we can expect new jobs and entirely new sectors of the economy to be created, even if we have no inkling today what those jobs and sectors might be.[106]

The same report also notes the importance of lifelong learning and continuing training an education preferably provided by unions to remain relevant in the labor market.

The status quo tendency among labor unions is not restricted to the US. In Germany, IG Metall Industrie 4.0 initiative focuses on providing job training in digital skills in emerging industries like renewable energy, cybersecurity and IT.[107] The Canadian branch of UFCW has called on the Canadian government and employers to promote the Future Skills initiative to support displaced workers in "lifelong training."[108]

US Political Discourse: Laissez Faire and Job Training

US political discourse on automation by presidents have been focused on two major themes: laissez faire and the need for job training. Political leaders in the laissez faire, conservative camp claim that technological unemployment is at most a temporary inconvenience and that the free enterprise private sector will be capable of accommodating all displaced workers without government interference. Political leaders, who are skeptical of the laissez faire framework and are liberal, believe that the government has to support displaced workers via job training and temporary social assistance programs. While the two policy visions appear different aligning with the big vs. small government ideologies, they are similar in the sense that none of these visions question the status quo of a market- and growth-based capitalist system that depends on human labor to function. What follows is a compilation of presidential statements since Herbert Hoover reflecting these two policy visions. Some presidents appear in both themes which suggests ambiguous views on this subject. Presidents may express laissez faire sentiments on automation policies in their speeches and statements, while their administration propose job training or social programs.

Laissez Faire: Market Forces Alone Will Lead to Job Creation.

President Herbert Hoover said in the 1930 AFL convention that technological displacement causes misery among some workers but over the long term new industries and new jobs in the service sector will absorb these laid off workers.[109] He said the nation's advance is made possible by labor-saving devices and any problems like technological unemployment can be corrected with minor economic adjustments.[110] The government's role is primarily to capture unemployment statistics, be "helpful in emergency", but leave the solution of technological unemployment to individual initiative,[111] and study the subject.[112] Hoover attacked a Congressional bill to fund a public works project, as providing pork barrel rather than employment because the public works projects created few jobs and were highly mechanized.[113]

President Dwight Eisenhower put a low priority on automation. He noted in a press conference that technology tends to create new jobs, but if it didn't he would support a commission to study it.[114] His administration promoted automation via the International Automation Congress and Exposition in 1958.[115] Toward the end of his presidency he took a more pessimistic note by claiming that coal automation could create employment problems which "take all the best brains that there are" to solve, but "arbitrary political action from the Federal Government is not going to do it".[116] While acknowledging technological displacement, he did not think it would rise to the occasion of political intervention.

In his 1968 presidential campaign, President Richard Nixon argued that displaced workers should be accommodated in a gradually expanding private sector economy, not government jobs.[117] He had the confidence that workers will be accommodated in new jobs without much government intervention.

President Gerald Ford was not concerned about automation at all. He celebrated the high productivity of American farmers using the most advanced technology (despite the small farm workforce) compared to the poorer, less efficient Soviet Union.[118] He also advocated for the deregulation of occupational licensing to encourage technological innovation.[119] Ford said that given the high oil prices in the wake of the Yom Kippur War, the US should promote domestic coal technology that reduce US dependence on foreign oil. This would create new coalmining jobs.[120] Thus, Ford associated technology with new jobs, not with the replacement of labor.

Similarly, Jimmy Carter did not find automation problematic and was concerned about the opposite concern of technological stagnation. He claimed that coal mining mechanization along with rising prices and new mining areas would relax labor-management conflicts in that industry.[121] Carter promoted the automation of processing paperwork for importers.[122] In a speech directed at unions, he argued that public works projects using the newest technology will fund many construction jobs.[123] Carter was concerned that automation was not happening fast enough given the economic "malaise" of the 1970s, which was reflected in high inflation and slow productivity growth.[124] Full employment could be restored with new technologies that create new industries.[125]

President Ronald Reagan thought that the private sector will generate enough jobs for workers. Economic growth by using high technology in the growing computer industry will also expand the service sector, which also lessens unemployment concerns.[126] He argued that the number of new service sector jobs created in the 1980s more than made up for the factory job losses happening at that time.[127]

George H.W. Bush agreed with the positive relationship between technology and jobs/skills: as automation becomes more pervasive more people needed to become 'smart workers' able to communicate, solve problems, design software and repair robots.[128] New jobs are created by "unleashing new technology".[129] He praised small businesses for developing new technology as well as new jobs.[130]

The Trump administration placed most of its emphasis on restrictive immigration and trade policies in line with the 'America first' agenda, thereby neglecting a focus on automation. The administration pointed out that in an era of automation and the disappearance of low-skilled jobs, immigrant worker visas have to be curtailed to improve job opportunities for low-skilled American workers.[131] The administration echoed the business concern of a lack of skilled workers, who can implement robots and technologies and advocates worker reskilling,[132] that is primarily sponsored by the private sector rather than the government.[133] The second term of the Trump administration continues the government minimalist approach to technology. The earlier mentioned J.D. Vance speech on AI promotion emphasized the geopolitical need of the US to innovate faster than China. It involved the deliberate disregard of social safeguards,[134] regarding data privacy, misinformation, algorithmic bias, or the risks of technological unemployment. The speech implies a deep belief that market forces will figure out how to make displaced workers useful in the labor market.

Government Intervention Is Necessary: Job Training and Social Programs

An alternative view is that the government needs to be more interventionist and assist displaced workers with job training and other social programs. In a speech in Little Rock, Arkansas, President Franklin Roosevelt argued that mechanization concentrates power in the hands of the few and the challenge is to spread the "fruits of this mechanization…to the people as a whole."[135] Roosevelt's State of the Union address in 1937 noted that "reckless overproduction", presumably from automation, was behind the depression-era unemployment.[136] In the 1940 state of the Union address, he claimed that technology-induced increases in efficiency has created surplus labor.[137] Thus, Roosevelt's redistributive demands fall somewhat outside what most presidents would have demanded, but such populist policies were meant to solidify popular support over the effects of automation on work rather than to challenge the capitalist system. Roosevelt came to power at the height of the Great Depression where socialist and communist movements were gaining political ground and Roosevelt's populist appeal weakened the political support for more left-wing policies.[138]

President Harry Truman found a positive connection between technology, rising productivity and jobs.[139] He argued that full employment can best be guaranteed if industries apply the newest scientific insights and technology.[140] As automation replaces industrial and agricultural workers, the federal government needed to invest more in education, health and social security as a provider of employment. Productivity rises could be converted into additional leisure time.[141] This remark is in line with the futurist automation discourse.

Eisenhower was open to education and job training as well but after the end of his presidency. He claimed that temporary dislocations from automation should not deter the country from pursuing it and education and training can reabsorb the laid off easily.[142]

President John Kennedy was worried about the negative effects of automation but was confident that it was a manageable problem. Replaced workers must be accommodated in new jobs via retraining,[143] improved unemployment benefits,[144] and lengthened education for the less skilled and the young.[145] If the government does not work to reduce unemployment, it will create economic losers who resist automation and thereby hinder progress and economic growth.[146]

President Lyndon Johnson supported government commissions to study labor displacement,[147] and advocated for tax cuts to stimulate the economy hoping to reduce unemployment.[148] He supported improvements in unemployment benefit[149] and viewed automation favorably for its potential to remove "dullness from the work of man".[150] He connected the 'War on Poverty' with providing training to upgrade worker skills and using the newest technology.[151] Before departing office in 1969, Johnson claimed that the low unemployment rate suggested that there was no longer any "scare talk of automation".[152] Thus, he did not believe that automation was a serious problem, but he supported federal workforce development policies.

President Richard Nixon told Labor Department officials that they were responsible for job training programs.[153] Nixon was concerned that farm mechanization shrunk the farm labor force and increase the urban-rural income gap.[154] He promoted economic assistance to states and communities impacted by structural economic changes that produced high poverty and unemployment.[155]

Reagan was generally supportive of job training programs to accommodate the laid-off from automation signing the Job Training Partnership Act in October 1982, but he was skeptical of his own program because the federal government was "wasting" money on programs that were not connected to jobs.[156]

President Bill Clinton believed in job training to respond to automation, but he was against expanding government jobs. Job training programs should kick in immediately upon layoff rather than when the unemployment benefits expire.[157] He promoted tax credits for businesses hiring disadvantaged youth.[158] He argued that his welfare-to-work scheme was a way to employ the poor.[159] Government automation is in line with his policy to shrink the size of the civil service.[160]

President George W. Bush created the *21'st Century Workforce Initiative*, where the government would study the effects of technological change on the workforce and the retraining and skills upgrading needs. He also promoted improvements in adult literacy.[161] Workers replaced by technology should be better educated so they can "shift with the technologies." He supported the Job Corps to provide job training for disadvantaged youth. He also favored R&D spending to generate new industries and jobs.[162] He believed that developing natural gas drilling and "clean coal" technology would generate jobs.[163] He also supported government-business-community college partnerships to train unemployed workers in growing health care and technology industries.[164] Community colleges "enable people to get the skills to work".[165] Bush favored the creation of an "unemployment account" of $3,000 to fund job training, relocation and child care for laid off workers.[166]

President Barack Obama argued that public investments in infrastructure building, solar and wind energy would create jobs for manufacturing workers displaced by automation.[167] R&D spending should increase to develop new industries.[168] He promoted the growth of the biomedical industry to provide medical cures.[169] He touted the creation of new industries like 3-D printing and advanced manufacturing, tax incentives to bring investments into declining manufacturing cities and training 2 million workers for new jobs.[170] He advocated AI and machine learning.[171] To develop AI, the government should provide a light-touch regulation, at least in the early exploratory phase.[172] Obama argued that automation should be dealt with by improving college access,[173] increasing federal education funding for K-12 schools in low-income neighborhoods,[174] and short job training programs.[175] He argued that higher minimum wage and collective bargaining restores worker leverage in a more automated workplace and spreads the productivity gains wider.[176] Higher corporate and marginal income taxes are also needed to spread the gains of technology.[177]

The Joe Biden administration in its official discourse has formulated positive views on the ability of AI, semiconductors and electric vehicle industries to create jobs,[178] but also acknowledged several downside risks to AI, including cybersecurity, privacy, civil rights, trust in democracy (deepfakes) and job displacement from automation.[179] Biden formulated a blueprint to invest in US supply chains, manufacturing, R&D and train people for well-paying, middle class jobs of the future.[180]

The second Trump administration's AI Action Plan that was released in the summer of 2025 states that the Department of Labor will distribute funding to states to retrain AI-displaced workers.[181]

Conclusion

The status quo discourse of automation states that new technologies should not be feared. Instead, they produce new job opportunities for workers while allowing shareholders and businesses to profit and governments to raise more tax revenues to support their operations. In the Schumpeterian theoretical framework, the stability of the capitalist system is dependent on technological innovation and rising labor productivity. Thus, the presumed economic disruption that comes from innovation is economically stabilizing. The lack of innovation rather than its presence is the threat to the social order. The status quo perspective is dismissive of the view that social disruptions from automation can become a serious problem, and they either believe in the power of the free market to generate jobs or call for job training and minor social assistance programs to respond to these concerns. The allure to the status quo discourse is that the historic track record of technological unemployment has been limited and new industries have arisen to accommodate displaced workers, but there are fair objections from the other perspectives, especially among activists and the resigned, on whether minor technocratic workforce development initiatives or social assistance programs are sufficient to ensure social stability. There are also objections about whether new technologies should only serve the interest of capital rather than broader humanity by delivering an increase in leisure time. This futurist vision is discussed in Chapter 6.

Notes

1 Vance, J.D. "Remarks by the Vice President at the Artificial Intelligence Action Summit in Paris, France." February 11, 2025. https://www.presidency.ucsb.edu/documents/remarks-the-vice-president-the-artificial-intelligence-action-summit-paris-france
2 Cobb, Charles W., and Paul H. Douglas. "A Theory of Production." *American Economic Review* 18 (Supplement: 1928): 139–65. Solow, Robert M. "A Contribution to the Theory of Economic Growth." *Quarterly Journal of Economics* 70, no. 1 (February 1956): 65–94.
3 Capitalism defenders will claim that Schumpeter was a status quo theorist, but that view is quite simplistic. Schumpeter believed in the eventual collapse of capitalism, but it would come from overbureaucratization and lack of innovation rather than working class upheaval as in the Marxist framework. It will end with a social implosion rather than a social explosion. Schumpeter, Joseph. *Capitalism, Socialism and Democracy*. New York: Harper and Brothers, 1942.
4 Comshaw-Arnold, Benjamin W. "Feudalism in Decline: The Influence of Technology on Society." Bachelor's Thesis, *Kent State University* (2014).
5 Business Roundtable. "Building America's Tomorrow-Ready Workforce." https://www.businessroundtable.org/policy-perspectives/building-americas-ever-ready-workforce

6 Business Roundtable. "Innovation Nation: An American Innovation Agenda for 2020." 2019. https://s3.amazonaws.com/brt.org/BRT-InnovationNation-Report.pdf
7 Business Roundtable. "Business Roundtable Roadmap for Responsible Artificial Intelligence." 2022. https://s3.amazonaws.com/brt.org/Business_Roundtable_Artificial_Intelligence_Roadmap_Jan2022_1.pdf
8 Business Roundtable. "Q&A: GM CEO Mary Barra on the Promise and Potential of AVs." May 6, 2019.
9 Business Roundtable. "Business Roundtable Releases Recommendations to Bolster American Leadership in Key Technologies." May 6, 2019. https://www.businessroundtable.org/business-roundtable-releases-recommendations-to-bolster-american-leadership-in-key-technologies
10 Business Roundtable. "ICYMI: United's Scott Kirby Joins Axios to Discuss Workforce Development." September 25, 2023. https://www.businessroundtable.org/icymi-uniteds-scott-kirby-joins-axios-to-discuss-workforce-development
11 Business Roundtable. "Revolutionizing Manufacturing." December 6, 2018. https://www.businessroundtable.org/brt-innovation-summit-revolutionizing-manufacturing
12 Business Roundtable. "Recap: Business Roundtable CEO Workforce Forum." July 18, 2025.
13 NAM. "Report: Automation Offers Manufacturing Opportunities." May 23, 2019.
14 NAM. "Rep. Joyce Touts Tax Reform Benefits at Rockwell Automation." August 13, 2018.
15 NAM. "2.1 Million Manufacturing Jobs Could Go Unfilled by 2030." May 4, 2021.
16 NAM. "Rep. Joyce Touts Tax Reform Benefits at Rockwell Automation." August 13, 2018.
17 NAM. "NAM Hails Manufacturing in California on State of Manufacturing Tour." February 27, 2019.
18 NAM. "A Hiring Engine: A Breakdown of the Job Openings in Manufacturing." 2019. Retrieved on March 18, 2021. https://www.themanufacturinginstitute.org/wp-content/uploads/2020/03/MI-Hiring-Engine-Job-Opening-Paper.pdf
19 NAM. "NAM Unveils Historic "Creators Wanted" Campaign Showcasing Modern Manufacturing." February 12, 2020. Creators Wanted. "Building the Workforce of Tomorrow." Retrieved on March 18, 2021.
20 Manufacturing Institute (NAMI). "Industrial Mobility: How Autonomous Vehicles Can Change Manufacturing." February 2018.
21 NAMI. "Small and Medium-Sized Manufacturers Survey: The 'New Normal' and Post-Pandemic Workforce Challenges." February 2021. Retrieved on March 18, 2021. https://www.themanufacturinginstitute.org/wp-content/uploads/2021/02/BKD-MI-Survey-Feb2021.pdf
22 NAMI and PwC. "Navigating the Fourth Industrial Revolution to the Bottom Line." 2019. Retrieved on March 18, 2021. https://www.themanufacturinginstitute.org/wp-content/uploads/2020/03/MI-Smart-Factory-4IR-Report.pdf
23 NAM. "Manufacturing Trends 2025." 2025 https://nam.org/wp-content/uploads/securepdfs/2025/01/NAM-2025-Manufacturing-Trends.pdf
24 NAM. "NAM and MI: AI Will Strengthen the Manufacturing Workforce." August 6, 2025. https://nam.org/nam-and-mi-ai-will-strengthen-the-manufacturing-workforce-34550/
25 NAM. "AI's Rising Power in Manufacturing Spurs Call for Smarter AI Policy Solutions." May 29, 2025. https://nam.org/ais-rising-power-in-manufacturing-spurs-call-for-smarter-ai-policy-solutions-34092/
26 U.S. Chamber of Commerce. "2025 Chamber Technology Priorities." 2025 https://www.uschamber.com/assets/documents/CTEC_2025_Technology-Priorities.pdf
27 Day, Tim. "U.S. Chamber Letter on the Hearing, "Highly Automated Vehicles: Federal Perspectives on the Deployment of Safety Technology"." *U.S. Chamber of Commerce*, November 19, 2019.

28 U.S. Chamber of Commerce. "C_TEC Submits Comments to DOT following the Autonomous Vehicle Policy Summit." March 9, 2018. U.S. Chamber of Commerce. "We Want the U.S. to Lead in Driverless Cars. Here's What Washington Can Do to Help." January 26, 2018.
29 Crenshaw, Jordan, and Julie Stitzel. "The Chamber Embraces Biden. And Republicans Are Livid." *Politico*, February 12, 2021.
30 U.S. Chamber of Commerce. "Commercial Construction Index, Q4 2018." 2018. https://www.uschamber.com/sites/default/files/cci_2018_q4_report.pdf
31 U.S. Chamber of Commerce. "Dear 45- A Letter on Innovation to Our Next President." November 9, 2016.
32 Kim, Harold. "Consumers Overwhelmingly Say Lawsuits Should Not "Regulate" New Technologies." *U.S. Chamber of Commerce*, April 18, 2018.
33 U.S. Chamber of Commerce. "U.S. Chamber Applauds Executive Order Promoting the Use of Artificial Intelligence in the Federal Government." December 4, 2020.
34 U.S. Chamber of Commerce. "U.S. Chamber Policy Priorities for 2020." January 9, 2020.
35 U.S. Chamber of Commerce. "U.S. Chamber Statement on President Obama's Announcement Regarding Municipal Broadband." January 14, 2015.
36 Quaadman, Tom. "How Technology Enables Small Business." *U.S. Chamber of Commerce*, July 29, 2020.
37 U.S. Chamber of Commerce. "Future of the Workforce." 2020.
38 Bradley, Neil L. "U.S. Chamber Letter on the Hearing, "The Future of Work: Preserving Worker Protections in the Modern Economy."" *U.S. Chamber of Commerce*, October 23, 2019.
39 U.S. Chamber of Commerce. "Future of the Workforce."
40 Donohue, Thomas. "An Attack on Entrepreneurship and Innovation." *U.S. Chamber of Commerce*, March 14, 2016.
41 U.S. Chamber of Commerce. "Future of the Workforce."
42 U.S. Chamber of Commerce. "Data Centers: Jobs & Opportunities in Communities Nationwide." June 15, 2017
43 Hackbarth, Sean. "The State of the App Economy Is Strong: 1.6 Million Jobs in 2015." *U.S. Chamber of Commerce*, January 12, 2016.
44 Marinaccio, Michael. "Jose Canseco Says Robots Are Stealing Our Jobs. Are They?" *U.S. Chamber of Commerce*, February 22, 2017
45 Donohue, Thomas J. "Maximizing the Promise of the New Economy." *U.S. Chamber of Commerce*, March 12, 2018.
46 U.S. Chamber of Commerce. "Commercial Construction Looks to Advanced Technologies to Alleviate Workforce Challenges and Improve Productivity." December 11, 2018.
47 Orrell, Brent. "AI and the Future of Work: Preparing the Workforce for an AI-Driven Economy." *U.S. Chamber of Commerce*, March 31, 2023.
48 U.S. Chamber of Commerce. "U.S. Chamber's Latest "Empowering Small Business" Report Shows Majority of Businesses in All 50 States Are Embracing AI." August 18, 2025. https://www.uschamber.com/technology/artificial-intelligence/u-s-chambers-latest-empowering-small-business-report-shows-majority-of-businesses-in-all-50-states-are-embracing-ai
49 Schiølin, Kasper. 2020. "Revolutionary Dreams: Future Essentialism and the Sociotechnical Imaginary of the Fourth Industrial Revolution in Denmark." *Social Studies of Science* 50, no. 4: 542–66.
50 Schiølin. "Revolutionary Dreams." p. 4.
51 This is criticized in the STS framework. See Haraway, Donna. *Simians, Cyborgs, and Women: The Reinvention of Nature*. New York: Routledge, 1991. Latour, Bruno. *We Have Never Been Modern*. Cambridge, MA: Harvard University Press, 1993.
52 Winner, Langdon. "Prophets of Inevitability." *MIT Technology Review* 101, no. 2 (1998): 62.

53 Wikipedia. "World Economic Forum." https://en.wikipedia.org/wiki/World_Economic_Forum
54 Monck, Adrian. "New Forum Center to Advance Global Cooperation on Fourth Industrial Revolution." *World Economic Forum*, October 10, 2016.
55 Schwab, Klaus. *The Fourth Industrial Revolution*. London: Geneva: World Economic Forum, 2016, pp. 11, 21. https://law.unimelb.edu.au/__data/assets/pdf_file/0005/3385454/Schwab-The_Fourth_Industrial_Revolution_Klaus_S.pdf
56 Schwab. *The Fourth Industrial Revolution*, p. 14.
57 Schwab. *The Fourth Industrial Revolution*, pp. 16–17.
58 Schwab. *The Fourth Industrial Revolution*, p. 49.
59 Schwab. *The Fourth Industrial Revolution*, p. 70.
60 Schwab. *The Fourth Industrial Revolution*, p. 88.
61 World Economic Forum. "The Future of Jobs Report 2020." October 20, 2020, p. 13. https://www.weforum.org/reports/the-future-of-jobs-report-2020
62 World Economic Forum. "The Future of Jobs Report 2020." pp. 36–37.
63 World Economic Forum. "The Future of Jobs Report 2020." p. 30.
64 World Economic Forum. "The Future of Jobs Report 2020." p. 3.
65 World Economic Forum. "The Future of Jobs Report 2020." p. 5.
66 World Economic Forum. "The Future of Jobs Report 2020." p. 6.
67 World Economic Forum. "The Future of Jobs Report 2020." p. 45.
68 World Economic Forum. "The Future of Jobs Report 2020." p. 48.
69 Schiølin. "Revolutionary Dreams."
70 Werr, Andreas, and Torbjörn Stjernberg. "Exploring Management Consulting Firms as Knowledge Systems." *Organization Studies* 24, no. 6 (2003): 881–908.
71 Hyman, Louis. *Temp: How American Work, American Business, and the American Dream Became Temporary*. New York: Viking, 2018.
72 About 5% of occupations are completely replaceable, but 60% of jobs have at least 30% of their tasks automatable. Manyika, James, Michael Chui, Anu Madgavkar, and Susan Lund. *Technology, Jobs and the Future of Work*. San Francisco, CA: McKinsey Global Institute, 2017.
73 McKinsey Global Institute. "A New Future of Work: The Race to Deploy AI and Raise Skills in Europe and Beyond." May 21, 2024. https://www.mckinsey.com/mgi/our-research/a-new-future-of-work-the-race-to-deploy-ai-and-raise-skills-in-europe-and-beyond
74 Hawksworth, John, Richard Berriman, and Saloni Goel. *Will Robots Really Steal Our Jobs? An International Analysis of the Potential Long Term Impact of Automation*. London: PricewaterhouseCoopers, 2018, p. 36.
75 Hawksworth et al. *Will Robots Really Steal Our Jobs? An International Analysis of the Potential Long Term Impact of Automation*, p. 7.
76 Hawksworth et al. *Will Robots Really Steal Our Jobs? An International Analysis of the Potential Long Term Impact of Automation*, p. 8.
77 Hawksworth et al. *Will Robots Really Steal Our Jobs? An International Analysis of the Potential Long Term Impact of Automation*, p. 34.
78 Hawksworth et al. *Will Robots Really Steal Our Jobs? An International Analysis of the Potential Long Term Impact of Automation*, p. 17.
79 Hawksworth et al. *Will Robots Really Steal Our Jobs? An International Analysis of the Potential Long Term Impact of Automation*, p. 22.
80 Deloitte. *Power Up: UK Skills*. London: Deloitte, 2018, p. 3.
81 Deloitte. *Power Up: UK Skills*, p. 6.
82 Deloitte. *Power Up: UK Skills*, p. 11.
83 Deloitte. *Power Up: UK Skills*, p. 23.
84 Strack, Rainer, Miguel Carrasco, Philipp Kolo, Nicholas Nouri, Michael Priddis, and Richard George. "The Future of Jobs in the Era of AI." *Boston Consulting Group,* March 18, 2021. https://www.bcg.com/publications/2021/impact-of-new-technologies-on-jobs

85 Unite Here. "Prepared for U.S. Senate AI Insight Forum: Workforce." November 1, 2023. https://www.schumer.senate.gov/imo/media/doc/Paul%20Schwalb%20-%20Statement.pdf
86 UAW. "2023 Special Bargaining Convention." 2023, p. 35. https://uaw.org/wp-content/uploads/2023/11/UAW_resolutions-2023_v2_plus_additions.pdf
87 Accelerator for America. "UBC General President Douglas Mccarron: High-Skilled Professionals Pouring Concrete? You Bet." *Medium*, November 26, 2018. Also see Carpenter Magazine. "Mechatronics: Up-to-the-Minute Training for a Booming Automation Industry." 2015, p. 22. https://www.carpenters.org/wp-content/uploads/2017/04/2015-Carpenter-Magazine-US-1.pdf
88 Robotics Business Review. "Built Robotics Partners with International Union of Operating Engineers for Training." June 12, 2020.
89 Simonite, Tom. "Construction Workers Embrace the Robots That Do Their Jobs." *Wired*, March 10, 2020. Also see Bergeron, Tom. "Local 825's Lalevee Says Automation Isn't Killing Union Jobs, It's Changing Them — So His Union Must Update Training, Too." *ROI-NJ.com*, January 16, 2020.
90 IUOE. "Training Programs." Retrieved on February 23, 2021. https://www.iuoe.org/training
91 McAdams, Deborah. "Digital Displacement: The State of Our Unions." *TV Technology*, September 13, 2003.
92 IATSE. "Training Need to Keep Projectionist Jobs." N.d.
93 IATSE. "Bulletin." Third Quarter, 2008. http://www.iatse8.com/Docs/pdf/Bulletin/621.pdf
94 IATSE. "Bulletin." Second Quarter, 2019. https://iatse.net/wp-content/uploads/2021/05/IATSE-2nd-2019-web.pdf
95 Robotics Tomorrow. "Construction Robotics Startup Canvas Announces Public Launch." November 20, 2020.
96 IUPAT. "Painters and Allied Trades Journal." Spring 2019. Retrieved March 7, 2019. https://iupat.org/wp-content/uploads/2019_Issue-1_January-March-1.pdf
97 Finishing First LMCI. "May 3: IFTI on VR Webinar Panel with Engineering News Record." May 3, 2018.
98 Automation Alley. "Washtenaw Community College, Ann Arbor Area Welcomes Ironworkers Back for Annual Instructor Training Program." July 17, 2019.
99 Worley, Lee. "Promoting Skilled Trades." *Iron Workers*, January 2019.
100 The Ironworker. November 2020. Retrieved on March 8, 2021. https://iwmagazine.iwintl.org/PdfView.aspx?Filename=%2fsites%2fIronworkersMagazine%2fShared+Documents%2f2020%2fThe+Ironworker+-+2020-11.pdf
101 Boilermakers. "L-D23 Boosts Education and Safety at Cemex Plant." January 2, 2020. https://boilermakers.org/news/locals/local-d23-boosts-education-and-safety-at-cemex-plant
102 Shuler, Liz. "Shuler to the Climate Jobs and Just Transition Summit: The Renewable Sector Must Be Unionized." *AFL-CIO*, September 22, 2020.
103 Garrett-Peltier, Heidi. "Green Versus Brown: Comparing the Employment Impacts of Energy Efficiency, Renewable Energy, and Fossil Fuels Using an Input-Output Model." *Economic Modelling* 61 (2017): 439–47.
104 AFL-CIO. "AFL-CIO Launches Technology Institute." January 11, 2021.
105 AFL-CIO. "Industry Matters: Smarter Energy Use Is Key for US Competitiveness, Jobs, and Climate Efforts." October 10, 2018.
106 AFL-CIO. "AFL-CIO Commission on the Future of Work and Unions." September 13, 2019.
107 Cogent Infotech. 2025. „Union Roles in AI Oversight: Ethical Workforce Transitions in Tech." June 17.
108 UFCW Canada. "Future Skills Initiative Should Focus on Needs of Workers." March 18, 2019. https://www.ufcw.ca/index.php?option=com_content&view=article&id=32226&catid=10042&lang=en

109 Bix, Amy Sue. *Inventing Ourselves Out of Jobs?* Baltimore, MD: Johns Hopkins University Press, 2000, p. 47.
110 Bix, *Inventing Ourselves,* p. 48.
111 Hoover, Herbert. "Address to the Chamber of Commerce of the United States, May 1, 1930." In *Public Papers of the Presidents of the United States 1930.* US Government Printing Office, 1976. https://hoover.archives.gov/sites/default/files/research/ebooks/b2v2_full.pdf .
112 Hoover, Herbert. "Statement on the Appointment of John R. Alpine to the United States Employment Service, March 13, 1931." In *Public Papers of the Presidents of the United States 1931.* US Government Printing Office, 1976. https://hoover.archives.gov/sites/default/files/research/ebooks/b2v3_full.pdf
113 Hoover, Herbert. "The President's News Conference of May 27, 1932." In *Public Papers of the Presidents of the United States 1932-3.* US Government Printing Office, 1977. https://hoover.archives.gov/sites/default/files/research/ebooks/b2v4_full.pdf
114 Eisenhower, Dwight D. "The President's News Conference." *UCSB American Presidency Project,* March 16, 1955. https://www.presidency.ucsb.edu/documents/the-presidents-news-conference-325
115 Eisenhower, Dwight D. "Proclamation 3240—Fourth International Automation Congress and Exposition." *UCSB American Presidency Project,* May 9, 1958. https://www.presidency.ucsb.edu/documents/proclamation-3240-fourth-international-automation-congress-and-exposition
116 Eisenhower, Dwight D. "The President's News Conference." *UCSB American Presidency Project,* March 25, 1959. https://www.presidency.ucsb.edu/documents/the-presidents-news-conference-230
117 Nixon, Richard M. "Remarks on the CBS Radio Network: "An Open Door for American Labor"." *UCSB American Presidency Project,* October 21, 1968. https://www.presidency.ucsb.edu/documents/remarks-the-cbs-radio-network-open-door-for-american-labor
118 Ford, Gerald R. "Remarks and a Question-and-Answer Session at Tyler Junior College, Tyler, Texas." *UCSB American Presidency Project,* April 28, 1976. https://www.presidency.ucsb.edu/documents/remarks-and-question-and-answer-session-tyler-junior-college-tyler-texas
119 Ford, Gerald R. "Annual Message to the Congress: The Economic Report of the President." *UCSB American Presidency Project,* January 18, 1977. https://www.presidency.ucsb.edu/documents/annual-message-the-congress-the-economic-report-the-president-0
120 Ford, Gerald R. "Remarks at a Republican Party Fundraising Dinner in Charleston." *UCSB American Presidency Project,* November 11, 1975. https://www.presidency.ucsb.edu/documents/remarks-republican-party-fundraising-dinner-charleston
121 Carter, Jimmy. "Interview with the President Question-and-Answer Session with a Group of Publishers, Editors, and Broadcasters." *UCSB American Presidency Project,* June 24, 1977. https://www.presidency.ucsb.edu/documents/interview-with-the-president-question-and-answer-session-with-group-publishers-editors-and
122 Carter, Jimmy. "Statement on Signing H.R. 8149 Into Law - Customs Procedural Reform and Simplification Act of 1978." *UCSB American Presidency Project,* October 4, 1978. https://www.presidency.ucsb.edu/documents/statement-signing-hr-8149-into-law-customs-procedural-reform-and-simplification-act-1978
123 Carter, Jimmy. "San Diego, California Remarks at the Annual Convention of the Building and Construction Trades Department, AFL-CIO." *UCSB American Presidency Project,* October 11, 1979. https://www.presidency.ucsb.edu/documents/san-diego-california-remarks-the-annual-convention-the-building-and-construction-trades

124 Carter, Jimmy. "Annual Message to the Congress: The Economic Report of the President." *UCSB American Presidency Project*, January 20, 1978. https://www.presidency.ucsb.edu/documents/annual-message-the-congress-the-economic-report-the-president-10
125 Carter, Jimmy. "The Nation's Economy Radio Address to the Nation." *UCSB American Presidency Project*, October 12, 1980. https://www.presidency.ucsb.edu/documents/the-nations-economy-radio-address-the-nation
126 Reagan, Ronald. "Remarks and a Question-and-Answer Session via Satellite to the Young Presidents Organization in Tucson, Arizona." *UCSB American Presidency Project*, February 14, 1983. https://www.presidency.ucsb.edu/documents/remarks-and-question-and-answer-session-via-satellite-the-young-presidents-organization
127 Reagan, Ronald. "Interview With Representatives of College Radio Stations." *UCSB American Presidency Project*, September 9, 1985. https://www.presidency.ucsb.edu/documents/interview-with-representatives-college-radio-stations
128 Bush, George H.W. "Remarks at the Presentation Ceremony for the American Success Awards." *UCSB American Presidency Project*, September 11, 1989. https://www.presidency.ucsb.edu/documents/remarks-the-presentation-ceremony-for-the-american-success-awards
129 Bush, George H.W. "Remarks at the Electronic Industries Association's Government-Industry Dinner." *UCSB American Presidency Project*, March 15, 1989. https://www.presidency.ucsb.edu/documents/remarks-the-electronic-industries-associations-government-industry-dinner
130 Bush, George H.W. "Proclamation 6289—Small Business Week, 1991." *UCSB American Presidency Project*, May 7, 1991. https://www.presidency.ucsb.edu/documents/proclamation-6289-small-business-week-1991
131 Trump, Donald J. "Press Briefing by Press Secretary Sarah Sanders and Senior Policy Advisor Stephen Miller." *UCSB American Presidency Project*, August 2, 2017. https://www.presidency.ucsb.edu/documents/press-briefing-press-secretary-sarah-sanders-and-senior-policy-advisor-stephen-miller
132 Trump, Donald J. "President Donald J. Trump's Administration Is Taking Action to Equip American Students and Workers with the Skills They Need to Succeed." *UCSB American Presidency Project*, July 29, 2018. https://www.presidency.ucsb.edu/documents/president-donald-j-trumps-administration-taking-action-equip-american-students-and-workers
133 Trump, Donald J. "Press Release – President Donald J. Trump's Commitment to Workforce Development Generates Training Opportunities for Millions of Americans." *UCSB American Presidency Project*, October 31, 2018. https://www.presidency.ucsb.edu/documents/press-release-president-donald-j-trumps-commitment-workforce-development-generates
134 Vance, J.D. "Remarks by the Vice President at the Artificial Intelligence Action Summit in Paris, France." *UCSB American Presidency Project*, February 11, 2025. https://www.presidency.ucsb.edu/documents/remarks-the-vice-president-the-artificial-intelligence-action-summit-paris-france
135 Roosevelt, Franklin D. "Address at Little Rock, Arkansas." *UCSB American Presidency Project*, June 10, 1936. https://www.presidency.ucsb.edu/documents/address-little-rock-arkansas
136 Bix, Amy Sue. *Inventing Ourselves out of Jobs?* Baltimore, MD: Johns Hopkins University Press, 2000, p. 62. Roosevelt, Franklin D. "Message to Congress - State of the Union (Speech File 1028), January 6, 1937." *FDR Library*. http://www.fdrlibrary.marist.edu/archives/collections/franklin/index.php?p=collections/findingaid&id=582
137 Bix, *Inventing Ourselves*, p. 73. "We have not yet found a way to employ the surplus of our labor which the efficiency of our industrial processes has created."

Roosevelt, Franklin D. "Message to Congress – State of the Union Address (Speech File 1262)," January 3, 1940.
138 Lipset, Seymour Martin. "Roosevelt and the Protest of the 1930s." *Minnesota Law Review* 2317 (1984). https://scholarship.law.umn.edu/mlr/2317
139 Truman, Harry S. "Special Message to the Congress: The President's Midyear Economic Report." July 19, 1952. https://www.trumanlibrary.gov/library/public-papers/215/special-message-congress-presidents-midyear-economic-report
140 Truman, Harry S. "Annual Message to the Congress: The President's Economic Report." *Truman Library*, January 14, 1953. https://www.trumanlibrary.gov/library/public-papers/376/annual-message-congress-presidents-economic-report
141 Truman, Harry S. "Excerpts from Annual Message: The President's Economic Report to the Congress." *Truman Library*, January 14, 1948. https://www.trumanlibrary.gov/library/public-papers/8/excerpts-annual-message-president-s-economic-report-congress
142 Eisenhower, Dwight D. "Speech at Life Insurance Association, New York City." *Eisenhower Library*, December 9, 1964. https://www.eisenhowerlibrary.gov/sites/default/files/file/post_presidential_speeches.pdf
143 Kennedy, John F. "Special Message to the Congress on Taxation." *UCSB American Presidency Project*, April 20, 1961. https://www.presidency.ucsb.edu/documents/special-message-the-congress-taxation
144 Kennedy, John F. "Letter to the President of the Senate and to the Speaker of the House on the Unemployment Compensation System." *UCSB American Presidency Project*, March 12, 1962. https://www.presidency.ucsb.edu/documents/letter-the-president-the-senate-and-the-speaker-the-house-the-unemployment-compensation
145 Kennedy, John F. "Remarks at a Civic Luncheon in Chicago." *UCSB American Presidency Project*, March 23, 1963. https://www.presidency.ucsb.edu/documents/remarks-civic-luncheon-chicago
146 Kennedy, John F. "Address and Question and Answer Period at the Economic Club of New York." *UCSB American Presidency Project*, December 14, 1962. https://www.presidency.ucsb.edu/documents/address-and-question-and-answer-period-the-economic-club-new-york
147 Johnson, Lyndon B. "Annual Message to the Congress: The Economic Report of the President." *UCSB American Presidency Project*, January 20, 1964. https://www.presidency.ucsb.edu/documents/annual-message-the-congress-the-economic-report-the-president-13
148 Johnson, Lyndon B. "Remarks in Atlantic City at the Convention of the United Auto Workers." *UCSB American Presidency Project*, March 23, 1964. https://www.presidency.ucsb.edu/documents/remarks-atlantic-city-the-convention-the-united-auto-workers
149 Johnson, Lyndon B. "Special Message to the Congress on Labor." *UCSB American Presidency Project*, May 18, 1965. https://www.presidency.ucsb.edu/documents/special-message-the-congress-labor
150 Johnson, Lyndon B. "Remarks upon Signing Bill Creating the National Commission on Technology, Automation, and Economic Progress." *UCSB American Presidency Project*, August 19, 1964. https://www.presidency.ucsb.edu/documents/remarks-upon-signing-bill-creating-the-national-commission-technology-automation-and
151 Johnson, Lyndon B. "Remarks in Atlantic City at the Convention of the United Auto Workers." *UCSBAmericanPresidencyProject*,March23,1964.https://www.presidency.ucsb.edu/documents/remarks-atlantic-city-the-convention-the-united-auto-workers
152 Johnson, Lyndon B. "Remarks to Members of the Business Council." *UCSB American Presidency Project*, December 4, 1968. https://www.presidency.ucsb.edu/documents/remarks-members-the-business-council-0

153 Nixon, Richard M. "Remarks to Top Officials at the Department of Labor." *UCSB American Presidency Project*, February 4, 1969. https://www.presidency.ucsb.edu/documents/remarks-top-officials-the-department-labor
154 Nixon, Richard M. "Special Message to the Congress on Rural Development." *UCSB American Presidency Project*, February 1, 1972. https://www.presidency.ucsb.edu/documents/special-message-the-congress-rural-development
155 Nixon, Richard M. "Annual Message to the Congress on the State of the Union." *UCSB American Presidency Project*, January 30, 1974. https://www.presidency.ucsb.edu/documents/annual-message-the-congress-the-state-the-union
156 Reagan, Ronald. "Question-and-Answer Session with High School Students on Domestic and Foreign Policy Issues." *UCSB American Presidency Project*, March 25, 1983. https://www.presidency.ucsb.edu/documents/question-and-answer-session-with-high-school-students-domestic-and-foreign-policy-issues-0
157 Clinton, William J. "Remarks in a Town Meeting in Sacramento." *UCSB American Presidency Project*, October 3, 1993. https://www.presidency.ucsb.edu/documents/remarks-town-meeting-sacramento
158 Clinton, William J. "Message to the Congress on Small Business." *UCSB American Presidency Project*, February 1, 1994. https://www.presidency.ucsb.edu/documents/message-the-congress-small-business-0
159 Clinton, William J. "Remarks and a Question-and-Answer Session with the Economic Club of Detroit in Detroit, Michigan." *UCSB American Presidency Project*, January 8, 1999. https://www.presidency.ucsb.edu/documents/remarks-and-question-and-answer-session-with-the-economic-club-detroit-detroit-michigan
160 Clinton, William J. "Remarks at a Town Meeting in San Diego." *UCSB American Presidency Project*, May 17, 1993. https://www.presidency.ucsb.edu/documents/remarks-town-meeting-san-diego
161 Bush, George W. "Executive Order 13218—21st Century Workforce Initiative." *UCSB American Presidency Project*, June 20, 2001. https://www.presidency.ucsb.edu/documents/executive-order-13218-21st-century-workforce-initiative
162 Bush, George W. "Remarks to Employees of the Cecil I. Walker Machinery Company in Belle." *UCSB American Presidency Project*, January 22, 2002. https://www.presidency.ucsb.edu/documents/remarks-employees-the-cecil-i-walker-machinery-company-belle
163 Bush, George W. "Remarks to the Greater Manchester Chamber of Commerce in Manchester, New Hampshire." *UCSB American Presidency Project*, October 9, 2003. https://www.presidency.ucsb.edu/documents/remarks-the-greater-manchester-chamber-commerce-manchester-new-hampshire
164 Bush, George W. "Remarks at Northern Virginia Community College in Annandale, Virginia." *UCSB American Presidency Project*, June 17, 2003. https://www.presidency.ucsb.edu/documents/remarks-northern-virginia-community-college-annandale-virginia
165 Bush, George W. "Remarks in a Discussion on Job Training in Arnold, Maryland." *UCSB American Presidency Project*, March 2, 2005. https://www.presidency.ucsb.edu/documents/remarks-discussion-job-training-arnold-maryland
166 Bush, George W. "Remarks in Livonia, Michigan." *UCSB American Presidency Project*, July 24, 2003. https://www.presidency.ucsb.edu/documents/remarks-livonia-michigan-0
167 Obama, Barack. "Remarks at Lehigh Carbon Community College and a Question-and-Answer Session in Allentown, Pennsylvania." *UCSB American Presidency Project*, December 4, 2009. https://www.presidency.ucsb.edu/documents/remarks-lehigh-carbon-community-college-and-question-and-answer-session-allentown
168 Obama, Barack. "Remarks at a Town Hall Meeting and a Question-and-Answer Session at Millennium Steel Service, LLC, in Princeton, Indiana." *UCSB American*

Presidency Project, October 3, 2014. https://www.presidency.ucsb.edu/documents/remarks-town-hall-meeting-and-question-and-answer-session-millennium-steel-service-llc

169 Obama, Barack. "The Budget Message of the President." *UCSB American Presidency Project*, February 2, 2015. https://www.presidency.ucsb.edu/documents/the-budget-message-the-president-20

170 Obama, Barack. "Remarks at the Facilities of the Linamar Corporation in Arden, North Carolina." *UCSB American Presidency Project*, February 13, 2013. https://www.presidency.ucsb.edu/documents/remarks-the-facilities-the-linamar-corporation-arden-north-carolina

171 Obama, Barack. "Press Release – ICYMI: White House Frontiers: Robots, Space Exploration, and the Future of American Innovation." *UCSB American Presidency Project*, October 7, 2016. https://www.presidency.ucsb.edu/documents/press-release-icymi-white-house-frontiers-robots-space-exploration-and-the-future-american

172 Obama, Barack. "Interview with Joi Ito of MIT and Scott Dadich of WIRED." *UCSB American Presidency Project*, August 24, 2016. https://www.presidency.ucsb.edu/documents/interview-with-joi-ito-mit-and-scott-dadich-wired

173 Obama, Barack. "Remarks at a Democratic National Committee Fundraiser in Philadelphia." *UCSB American Presidency Project*, June 30, 2011. https://www.presidency.ucsb.edu/documents/remarks-democratic-national-committee-fundraiser-philadelphia

174 Obama, Barack. "Remarks and a Question-and-Answer Session at a Town Hall Meeting at McKinley Senior High School in Baton Rouge, Louisiana." *UCSB American Presidency Project*, January 14, 2016. https://www.presidency.ucsb.edu/documents/remarks-and-question-and-answer-session-town-hall-meeting-mckinley-senior-high-school

175 Obama, Barack. "Remarks and a Question-and-Answer Session at a Young Leaders of the Americas Initiative Town Hall Meeting in Lima, Peru." *UCSB American Presidency Project*, November 19, 2016. https://www.presidency.ucsb.edu/documents/remarks-and-question-and-answer-session-young-leaders-the-americas-initiative-town-hall

176 Obama, Barack. "Interview with Steve Inskeep of National Public Radio." *UCSB American Presidency Project*, June 27, 2016. https://www.presidency.ucsb.edu/documents/interview-with-steve-inskeep-national-public-radio-4

177 Obama, Barack. "Farewell Address to the Nation from Chicago, Illinois." *UCSB American Presidency Project*, January 10, 2017. https://www.presidency.ucsb.edu/documents/farewell-address-the-nation-from-chicago-illinois

178 Biden, Joseph R. Jr. "Statement on Senate Passage of the United States Innovation and Competition Act." *UCSB American Presidency Project*, June 8, 2021. https://www.presidency.ucsb.edu/documents/statement-senate-passage-the-united-states-innovation-and-competition-act

179 Biden, Joseph R. Jr. "Background Press Call by a Senior Administration Official on New Artificial Intelligence Announcements." *UCSB American Presidency Project*, May 3, 2023. https://www.presidency.ucsb.edu/documents/background-press-call-senior-administration-official-new-artificial-intelligence

180 Biden, Joseph R. Jr. „FACT SHEET: The American Jobs Plan." *UCSB American Presidency Project*, March 31, 2021. https://www.presidency.ucsb.edu/documents/fact-sheet-the-american-jobs-plan

181 Trump White House. "Winning the Race: America's AI Action Plan." July 2025. https://www.whitehouse.gov/wp-content/uploads/2025/07/Americas-AI-Action-Plan.pdf

References

Accelerator for America. "UBC General President Douglas McCarron: High-Skilled Professionals Pouring Concrete? You Bet." *Medium*, November 26, 2018.

AFL-CIO. "Industry Matters: Smarter Energy Use Is Key for U.S. Competitiveness, Jobs, and Climate Efforts." October 10, 2018.

AFL-CIO. "AFL-CIO Commission on the Future of Work and Unions." September 13, 2019.

AFL-CIO. "AFL-CIO Launches Technology Institute." January 11, 2021.

Automation Alley. "Washtenaw Community College, Ann Arbor Area Welcomes Ironworkers Back for Annual Instructor Training Program." July 17, 2019.

Bergeron, Tom. "Local 825's Lalevee Says Automation Isn't Killing Union Jobs, It's Changing Them — So His Union Must Update Training, Too." *ROI-NJ.com*, January 16, 2020.

Biden, Joseph R., Jr. "FACT SHEET: The American Jobs Plan." *American Presidency Project*, March 31, 2021.

Biden, Joseph R., Jr. "Statement on Senate Passage of the United States Innovation and Competition Act." *American Presidency Project*, June 8, 2021.

Biden, Joseph R., Jr. "Background Press Call by a Senior Administration Official on New Artificial Intelligence Announcements." *American Presidency Project*, May 3, 2023.

Bix, Amy Sue. *Inventing Ourselves Out of Jobs? America's Debate over Technological Unemployment, 1929–1981*. Baltimore, MD: Johns Hopkins University Press, 2000.

Boilermakers. "L-D23 Boosts Education and Safety at Cemex Plant." January 2, 2020.

Bradley, Neil L. "U.S. Chamber Letter on the Hearing, 'The Future of Work: Preserving Worker Protections in the Modern Economy.'" U.S. Chamber of Commerce, October 23, 2019.

Bush, George H.W. "Remarks at the Electronic Industries Association's Government-Industry Dinner." *UCSB American Presidency Project*, March 15, 1989. https://www.presidency.ucsb.edu/documents/remarks-the-electronic-industries-associations-government-industry-dinner

Bush, George H.W. "Remarks at the Presentation Ceremony for the American Success Awards." *UCSB American Presidency Project*, September 11, 1989. https://www.presidency.ucsb.edu/documents/remarks-the-presentation-ceremony-for-the-american-success-awards

Bush, George H.W. "Proclamation 6289—Small Business Week, 1991." *UCSB American Presidency Project*, May 7, 1991. https://www.presidency.ucsb.edu/documents/proclamation-6289-small-business-week-1991

Bush, George W. "Executive Order 13218—21st Century Workforce Initiative." *UCSB American Presidency Project*, June 20, 2001. https://www.presidency.ucsb.edu/documents/executive-order-13218-21st-century-workforce-initiative

Bush, George W. "Remarks to Employees of the Cecil I. Walker Machinery Company in Belle." *UCSB American Presidency Project*, January 22, 2002. https://www.presidency.ucsb.edu/documents/remarks-employees-the-cecil-i-walker-machinery-company-belle

Bush, George W. "Remarks at Northern Virginia Community College in Annandale, Virginia." *UCSB American Presidency Project*, June 17, 2003. https://www.presidency.ucsb.edu/documents/remarks-northern-virginia-community-college-annandale-virginia

Bush, George W. "Remarks in Livonia, Michigan." *UCSB American Presidency Project*, July 24, 2003. https://www.presidency.ucsb.edu/documents/remarks-livonia-michigan-0

Bush, George W. "Remarks to the Greater Manchester Chamber of Commerce in Manchester, New Hampshire." *UCSB American Presidency Project*, October 9, 2003. https://www.presidency.ucsb.edu/documents/remarks-the-greater-manchester-chamber-commerce-manchester-new-hampshire

Bush, George W. "Remarks in a Discussion on Job Training in Arnold, Maryland." *UCSB American Presidency Project*, March 2, 2005. https://www.presidency.ucsb.edu/documents/remarks-discussion-job-training-arnold-maryland

Business Roundtable. "Revolutionizing Manufacturing." December 6, 2018.

Business Roundtable. *Innovation Nation: An American Innovation Agenda for 2020*. 2019.

Business Roundtable. "Business Roundtable Releases Recommendations to Bolster American Leadership in Key Technologies." May 6, 2019.

Business Roundtable. "Q&A: GM CEO Mary Barra on the Promise and Potential of AVs." May 6, 2019.

Business Roundtable. "Business Roundtable Roadmap for Responsible Artificial Intelligence." 2022.

Business Roundtable. "ICYMI: United's Scott Kirby Joins Axios to Discuss Workforce Development." September 25, 2023.

Business Roundtable. "Recap: Business Roundtable CEO Workforce Forum." July 18, 2025.

Business Roundtable. "Building America's Tomorrow-Ready Workforce." N.d. https://www.businessroundtable.org/policy-perspectives/building-americas-ever-ready-workforce

Carpenter Magazine. "Mechatronics: Up-to-the-Minute Training for a Booming Automation Industry." 2015, p. 22. https://www.carpenters.org/wp-content/uploads/2017/04/2015-Carpenter-Magazine-US-1.pdf

Carter, Jimmy. "Interview with the President Question-and-Answer Session with a Group of Publishers, Editors, and Broadcasters." *UCSB American Presidency Project*, June 24, 1977. https://www.presidency.ucsb.edu/documents/interview-with-the-president-question-and-answer-session-with-group-publishers-editors-and

Carter, Jimmy. "Annual Message to the Congress: The Economic Report of the President." *UCSB American Presidency Project*, January 20, 1978. https://www.presidency.ucsb.edu/documents/annual-message-the-congress-the-economic-report-the-president-10

Carter, Jimmy. "Statement on Signing H.R. 8149 Into Law - Customs Procedural Reform and Simplification Act of 1978." *UCSB American Presidency Project*, October 4, 1978. https://www.presidency.ucsb.edu/documents/statement-signing-hr-8149-into-law-customs-procedural-reform-and-simplification-act-1978

Carter, Jimmy. "San Diego, California Remarks at the Annual Convention of the Building and Construction Trades Department, AFL-CIO." *UCSB American Presidency Project*, October 11, 1979. https://www.presidency.ucsb.edu/documents/san-diego-california-remarks-the-annual-convention-the-building-and-construction-trades

Carter, Jimmy. "The Nation's Economy Radio Address to the Nation." *UCSB American Presidency Project*, October 12, 1980. https://www.presidency.ucsb.edu/documents/the-nations-economy-radio-address-the-nation

Clinton, William J. "Remarks at a Town Meeting in San Diego." *UCSB American Presidency Project*, May 17, 1993. https://www.presidency.ucsb.edu/documents/remarks-town-meeting-san-diego

Clinton, William J. "Remarks in a Town Meeting in Sacramento." *UCSB American Presidency Project*, October 3, 1993. https://www.presidency.ucsb.edu/documents/remarks-town-meeting-sacramento

Clinton, William J. "Message to the Congress on Small Business." *UCSB American Presidency Project*, February 1, 1994. https://www.presidency.ucsb.edu/documents/message-the-congress-small-business-0

Clinton, William J. "Remarks and a Question-and-Answer Session with the Economic Club of Detroit in Detroit, Michigan." *UCSB American Presidency Project*, January 8, 1999. https://www.presidency.ucsb.edu/documents/remarks-and-question-and-answer-session-with-the-economic-club-detroit-detroit-michigan

Cobb, Charles W., and Paul H. Douglas. "A Theory of Production." *American Economic Review* 18 (Supplement) (1928): 139–65.

Cogent Infotech. "Union Roles in AI Oversight: Ethical Workforce Transitions in Tech." June 17, 2025.

Comshaw-Arnold, Benjamin W. "Feudalism in Decline: The Influence of Technology on Society." Bachelor's thesis, Kent State University, 2014.

Crenshaw, Jordan, and Julie Stitzel. "The Chamber Embraces Biden. And Republicans Are Livid." *Politico*, February 12, 2021.

Day, Tim. "U.S. Chamber Letter on the Hearing, 'Highly Automated Vehicles: Federal Perspectives on the Deployment of Safety Technology.'" U.S. Chamber of Commerce, November 19, 2019.

Deloitte. *Power Up: UK Skills.* London: Deloitte, 2018.

Donohue, Thomas. "An Attack on Entrepreneurship and Innovation." U.S. Chamber of Commerce, March 14, 2016.

Donohue, Thomas J. "Maximizing the Promise of the New Economy." *U.S. Chamber of Commerce*, March 12, 2018.

Eisenhower, Dwight D. "The President's News Conference." *UCSB American Presidency Project*, March 16, 1955. https://www.presidency.ucsb.edu/documents/the-presidents-news-conference-325

Eisenhower, Dwight D. "Proclamation 3240—Fourth International Automation Congress and Exposition." *UCSB American Presidency Project*, May 9, 1958. https://www.presidency.ucsb.edu/documents/proclamation-3240-fourth-international-automation-congress-and-exposition

Eisenhower, Dwight D. "The President's News Conference." *UCSB American Presidency Project*, March 25, 1959. https://www.presidency.ucsb.edu/documents/the-presidents-news-conference-230

Eisenhower, Dwight D. "Speech at Life Insurance Association, New York City." *Eisenhower Library*, December 9, 1964. https://www.eisenhowerlibrary.gov/sites/default/files/file/post_presidential_speeches.pdf

Finishing First LMCI. "May 3: IFTI on VR Webinar Panel with Engineering News Record." May 3, 2018.

Ford, Gerald R. "Remarks at a Republican Party Fundraising Dinner in Charleston." *UCSB American Presidency Project*, November 11, 1975. https://www.presidency.ucsb.edu/documents/remarks-republican-party-fundraising-dinner-charleston

Ford, Gerald R. "Remarks and a Question-and-Answer Session at Tyler Junior College, Tyler, Texas." *UCSB American Presidency Project*, April 28, 1976. https://www.presidency.ucsb.edu/documents/remarks-and-question-and-answer-session-tyler-junior-college-tyler-texas

Ford, Gerald R. "Annual Message to the Congress: The Economic Report of the President." January 18, 1977. *American Presidency Project.*

Frey, Carl Benedikt, and Michael A. Osborne. *The Future of Employment: How Susceptible Are Jobs to Computerisation?* Oxford: Oxford Martin School, 2017.

Garrett-Peltier, Heidi. "Green Versus Brown: Comparing the Employment Impacts of Energy Efficiency, Renewable Energy, and Fossil Fuels Using an Input-Output Model." *Economic Modelling* 61 (2017): 439–47.

Hackbarth, Sean. "The State of the App Economy Is Strong: 1.6 Million Jobs in 2015." *U.S. Chamber of Commerce*, January 12, 2016.

Haraway, Donna. *Simians, Cyborgs, and Women: The Reinvention of Nature.* New York: Routledge, 1991.

Hawksworth, John, Richard Berriman, and Saloni Goel. *Will Robots Really Steal Our Jobs? An International Analysis of the Potential Long-Term Impact of Automation.* London: PricewaterhouseCoopers, 2018.

Hoover, Herbert. "Address to the Chamber of Commerce of the United States, May 1, 1930." In *Public Papers of the Presidents of the United States 1930.* US Government Printing Office, 1976. https://hoover.archives.gov/sites/default/files/research/ebooks/b2v2_full.pdf.

Hoover, Herbert. "Statement on the Appointment of John R. Alpine to the United States Employment Service, March 13, 1931." In *Public Papers of the Presidents of the United States 1931.* US Government Printing Office, 1976. https://hoover.archives.gov/sites/default/files/research/ebooks/b2v3_full.pdf

Hoover, Herbert. "The President's News Conference of May 27, 1932." In *Public Papers of the Presidents of the United States 1932-3.* US Government Printing Office, 1977. https://hoover.archives.gov/sites/default/files/research/ebooks/b2v4_full.pdf

Hyman, Louis. *Temp: How American Work, American Business, and the American Dream Became Temporary.* New York: Viking, 2018.

IATSE. "Bulletin." Third Quarter, 2008. https://www.iatse8.com/Docs/pdf/Bulletin/621.pdf

IATSE. "Bulletin." Second Quarter, 2019. https://iatse.net/wp-content/uploads/2021/05/IATSE-2nd-2019-web.pdf

IATSE. "Training Need to Keep Projectionist Jobs." N.d.

IUOE. "Training Programs." Retrieved on February 23, 2021. https://www.iuoe.org/training

IUPAT. "Painters and Allied Trades Journal." Spring 2019. Retrieved March 7, 2019. https://iupat.org/wp-content/uploads/2019_Issue-1_January-March-1.pdf

Johnson, Lyndon B. "Annual Message to the Congress: The Economic Report of the President." *UCSB American Presidency Project*, January 20, 1964. https://www.presidency.ucsb.edu/documents/annual-message-the-congress-the-economic-report-the-president-13

Johnson, Lyndon B. "Remarks in Atlantic City at the Convention of the United Auto Workers." *UCSB American Presidency Project*, March 23, 1964. https://www.presidency.ucsb.edu/documents/remarks-atlantic-city-the-convention-the-united-auto-workers

Johnson, Lyndon B. "Remarks Upon Signing Bill Creating the National Commission on Technology, Automation, and Economic Progress." *UCSB American Presidency Project*, August 19, 1964. https://www.presidency.ucsb.edu/documents/remarks-upon-signing-bill-creating-the-national-commission-technology-automation-and

Johnson, Lyndon B. "Special Message to the Congress on Labor." *UCSB American Presidency Project*, May 18, 1965. https://www.presidency.ucsb.edu/documents/special-message-the-congress-labor

Johnson, Lyndon B. "Remarks to Members of the Business Council." *UCSB American Presidency Project*, December 4, 1968. https://www.presidency.ucsb.edu/documents/remarks-members-the-business-council-0

Kennedy, John F. "Special Message to the Congress on Taxation." April 20, 1961. *American Presidency Project.*

Kennedy, John F. "Letter to the President of the Senate and to the Speaker of the House on the Unemployment Compensation System." *UCSB American Presidency Project*, March 12, 1962. https://www.presidency.ucsb.edu/documents/letter-the-president-the-senate-and-the-speaker-the-house-the-unemployment-compensation

Kennedy, John F. "Address and Question and Answer Period at the Economic Club of New York." *UCSB American Presidency Project*, December 14, 1962. https://www.presidency.ucsb.edu/documents/address-and-question-and-answer-period-the-economic-club-new-york

Kennedy, John F. "Remarks at a Civic Luncheon in Chicago." *UCSB American Presidency Project*, March 23, 1963. https://www.presidency.ucsb.edu/documents/remarks-civic-luncheon-chicago

Kim, Harold. "Consumers Overwhelmingly Say Lawsuits Should Not "Regulate" New Technologies." *U.S. Chamber of Commerce*, April 18, 2018.

Latour, Bruno. *We Have Never Been Modern.* Cambridge, MA: Harvard University Press, 1993.

Lipset, Seymour Martin. "Roosevelt and the Protest of the 1930s" *Minnesota Law Review* 2317 (1984). https://scholarship.law.umn.edu/mlr/2317

Manufacturing Institute (NAMI). "Industrial Mobility: How Autonomous Vehicles Can Change Manufacturing." February 2018.

Manyika, James, Michael Chui, Anu Madgavkar, and Susan Lund. *Technology, Jobs, and the Future of Work.* San Francisco, CA: McKinsey Global Institute, 2017.

Marinaccio, Michael. "Jose Canseco Says Robots Are Stealing Our Jobs. Are They?" *U.S. Chamber of Commerce,* February 22, 2017

McAdams, Deborah. "Digital Displacement: The State of Our Unions." *TV Technology,* September 13, 2003.

McKinsey Global Institute. "A New Future of Work: The Race to Deploy AI and Raise Skills in Europe and Beyond." May 21, 2024.

Monck, Adrian. "New Forum Center to Advance Global Cooperation on Fourth Industrial Revolution." *World Economic Forum*, October 10, 2016.

NAM. "Rep. Joyce Touts Tax Reform Benefits at Rockwell Automation." August 13, 2018.

NAM. "NAM Hails Manufacturing in California on State of Manufacturing Tour." February 27, 2019.

NAM. "Report: Automation Offers Manufacturing Opportunities." May 23, 2019.

NAM. "A Hiring Engine: A Breakdown of the Job Openings in Manufacturing." 2019. Retrieved on March 18, 2021. https://www.themanufacturinginstitute.org/wp-content/uploads/2020/03/MI-Hiring-Engine-Job-Opening-Paper.pdf

NAM. "NAM Unveils Historic "Creators Wanted" Campaign Showcasing Modern Manufacturing." February 12, 2020. Creators Wanted. "Building the Workforce of Tomorrow." Retrieved on March 18, 2021.

NAM. "2.1 Million Manufacturing Jobs Could Go Unfilled by 2030." May 4, 2021.

NAM. "Manufacturing Trends 2025." 2025 https://nam.org/wp-content/uploads/securepdfs/2025/01/NAM-2025-Manufacturing-Trends.pdf

NAM. "AI's Rising Power in Manufacturing Spurs Call for Smarter AI Policy Solutions." May 29, 2025. https://nam.org/ais-rising-power-in-manufacturing-spurs-call-for-smarter-ai-policy-solutions-34092/

NAM. "NAM and MI: AI Will Strengthen the Manufacturing Workforce." August 6, 2025. https://nam.org/nam-and-mi-ai-will-strengthen-the-manufacturing-workforce-34550/

NAMI. "Small and Medium-Sized Manufacturers Survey: The 'New Normal' and Post-Pandemic Workforce Challenges." February 2021. Retrieved on March 18, 2021. https://www.themanufacturinginstitute.org/wp-content/uploads/2021/02/BKD-MI-Survey-Feb2021.pdf

NAMI and PwC. "Navigating the Fourth Industrial Revolution to the Bottom Line." 2019. Retrieved on March 18, 2021. https://www.themanufacturinginstitute.org/wp-content/uploads/2020/03/MI-Smart-Factory-4IR-Report.pdf

Nixon, Richard M. "Remarks on the CBS Radio Network: "An Open Door for American Labor"." *UCSB American Presidency Project*, October 21, 1968. https://www.presidency.ucsb.edu/documents/remarks-the-cbs-radio-network-open-door-for-american-labor

Nixon, Richard M. "Remarks to Top Officials at the Department of Labor." *UCSB American Presidency Project*, February 4, 1969. https://www.presidency.ucsb.edu/documents/remarks-top-officials-the-department-labor

Nixon, Richard M. "Special Message to the Congress on Rural Development." *UCSB American Presidency Project*, February 1, 1972. https://www.presidency.ucsb.edu/documents/special-message-the-congress-rural-development

Nixon, Richard M. "Annual Message to the Congress on the State of the Union." *UCSB American Presidency Project*, January 30, 1974. https://www.presidency.ucsb.edu/documents/annual-message-the-congress-the-state-the-union

Obama, Barack. "Remarks at Lehigh Carbon Community College and a Question-and-Answer Session in Allentown, Pennsylvania." *UCSB American Presidency Project*, December 4, 2009. https://www.presidency.ucsb.edu/documents/remarks-lehigh-carbon-community-college-and-question-and-answer-session-allentown

Obama, Barack. "Remarks at a Democratic National Committee Fundraiser in Philadelphia." *UCSB American Presidency Project*, June 30, 2011. https://www.presidency.ucsb.edu/documents/remarks-democratic-national-committee-fundraiser-philadelphia

Obama, Barack. "Remarks at the Facilities of the Linamar Corporation in Arden, North Carolina." *UCSB American Presidency Project*, February 13, 2013. https://www.presidency.ucsb.edu/documents/remarks-the-facilities-the-linamar-corporation-arden-north-carolina

Obama, Barack. "Remarks at a Town Hall Meeting and a Question-and-Answer Session at Millennium Steel Service, LLC, in Princeton, Indiana." *UCSB American Presidency Project*, October 3, 2014. https://www.presidency.ucsb.edu/documents/remarks-town-hall-meeting-and-question-and-answer-session-millennium-steel-service-llc

Obama, Barack. "The Budget Message of the President." *UCSB American Presidency Project*, February 2, 2015. https://www.presidency.ucsb.edu/documents/the-budget-message-the-president-20

Obama, Barack. "Remarks and a Question-and-Answer Session at a Town Hall Meeting at McKinley Senior High School in Baton Rouge, Louisiana." *UCSB American Presidency Project*, January 14, 2016. https://www.presidency.ucsb.edu/documents/remarks-and-question-and-answer-session-town-hall-meeting-mckinley-senior-high-school

Obama, Barack. "Interview with Steve Inskeep of National Public Radio." *UCSB American Presidency Project*, June 27, 2016. https://www.presidency.ucsb.edu/documents/interview-with-steve-inskeep-national-public-radio-4

Obama, Barack. "Interview with Joi Ito of MIT and Scott Dadich of WIRED." *UCSB American Presidency Project*, August 24, 2016. https://www.presidency.ucsb.edu/documents/interview-with-joi-ito-mit-and-scott-dadich-wired

Obama, Barack. "Press Release – ICYMI: White House Frontiers: Robots, Space Exploration, and the Future of American Innovation." *UCSB American Presidency Project*, October 7, 2016. https://www.presidency.ucsb.edu/documents/white-house-press-release-icymi-white-house-frontiers-robots-space-exploration-and-the

Obama, Barack. "Remarks and a Question-and-Answer Session at a Young Leaders of the Americas Initiative Town Hall Meeting in Lima, Peru." *UCSB American Presidency Project*, November 19, 2016. https://www.presidency.ucsb.edu/documents/remarks-and-question-and-answer-session-young-leaders-the-americas-initiative-town-hall

Obama, Barack. "Farewell Address to the Nation from Chicago, Illinois." January 10, 2017. *American Presidency Project.*

Orrell, Brent. "AI and the Future of Work: Preparing the Workforce for an AI-Driven Economy." *U.S. Chamber of Commerce*, March 31, 2023.

Quaadman, Tom. "How Technology Enables Small Business." *U.S. Chamber of Commerce*, July 29, 2020.

Reagan, Ronald. "Remarks and a Question-and-Answer Session via Satellite to the Young Presidents Organization in Tucson, Arizona." *UCSB American Presidency Project*, February 14, 1983. https://www.presidency.ucsb.edu/documents/remarks-and-question-and-answer-session-via-satellite-the-young-presidents-organization

Reagan, Ronald. "Question-and-Answer Session with High School Students on Domestic and Foreign Policy Issues." *UCSB American Presidency Project*, March 25, 1983. https://www.presidency.ucsb.edu/documents/question-and-answer-session-with-high-school-students-domestic-and-foreign-policy-issues-0

Reagan, Ronald. "Interview with Representatives of College Radio Stations." *UCSB American Presidency Project*, September 9, 1985. https://www.presidency.ucsb.edu/documents/interview-with-representatives-college-radio-stations

Robotics Business Review. "Built Robotics Partners with International Union of Operating Engineers for Training." June 12, 2020.

Robotics Tomorrow. "Construction Robotics Startup Canvas Announces Public Launch." November 20, 2020.

Roosevelt, Franklin D. "Address at Little Rock, Arkansas." June 10, 1936. *American Presidency Project.*

Roosevelt, Franklin D. "Message to Congress – State of the Union (Speech File 1028), January 6, 1937." *FDR Library.* http://www.fdrlibrary.marist.edu/_resources/images/msf/msf01057

Roosevelt, Franklin D. "Message to Congress – State of the Union Address (Speech File 1262)." January 3, 1940.

Schiølin, Kasper. "Revolutionary Dreams: Future Essentialism and the Sociotechnical Imaginary of the Fourth Industrial Revolution in Denmark." *Social Studies of Science* 50, no. 4 (2020): 542–66.

Schumpeter, Joseph A. *Capitalism, Socialism and Democracy.* New York: Harper and Brothers, 1942.

Schwab, Klaus. *The Fourth Industrial Revolution.* Geneva: World Economic Forum, 2016.

Shuler, Liz. "Shuler to the Climate Jobs and Just Transition Summit: The Renewable Sector Must Be Unionized." *AFL-CIO*, September 22, 2020.

Simonite, Tom. "Construction Workers Embrace the Robots That Do Their Jobs." *Wired*, March 10, 2020.

Solow, Robert M. "A Contribution to the Theory of Economic Growth." *Quarterly Journal of Economics* 70, no. 1 (1956): 65–94.

Strack, Rainer, Miguel Carrasco, Philipp Kolo, Nicholas Nouri, Michael Priddis, and Richard George. "The Future of Jobs in the Era of AI." Boston Consulting Group, March 18, 2021.

The Ironworker. November 2020. Retrieved on March 8, 2021. https://iwmagazine.iwintl.org/PdfView.aspx?Filename=%2fsites%2fIronworkersMagazine%2fShared+Documents%2f2020%2fThe+Ironworker+-+2020-11.pdf

Truman, Harry S. "Excerpts from Annual Message: The President' s Economic Report to the Congress." *Truman Library*, January 14, 1948. https://www.trumanlibrary.gov/library/public-papers/8/excerpts-annual-message-president-s-economic-report-congress

Truman, Harry S. "Special Message to the Congress: The President's Midyear Economic Report." July 19, 1952. https://www.trumanlibrary.gov/library/public-papers/215/special-message-congress-presidents-midyear-economic-report

Truman, Harry S. "Annual Message to the Congress: The President's Economic Report." *Truman Library,* January 14, 1953. https://www.trumanlibrary.gov/library/public-papers/376/annual-message-congress-presidents-economic-report

Trump, Donald J. "Press Briefing by Press Secretary Sarah Sanders and Senior Policy Advisor Stephen Miller." *UCSB American Presidency Project*, August 2, 2017. https://www.presidency.ucsb.edu/documents/press-briefing-press-secretary-sarah-sanders-and-senior-policy-advisor-stephen-miller

Trump, Donald J. "President Donald J. Trump's Administration Is Taking Action to Equip American Students and Workers with the Skills They Need to Succeed." *UCSB American Presidency Project*, July 29, 2018. https://www.presidency.ucsb.edu/documents/president-donald-j-trumps-administration-taking-action-equip-american-students-and-workers

Trump, Donald J. "Press Release – President Donald J. Trump's Commitment to Workforce Development Generates Training Opportunities for Millions of Americans." *UCSB American Presidency Project*, October 31, 2018. https://www.presidency.ucsb.edu/documents/white-house-press-release-president-donald-j-trumps-commitment-workforce-development

Trump White House. *Winning the Race: America's AI Action Plan.* July 2025.

UFCW Canada. "Future Skills Initiative Should Focus on Needs of Workers." March 18, 2019. https://www.ufcw.ca/index.php?option=com_content&view=article&id=32226&catid=10042&lang=en

Unite Here. "Prepared for U.S. Senate AI Insight Forum: Workforce." November 1, 2023.

United Auto Workers (UAW). *2023 Special Bargaining Convention.* 2023.

U.S. Chamber of Commerce. "U.S. Chamber Statement on President Obama's Announcement Regarding Municipal Broadband." January 14, 2015.

U.S. Chamber of Commerce. "Dear 45- A Letter on Innovation to Our Next President." November 9, 2016.

U.S. Chamber of Commerce. "Data Centers: Jobs & Opportunities in Communities Nationwide." June 15, 2017

U.S. Chamber of Commerce. "We Want the U.S. to Lead in Driverless Cars. Here's What Washington Can Do to Help." January 26, 2018.
U.S. Chamber of Commerce. "C_TEC Submits Comments to DOT following the Autonomous Vehicle Policy Summit." March 9, 2018.
U.S. Chamber of Commerce. "Commercial Construction Looks to Advanced Technologies to Alleviate Workforce Challenges and Improve Productivity." December 11, 2018.
U.S. Chamber of Commerce. "Commercial Construction Index, Q4 2018." 2018. https://www.uschamber.com/assets/documents/cci_2018_q4_report.pdf
U.S. Chamber of Commerce. *Future of the Workforce.* 2020.
U.S. Chamber of Commerce. "U.S. Chamber Policy Priorities for 2020." January 9, 2020
U.S. Chamber of Commerce. "U.S. Chamber Applauds Executive Order Promoting the Use of Artificial Intelligence in the Federal Government." December 4, 2020.
U.S. Chamber of Commerce. *2025 Chamber Technology Priorities.* 2025.
U.S. Chamber of Commerce. "U.S. Chamber's Latest "Empowering Small Business" Report Shows Majority of Businesses in All 50 States Are Embracing AI." August 18, 2025. https://www.uschamber.com/technology/artificial-intelligence/u-s-chambers-latest-empowering-small-business-report-shows-majority-of-businesses-in-all-50-states-are-embracing-ai
Vance, J.D. "Remarks by the Vice President at the Artificial Intelligence Action Summit in Paris, France." *American Presidency Project*, February 11, 2025. https://www.presidency.ucsb.edu/documents/remarks-the-vice-president-the-artificial-intelligence-action-summit-paris-france
Werr, Andreas, and Torbjörn Stjernberg. "Exploring Management Consulting Firms as Knowledge Systems." *Organization Studies* 24, no. 6 (2003): 881–908.
Wikipedia. "World Economic Forum." https://en.wikipedia.org/wiki/World_Economic_Forum
Winner, Langdon. "Prophets of Inevitability." *MIT Technology Review* 101, no. 2 (1998): 62–68.
World Economic Forum. *The Future of Jobs Report 2020.* Geneva: World Economic Forum, 2020.
Worley, Lee. "Promoting Skilled Trades." *Iron Workers,* January 2019.

6

THE FUTURISTS

Gene Roddenberry's *Star Trek* is a science fiction television series, which envisioned a starship going on voyages in outer space encountering alien creatures like Ferengi or Klingons, while the humans on the starship do not have to work. Computer technology such as replicators provides them with the necessities of life such as food and cures their diseases. The Federation is the interstellar world government that runs on the universal principles of liberty, civil rights and equality. The Federation has eliminated the need for money and poverty. Some people still work in the Starfleet, where they engage in arts, science and space exploration, but this is done by individual choice and passion rather than economic compulsion. By removing the need for money, social class distinctions no longer exist. There are no restrictions on who can join Starfleet. Humans have evolved culturally to no longer engage in war, greed and prejudice.[1] This Star Trek future is expressed in the quote of the fictional character Jean-Luc Picard,

> The economics of the future are somewhat different. You see, money doesn't exist in the 24th century. The acquisition of wealth is no longer the driving force in our lives. We work to better ourselves and the rest of Humanity.[2]

The above outlined Star Trek future poses a major challenge to the paradigm of unrestricted accumulation of capital and the perennial existential anxiety of workers losing their livelihood due to innovation. The futurist agenda is both post-capitalist and post-work and embraces the leisure society model. What are futurism and leisure society?

DOI: 10.4324/9781003780236-7

The Futurist Perspective

Futurists believe that many jobs are most likely to be displaced and find a workless world desirable. They agree that to make such an outcome palatable to the public social welfare must increase, including solutions like universal basic income (UBI), universal basic services (UBS) or the cost of living should approach zero. In a UBI, all residents in a country receive a flat-rate cash payment at regular intervals, while in UBS, all residents qualify for nationally supplied social programs like health care, education, or housing. These policies should become easier to implement over time because robots do not need to be paid a salary.[3]

In that view, humans can realize the ancient dream of a workless future with the only enemy being boredom. For Schopenhauer, life is a pendulum swinging between boredom and pain. Work is about the struggle to survive, and a form of suffering caused by unfulfilled desire and want. Once they are satisfied, people will become bored, contemplating their meaning in life. This view suggests that true happiness is impossible to achieve permanently. However, people with a rich inner life and mental stimulation can overcome both negative states.[4] The implied lack of a rich inner life could result in the unemployed dystopia of Marienthal described in Chapter 4, while a very self-motivated leisure would be a futurist ideal.

Futurism is a derivative of the belief in Moore's Law, the doubling in the number of transistors every two years and rising computational power. AI has a similarly exponential time trend, where the length and complexity of AI tasks keep on doubling every seven months. AI researchers measure model performance based on the ability of AI to mimic human professionals in their tasks. For instance, it measures a lawyer's speed and efficiency in analyzing legal documents.[5] If one extrapolates an exponential trend of AI taking over human tasks, then human workers will have a diminishing share of total tasks and their leisure time will increase, though it is not clear whether these productivity gains will be broadly shared in society. Futurists assume that such an income redistribution is a manageable technicality that will be implemented by responsive political leaders. I explore the critique of futurism in more detail in the conclusion.

There are still very few futurists, but it tends to be quite common among technology company leaders located in Silicon Valley, academics in institutions that are closest to cutting-edge technological development, politicians who are influenced by technologist thinking and free-thinking intellectuals. The vision of a workless future is nested within the literature on leisure society.

Leisure Society

A.J. Veal conceptualizes leisure society as one in which cultural and economic life centers around leisure rather than work, distinguishing it from earlier social formations such as agrarian and industrial societies.[6] *Bull et al.* similarly describe it as a society where "leisure would replace work as the central motivating force in people's lives."[7] Leisure society can be understood both quantitatively, through the reduction of working hours compared to industrial society and qualitatively, in terms of individuals gaining greater autonomy to pursue activities that foster personal fulfillment, creativity and social connection.[8] Another approach is to analyze leisure through its constituent activities, including rest and recovery, entertainment, family time and other pursuits such as sports, camping, fishing and music.[9]

A second key dimension of the leisure society is the idea of play as a counterweight to work. Drawing on Johan Huizinga, play can be understood as a foundational element of human culture, not confined to free time but operating as a central force in cultural creation and meaning-making.[10] In his view, play is voluntary rather than compelled, distinct from ordinary life, structured by its own rules, intrinsically rewarding, imaginative and largely independent of material gain or profit. On this basis, the moral case for a leisure society rest on elevating play and correspondingly diminishing work as the principal organizing value of culture.

Karl Marx believed that increasing automation reduces necessary labor time, which is the prerequisite to human freedom and overcoming alienated labor, where people work to accumulate capital for capitalists. In *Grundrisse*, Marx points out,

> Through this process, the amount of labour necessary for the production of a given object is indeed reduced to a minimum, but only in order to realize a maximum of labour in the maximum number of such objects. The first aspect is important, because capital here - quite unintentionally - reduces human labour, expenditure of energy, to a minimum. This will redound to the benefit of emancipated labour, and is the condition of its emancipation.[11]

But the condition for emancipation is not a guarantee for emancipation. For Marx, the attainment of freedom presupposes overcoming capitalism and realizing socialism. Contrary to the resigned view described in Chapter 4, Marx believed that leisure time is not passive rest but opens the doors for people to actively engage in artistic, scientific and social pursuits that are ends in themselves rather than subject to external economic pressures. The increase in leisure time is the prerequisite to human flourishing.[12]

The notion of a leisure society directly challenges the traditional Protestant work ethic.[13] In Max Weber's interpretation of Protestantism, individuals have a spiritual obligation to work diligently, save money and earn wealth. Doing so will earn them salvation and proximity to God.[14] This cultural disposition is the starting point of industrialization, capitalism and the innovation-based economy. Leisure society proponents agree that technological advancements inherent to capitalism are broadly beneficial to humanity but that the excessive focus on economic growth prevents the deployment of technologies for an increase in leisure time and a reduction of work hours. It is not clear whether the pursuit of increased leisure implies an end to capitalism given that a shorter workweek by itself does not end wage labor. However, the elimination of wage labor at the more extreme end of leisure society, as depicted in the Star Trek movies, is profoundly anti-capitalist given that wage labor is an integral part of it. Ironically, it is the industrial titans in Silicon Valley, who are promoting a post-work vision in their automation discourse. This tech business discourse is quite different from the mainstream business view presented in Chapter 5.

Silicon Valley's Futurism

Silicon Valley leads the contemporary futurist narrative with their calls to reduce or eliminate wage labor and an expansion of the social safety net, including UBI. By severing the link between work and income, a post-work future becomes feasible. Mark Zuckerberg, the founder of one of the biggest technology companies Facebook/Meta, argued in his graduation speech at Harvard University that automation will eliminate many jobs and that human purpose cannot exclusively be found in wage work. He said,

> Our generation will have to deal with tens of millions of jobs replaced by automation like self-driving cars and trucks... Purpose doesn't only come from work... [W]e can create a sense of purpose for everyone... by building community.[15]

Note that Zuckerberg is quite nebulous in laying out what the desirable 'community' entails, but it stands to reason that it would require having access to a Facebook account. In that same graduation speech, he endorsed UBI that will give people a cushion to try new ideas. He endorsed childcare and education funded by the very wealthy like himself.[16]

Elon Musk, Tesla car company and X social media company owner, tweeted that "Universal [basic] income will be necessary over time if AI takes over most human jobs."[17] Musk doubled down in a 2025 statement, where he promoted a universal "high" income because people no longer need to work.[18] Ironically, in 2018 Musk noted the limitations of existing automation in Tesla car factories. He said that "excessive automation at Tesla was a mistake."[19] Robots could not deal with unexpected orientations of objects like nuts and bolts or maneuvering between car frames. If a robot failed to handle the object the assembly line would stop, thus making the use of humans more efficient.[20] On the other hand, 75% of the Tesla factory is automated. Selected tasks like wire harnesses and general assembly are still done manually.[21] An electric car has 3.7 man hours compared to 6.2 for combustion engine cars. Thus, Tesla is more labor-saving than conventional car companies.[22] In his own government work as part of the Department of Government Efficiency (DOGE) in early 2025, he was largely silent on universal high income and instead pushed for draconian US federal budget cuts and mass layoffs in federal agencies due to the high federal debt.[23] This indicates a scarcity rather than an abundance logic. There is an apparent disconnect between Musk's ideological aspirations and actions as a capitalist and government adviser.

Sam Altman is the co-founder of OpenAI, the leading AI company. Elon Musk is another co-founder. Altman is also the co-founder of Y Combinator, which funds basic income experiments. His company's large language model called Chat-GPT was unveiled to the public in November 2022 and has coincided with a reduction of jobs for freelance writing jobs.[24] He argued that AI will replace most current jobs except teaching or social care. He found that society must figure out "how people find meaning and community, but a lack of material abundance will not be a problem." The fact that he is funding UBI pilot projects, reflects his underlying belief that technology will reduce employment.[25] Altman believes that the AI productivity increase is so substantial that it could easily fund an American Equity Fund to pay $13,500 per year to every US adult.[26] Altman promotes universal basic compute (UBC), where his Chat-GPT users receive compute, which they can use, sell for money or donate for computational tasks they care about. UBC works like an internal currency that would make people more dependent on his AI platform.[27]

Chris Hughes is a co-founder of Facebook who quit the company to become its chief critic. He demanded a break-up of Facebook subsidiaries and the creation of social media public utilities. He argued that technology is "going to continue to destroy work." He notes that gig economy workers (Uber, Lyft, Postmates etc.) face uncertain incomes. He favors a monthly basic income of $500, but only for workers earning less than $50,000, which is akin to an expansion of the earned income tax credit, an existing US federal program.[28] He also favors the expansion of the definition of work to revalue social care workers, presumably among the few remaining occupations that are remunerated in a highly automated economy.[29] As a founder of the Economic Security Project, his foundation has spent $10 million on city-led basic income pilots in Stockton, CA and Jackson, MS and elsewhere.[30]

Jack Dorsey, founder of Twitter and Square, argues that automation will not only replace manual workers but also computer programmers. Machine learning and deep learning would ensure that software could write itself and thereby replace entry-level programmers. Dorsey advocates a UBI, which would give workers peace of mind, be a floor for people to stand on and allow laid-off workers to acquire new skills.[31] Dorsey has donated $15 million in December 2020 to Mayors for a Guaranteed Income that distributes funding for local basic income experiments.[32]

Vinod Khosla, a venture capitalist, who has backed OpenAI and other AI firms, is convinced that every job "will be doable by AI by 2030". His views are aligned with the utopian vision, where AI will be liberating and allow humans to flourish by pursuing art, caregiving, or gardening. Work will not disappear but become optional. The drudgery of manual labor and professional expertise will be replaced by AI.[33] Khosla endorses a UBI to ensure "equitable wealth distribution."[34]

Silicon Valley's views affect mainstream corporate CEO views as well. Jamie Dimon, JP Morgan CEO, predicted that due to AI the work week of bankers will decrease from 5 days to 3.5 days.[35] Similar predictions about a shorter work week were made by Eric Yuan, the CEO of Zoom, Bill Gates, the co-founder of Microsoft, Jensen Huang, the CEO of NVIDIA.[36] It is mainly business leaders that are closely connected to the tech industry that promote a futurist outlook, while the other mainstream corporate executives hold onto the status quo vision of continued job growth and worker reskilling.

There are selected voices in the tech industry that have more pessimistic resigned views on predicted AI effects on jobs. Dario Amadei, the CEO of Anthropic, believes that the rise of autonomous AI agents will result in significant disruption and displacement across industries but especially in knowledge work. While he believes that UBI is better than nothing, it would amount to a dystopian future where a small group of elites continue to accumulate wealth while the unemployed public struggles to get by with minimal welfare.[37] There is a fair critique about the tech leaders' philanthropy on basic income pilots. Current basic income trials are highly selective rather than universal, thus limiting their societal scope. It also cannot compensate for the lack of a state-funded welfare system.[38]

Given that tech owners and their engineers are the most relevant "human resource" in the automation wave and they control many of the capital flows toward technologies, these futurists are, ironically, the least susceptible to automation while their innovations cause displacement across swathes of the workforce. Hence, at present futurists face legitimacy challenges in selling their workless future to the broader public. The tech owners also have a vested material interest in promoting the automation narrative even if it takes some time before labor market effects of AI are felt. This narrative keeps them socially relevant and attracts more customer spending and investor funding, thus allowing them to accumulate more capital and reinforce the Schumpeterian capitalist status quo described in Chapter 5. Thus, it stays ambiguous whether the tech leaders are genuine futurists or pragmatic capitalists.

Academic Futurists

There is a long history of academics and intellectuals who have a futurist leisure society orientation. As noted in the introduction, John Maynard Keynes wrote his futurist vision in the depth of the Great Depression when breadlines were long, and destitution was acute. He believed that the economic problems were only short-term and that over the long-term technological advancement is going to solve the economic problem of scarcity. He sketched the vision of a future with 15-hour work weeks and material abundance. The main issue would be how to keep society together without wage work. As an optimist, he thought this would be less challenging than achieving an end to scarcity. He wrote,

> Thus [due to technological progress] for the first time since his creation man will be faced with his real, his permanent problem – how to use his freedom from pressing economic cares, how to occupy the leisure, which science and compound interest will have won for him, to live wisely and agreeably and well.[39]

The British philosopher Bertrand Russell had a decidedly more explicit anti-work ideology. While for Keynes the reduction in work hours is the result of a technocratic decision to redistribute the surplus wealth that is produced by technology, Russell questions the ideology of work itself. Historically, rulers (kings, landlords) have enforced labor on peasants, serfs and slaves and lived off any surplus they produced. In a capitalist economy, the servitude of the common population is extended in the wage work relationship, in which workers are expected to spend most of their waking hours at a job, while "the rest were left to starve as unemployed" as technological progress continued to improve labor productivity.[40] Russell opposed the obsession with work, arguing that much of civilization, including art, literature, philosophy etc., has been created by idle aristocrats who were subsidized by society. With technological progress, it should be simple to remove the work compulsion and allow most people to pursue their passion, while minimizing the socially necessary labor. Removing the work compulsion will make people happier; allow brilliant people to produce more great works without having to conform to the opinion of elderly pundits; and lessen suspicion and anxiety, which are at the heart of wars.[41]

Andre Gorz, an Austrian French philosopher, argued that technological abundance could diminish the realm of necessity while increasing the realm of freedom for the individual to pursue activities they enjoy. However, unlike Karl Marx, who thought that human liberation from work and productivism comes from a self-conscious working class, Gorz believed that only a 'non-class of non-producers' is capable of overcoming the societal obsession with productivism/capital accumulation as an end in itself.[42] These are individuals that are ejected from the labor market or work jobs that are highly insecure. These include the long-term unemployed and welfare recipients. Capitalists prefer high unemployment caused by technology, because it would keep the shrinking workforce hard-working and submissive. In contrast, reducing work hours would threaten the established order of labor discipline. Capitalists must avoid this outcome.[43] Presumably, automation will increase the size of the non-class and raise the potential for anti-productive, anti-work movements. Gorz writes,

> Whatever the number of jobs remaining in industry and the service sector once automation has been fully achieved, they will be incapable of providing identity, meaning and power for those who fill them.[44]

In contrast to the non-producers, the traditional working class is too disorganized to take over the commanding heights of the economy from capitalists, and their subjective perception is that their well-being is tied up with capital accumulation and economic growth rather than socialist liberation.

The futurist architect, Buckminster Fuller, stated that society should get rid of the "absolutely specious notion that everybody has to earn a living." He argued that people should no longer have to justify their right to exist because technology is sufficient to support the living expenses of most of the population. He criticizes the creation of unnecessary, unproductive jobs to keep people employed. People should use their free time to pursue their childhood passions without fear of not being able to earn a living.[45] Whatever the reasoning these thinkers use, futurists predict a future without work and, unlike the resigned view, desire it as well.

Selected academics that are at the forefront of AI applications also have a futurist outlook. Max Tegmark, an MIT-based AI researcher, summarized the debate between job optimists and job pessimists in his book *Life 3.0*, but then discusses a section titled, 'Giving People Purpose Without Jobs.' He concedes that jobs can give meaning and structure but argues that these things can be provided outside the workplace. Non-work activities include sports, hobbies, clubs, schools, religious organizations, political movements. "It should be possible to make everyone as happy as if they had their personal dream job, but once one breaks free of the constraint that everyone's activities must generate income, the sky's the limit."[46] Thus, Tegmark's position is that it is not essential to have jobs and that justifies the continued growth of AI.

The economist Daniel Susskind specializes in the impacts of automation on workers. He predicted that technological unemployment would become more pervasive. He believes that the state must promote leisure policies, such as more education, sports, cultural activities and volunteer work.[47] The journalist and historian, Rutger Bregman, opposes the dogma of having to work to earn a living. He argues that the rich industrialized countries can already afford UBI and less attachment to labor, but instead there is a growth in socially useless jobs to keep people busy. The dovetails the bull-shit jobs discussion in Chapter 1. A realistic utopia would involve a UBI that frees people to pursue their passions and gain personal satisfaction and meaning. He rejects the notion that a future without work is dystopian and filled with boredom but is rather empowering as financial security enables people to pursue their true passion.[48]

Socialist futurists take their ideas from Marx' premise on technology reducing necessary labor time while increasing people's realm of freedom. Srnicek and Williams also advocate for a future characterized by full automation, a shorter work week and UBI. Higher labor costs would create a positive feedback loop of more technological advancement.[49] Bastani describes a post-scarcity future based on technological progress and welfare state redistribution, which he calls "fully automated luxury communism".[50] Mason believes that because many online commodities such as software, education, music and designs for objects, are reproduced at zero marginal cost the economic theory of scarcity is becoming increasingly irrelevant. The de facto elimination of the profit-based model will make it easier for an expansion of leisure time. He does not think that capitalism will implode by itself and advocates for a socialist program to break up economic monopolies and implement welfare state redistribution.[51] The intellectual Noam Chomsky is in favor of automation to release people from "routine and dangerous work and liberate them for more creative endeavors." He is in favor of UBI, but he believes that UBI is a crude instrument compared to more radical proposals to collectivize or nationalize the means of production.[52]

The academic advocacy for UBI has long preceded the rise of AI or technological unemployment discourse. Early advocates of UBI were Thomas Paine, Thomas Spence, Joseph Charlier and Henry George. The nineteenth century versions of UBI were focused on taxing land and providing cash payments to the people, while later proposals are about taxing economic capital more generally. Academic activism around UBI was reinvigorated beginning in 1986, when the philosopher Philippe Van Parijs and the economist Guy Standing founded the Basic Income European Network (BIEN). In 1999, US activists founded US Basic Income Guarantee (USBIG). In 2004, BIEN was renamed to Basic Income Earth Network to reflect the growing number of non-European basic income scholars and activists.[53]

Van Parijs and Vanderborght argue that UBI gives individuals the freedom to pursue their opportunities and the power to shape their own lives. Real freedom presumes the absence of coercion and economic dependence on others. A wage worker, a serf or slave are, by definition, not free from the coercion to work, while UBI recipients are free to escape poverty, pursue meaningful work, creativity and social participation outside of economic necessity. UBI sidesteps the inefficiencies, complexities and social exclusion coming from selective or conditional welfare programs. Instead of reducing work incentives, it is neutral on work incentives given that higher incomes do not result in the loss of UBI.[54] Thus, in the classic philosophical defense of UBI the increase of individual freedom is primary, while automation and economic abundance are secondary. But freedom and abundance from technology are quite complementary within a futurist vision given that abundance makes freedom easier to support financially. Indeed, Van Parijs and Vanderborght refer to UBI as a solution to manage the labor market disruptions that come from technology. Other writers in the UBI literature have related their advocacy to rapid technological changes as well.[55] Widerquist argues that UBI protects people not just from a future without jobs, but from smaller automation-related bouts of unemployment throughout the history of capitalism. UBI redistributes the technological gains back to the workers and gives them more leverage in collective bargaining with their employers.[56]

Political Futurists

UBI Advocacy

Political leaders in the US have engaged in advocacy of UBI. In the 1930s, the Louisiana senator Huey Long promoted a basic income plan based on his 'Share our Wealth' program. In the 1960s, Martin Luther King Jr., the civil rights leader, and Milton Friedman, the libertarian economist, each supported a Guaranteed Income, while the Nixon administration had proposed a Family Assistance Plan, which failed to pass Congress in the early-1970s. Outside the US, there was a 2016 failed Swiss Referendum and various basic income trials in countries as diverse as Finland, Canada, Kenya, Netherlands, Germany, Namibia and India.[57]

UBI has attracted attention in the more recent political era. The entrepreneur Andrew Yang became a US presidential candidate in the 2020 election cycle. Earlier in his career he was directing his start-up 'Venture for America' which provides small entrepreneurs with seed funding and technical training. He realized that such initiatives did not create a lot of jobs. He took Silicon Valley's mass job destruction prediction seriously and demanded a UBI as part of his presidential campaign. It became the centerpiece of his political agenda. During the pandemic, he was an advocate of recurring stimulus payments to households and predicted that many jobs lost during the pandemic are not coming back due to accelerated automation. He argued that UBI would subsidize a 'caring economy', focused on health care, education and social care for the old.[58] Even as he lost the presidential election, he unsuccessfully ran for mayor of New York City in 2021 with the promise of a slimmed down basic income plan for the poorest New Yorkers funded by landlords that benefit from tax exempt status.[59] The former Stockton, CA mayor, Michael Tubbs, has administered a basic income experiment in his town between 2019 and 2020, citing the economic insecurity that plagued many low-income residents in his town.[60] Mayors for a Guaranteed Income is a coalition of over 100 US municipal leaders, who work with donors to fund and organize local basic income trials.[61]

Congresswoman Alexandria Ocasio-Cortez (AOC) is a progressive advocate who was elected to Congress in 2018. In an interview, she argued that society should not be "haunted by the specter of being automated out of work." Instead,

> We should be excited about automation because what it could potentially mean is more time to educate ourselves, more time creating art, more time investing in and investigating the sciences, more time focused on invention, more time going to space, more time enjoying the world that we live in. Because not all creativity needs to be bonded by wage.[62]

AOC has endorsed UBI as a temporary measure for Covid pandemic economic relief.[63] But she has not made UBI a centerpiece of her political agenda. Earlier, she had promoted a job guarantee as a part of the Green New Deal, the investment in the US renewable energy transition.[64] The job guarantee could be supported by activist unions as an effective response to economic insecurity from automation, but it is not quite futurist given the normative focus on preserving wage work.

Shorter Work Week Advocacy

UBI is not the only policy proposal in the futurist repertoire. Another futurist policy is the reduction of the standard work week. This political demand is an integral part of leisure society.[65] Historically, the shortening of the work week has been the result of labor struggles against employers, who refused such demands. In the nineteenth century, industrial workers engaged in over 80-hour work weeks. The demand for the eight-hour day was first made by the Welsh manufacturer and social reformer, Robert Owen, which the labor movement popularized and adopted in its program. The National Labor Union petitioned Congress to introduce an eight-hour day. In 1869, President Ulysses Grant instituted an eight-hour day for federal employees. In 1886, Illinois mandated an eight-hour workday, but the employers resisted the policy. The workers organized a rally that resulted in the Haymarket riot. Nationally, the Adamson Act of 1916 created an eight-hour workday for railroad workers. In 1926, Henry Ford popularized the 40-hour workweek in his car plants because he assumed that loyalty, morale and productivity would increase. In the context of the New Deal, the Fair Labor Standards Act of 1938 set 44-hours as standard work week, which was lowered to 40 in 1940. Above that threshold, workers need to be paid a higher overtime wage rate.[66]

While the 40-hour work week is a significant reduction of standard work hours in labor history, no further work week reductions were formally implemented despite a continuous rise in labor productivity. Productivity rises were diverted to increasing consumerism.[67] The rise of precarious work forces low-wage workers to take on multiple jobs that stretches beyond a 40-hour work week. Corporate downsizing not only displace some workers but also increase the work hours for remaining workers.[68] Weaker unions also mean that workers are not in a bargaining position to demand a shorter work week.

Automation renews the demand for a shorter work week. The progressive US senator, Bernie Sanders, supports a 32 hour standard work week to address the spread of automation.[69] Sanders' legislation is co-sponsored by the California Representative Mark Takano and is endorsed by various labor unions like AFL-CIO, SEIU and UFCW.[70] Massachusetts and California legislatures have proposed bills to provide tax credits to companies that introduce four-day work weeks without pay reductions.[71] Unions like UAW have been campaigning for a shorter work week referring to the AI-related productivity gains. They attempted to obtain the 32-hour standard work week without pay cuts in their 2023 contract negotiations but failed in that effort. Ford management rejected the union demands, claiming that it would produce economic losses.[72] In France, the trade union federation (CGT) had called for the introduction of a 32 hour work week.[73] On the issue of the shorter work week, the activists and futurists find themselves in agreement, although for futurists the end goal is the abolition of work, which not all activists within the labor movement, politics or civil society would want.

Selected companies have experimented with a shorter work week. DiamondBack, a Pennsylvania-based manufacturing company, has introduced a 35-hour work week spaced over four days without cuts in pay. Buffer, a US tech company, offers a 32-hour work week, where the employees choose whether to work four or five days. Perpetual Guardian, a New Zealand estate planning company, introduced a 30-hour week in four days.[74] Such work reduction experiments work very well in high productivity industries, where even low hours generate sufficient profits, but to benefit all workers, legislation is required.

Other countries have already implemented workweek shortening legislation. In May 2025, Spain reduced the standard workweek from 40 to 37.5 hours. Belgium already has a 38-hour workweek, and in 2022, they gave workers the flexibility to spread their schedule over four days of the week. Iceland has introduced a standard 36 hour workweek in 2019.[75] The Netherlands formally retains a 40-hour workweek, but many workplaces give a lot of schedule flexibility such that with 32 hours the Dutch have the shortest European workweek.[76] Japan is a country with the notoriety of many deaths from overwork (karoshi). The Tokyo city government introduced a four-day workweek for public sector employees.[77] Countries like Poland and Portugal have been running four-day workweek voluntary pilot programs for private-sector employers.[78] We can expect that list to grow further in the future.

The shorter workweek is a gradual approach toward achieving a leisure society. Futurists see the reduction of working time as the dividend afforded by technological progress in the AI era.

Cultural Depictions of a Future without Work

The academic vision of a workless future and the policy demand of UBI and a shorter work week do not reveal in much detail how that workless technological utopia will actually look like. There are many more examples than *Star Trek*. Various novels, movies and TV shows have given a spark to our imagination on a utopian future without work. They form a sharp contrast to the undesirable technological unemployment depicted in the resigned discourse in Chapter 4.

In *Men Like Gods* by H.G. Wells, the main character Mr. Barnstaple is transported into a parallel universe 3,000 years ahead of his time. Advanced science and technologies have defeated disease, poverty and war. There is no formal government. Telepathy has replaced the spoken language as primary mode of communication. The utopians operate according to five principles of liberty, which include privacy, free movement, unlimited knowledge, truthfulness and free discussion.

In *Island* by Aldous Huxley, the fictional island society of Pala has integrated modern science and technology to serve human and environmental well-being. The focus is on improving health and food security, and the minimal work that is left on the island is focused on fulfilling and creative tasks for people. Mindless consumption is frowned on, and people consume 'moksha medicine,' which is a drug that provides spiritual insights. The only threat to the islanders comes from outside civilization that could invade them and forcefully reintegrate them into capitalist civilization.

In *Ecotopia* by Ernest Callenbach, the liberal US west coast states have declared their independence calling themselves Ecotopia and organize an ecologically sustainable nation powered by renewable energy. There is no economic growth in Ecotopia. It retains nuclear weapons to guard against a US military invasion. It utilizes advanced recycling and mass transit. It opposes mass media entertainment and favors community-based arts and participatory activities. There is a standard 20-hour workweek, and inhabitants do not feel significant work stress.

In *The Culture Series* by Iain M. Banks, the Culture is a post-scarcity, pan-galactic, anarchistic-utopian civilization. Humanoid species are free to pursue their own passions, while the material work is taken over by Minds, which are AI drones. The humanoids no longer must compete or accumulate capital. Minds are much more intelligent than the biological humanoids and are organizing society, resources and travel. Life-enhancing technologies involve genetic modification for longevity and physical customization, neural implants that allow humanoids to access all the information they want, consciousness backups that record and store the minds of humanoids so they can continue living after the death of their physical bodies. The latter technology implies immortality. The Culture lives in artificial habitats in rotating Orbitals or vast General Systems Vehicles (GSV) that travel the galaxy.

In *Andromeda* by Ivan Yefremov, life on earth is an advanced communist society where social ills and diseases are eradicated. Technologies are used for the common good and with an eye to respect the environment. People are energetic, educated and eager to pursue new challenges. All work is done voluntarily and with an eye to the common good. People pursue intellectual, artistic and athletic pursuits. The downside is that Andromeda's civilization still has "bulls" who are people who want to dominate and control others and rules are in place to limit their ability to exploit others.

In *Walkaway* by Cory Doctorow, there is a split future between a hyper-capitalist 'Default' and a post-scarcity world in 'walkaway.' In the latter world, technologies produce nearly all the goods and services. Work is voluntary and no one works for pay. In Default, most people are precarious and highly surveilled gig economy workers, who can barely make a living while the technologies produce more riches and power for the capital owners. The mixed vision produces a contrast between a desirable futurism and a dystopian resigned future.

There are movies and TV productions that depict a utopian future without work. In *Things to Come* (1936), which is based on H.G. Wells novel *The Shape of Things to Come*, humanity evolves to a state where a technocratic elite uses advanced engineering to produce an automated underground city where people no longer must work for a living. People living in the underground city have a lot of leisure time and pursue their own interests. There is some tension because some artists think that a life freed from necessity removes purpose.

In *Black Panther* (2018), the fictional African nation of Wakanda is a technologically advanced post-scarcity society. The extraterrestrial metal Vibranium enables Wakanda to develop advanced technology, which frees most Wakandans from traditional jobs. They are free to pursue creative, scientific and cultural activities. They intend to hide this technology from the world, but there is a struggle to spread it to the world.

The television series *The Jetsons* in the early-1960s and in the mid-1980s revolves around the Jetson family and their robot maid Rosie, who performs the household chores. George Jetson, the main character, only works an hour a day, two days a week as an employee of a high-tech equipment manufacturing firm, pushing a few buttons as the main task. The work is done to keep him employed, not to produce more output. Capitalists continue to compete with each other, which is more in line with the status quo than the futurist vision, but the reduction in working hours is quite futurist. Commutes happen in flying cars and moving sidewalks. Video calls are common. Food is generated by replicators, and dressing/grooming is automated as well. The family lives in a house in orbit. In this world, humans have long ago taken over outer space. Daily life is leisurely, but the labor-saving devices occasionally break down providing some comedic value. The characters complain about living with the remaining inconveniences of life.

There have been many cultural depictions showing that humans could find and obtain purpose if their life is no longer tied to wage work. Technological unemployment could be a futurist utopia.

Conclusion

The future of work is about reducing if not eliminating wage work. The futurist discourse anticipates that automation enables more and more people to escape the oppressive nature of wage work. Paid wage work is not a source of meaning but rather constitutes a burden that could be minimized by greater reliance on technological tools. Futurists cover a large number of actors, such as the owners of major technology companies, who are overseeing the AI products that automate tasks and occupations, left-wing intellectuals, who have a commitment to human freedom and the abolition of wage work, and political leaders, who are doing UBI or work reduction advocacy. With the ongoing craze for AI, the futurist discourse is on the ascendance.

Notes

1 Rosenfield, Eric. "Star Trek into Socialism." *Literate Machine*, April 12, 2023. https://literatemachine.com/2023/04/12/star-trek-into-socialism/
2 Star Trek. First Contact (1996). Movie transcript: http://www.chakoteya.net/movies/movie8.html
3 A more cynical Marxist take is that in a profit-driven economy, substantial price cuts would result in investment cuts, whose depressing economic effects could make it harder to fund the welfare state. Such investment cuts would not be an issue if the means of production were commonly owned. Futurists tend to neglect this sociological relationship between technology and capitalism.
4 Schopenhauer, Arthur. *Wisdom of Life*. New York: M.W. Dunne, 1901.
5 Schrittwieser, Julian. "Failing to Understand the Exponential, Again." *Blog*, September 27, 2025. https://www.julian.ac/blog/2025/09/27/failing-to-understand-the-exponential-again/
6 Veal, A. J. "The Elusive Leisure Society." *University of Technology, Sydney*, Working Paper No. 9 (2009). https://opus.lib.uts.edu.au/bitstream/10453/19821/1/lstwp9.pdf
7 Bull, Chris, Jayne Hoose, and Mike Weed. *An Introduction to Leisure Studies*. Hoboken: Prentice Hall, 2003, p. 282.
8 Veal, A. J. "The Leisure Society II: The Era of Critique, 1980–2011." *World Leisure Journal* 54, no. 2 (2012): 99–140. Veal, A. J. *Whatever Happened to the Leisure Society?* London: Routledge, 2018.
9 Veal. *Whatever Happened to the Leisure Society?*.
10 Huizinga, Johan. *Homo Ludens: A Study of the Play-Element of Culture*. London: Routledge & Kegan Paul, 1949.
11 Marx, Karl. *Grundrisse: Foundations of the Critique of Political Economy*. Translated by Martin Nicolaus. London: Penguin Books, 1973, p. 701. https://thenewobjectivity.com/pdf/marx.pdf
12 Goldstraw, Simeon. "Marx on Leisure: An Aristotelian Interpretation." *Canadian Journal of Political Science/Revue canadienne de science politique* 57, no. 2 (2024): 325–43.

13 Odell, Jenny. *How to Do Nothing: Resisting the Attention Economy.* New York: Melville House, 2019.
14 Weber, Max. *The Protestant Ethic and the "Spirit" of Capitalism and Other Writings.* London: Penguin, 2002.
15 Harvard Gazette. "Mark Zuckerberg's Commencement Address at Harvard." May 25, 2017.
16 Harvard Gazette. "Mark Zuckerberg's Commencement Address at Harvard." May 25, 2017.
17 Twitter, @elonmusk, June 15, 2018 https://twitter.com/elonmusk/status/1007762646182047744
18 Mancini, Jeanine. "'There Will Be Universal High Income': Elon Musk Predicts with 80% Certainty That 'None of Us' Will Have Jobs, but Bill Gates Says It's Too Soon." *Benzinga*, June 13, 2025.
19 Twitter, @elonmusk, April 13, 2018. https://twitter.com/elonmusk/status/984882630947753984
20 Kottenstette, Ryan. "Elon Musk Wasn't Wrong about Automating the Model 3 Assembly Line: He Was Just Ahead of His Time." *TechCrunch*, March 5, 2019.
21 Twitter, @elonmusk, October 12, 2020. https://twitter.com/elonmusk/status/1315751528511094784
22 Eisenstein, Paul. "Electric Vehicles Pose 'Real Risk' For Autoworkers, with Fewer Parts and Jobs Required." *NBC News*, October 3, 2019.
23 Gilder, Lucy, and Jake Horton. "How Much Has Elon Musk's Doge Cut from US Government Spending?" *BBC*, April 25, 2025. https://www.bbc.com/news/articles/cn4j33klz33o
24 Hui, Xiang, Oren Reshef, and Luofeng Zhou. "Artificial Intelligence and Its Short-Term Effects on Employment." *VoxEU*, December 1, 2023.
25 Rosoff, Matt. "A.I. May Replace Most of Today's Jobs, but This Start-up Investor Sees Global GDP Increasing 50 Percent a Year Within Decades." *CNBC*, February 26, 2019.
26 Clifford, Catherine. "OpenAI's Sam Altman: Artificial Intelligence Will Generate Enough Wealth to Pay Each Adult $13,500 a Year." *CNBC*, March 17, 2021.
27 Rajaratnam, Vaikunthan. "Universal Basic Compute Instead of Universal Basic Income." *LinkedIn*, May 13, 2024.
28 Belvedere, Matthew J. "Facebook Co-founder Hughes: The Digital Economy Is 'Going to Continue to Destroy' Jobs in America." *CNBC*, February 20, 2018.
29 Matthews, Dylan. "Chris Hughes Wants Another Chance." *Vox*, January 22, 2020.
30 Economic Security Project. "Guaranteed Income." https://www.economicsecurityproject.org/guaranteedincome/
31 Clifford, Catherine. "Twitter Billionaire Jack Dorsey: Automation Will Even Put Tech Jobs in Jeopardy." *CNBC*, May 22, 2020.
32 Konish, Lorie. "Twitter CEO Jack Dorsey Donates $15 Million to Help Cities Provide Guaranteed Income to Their Residents." *CNBC*, December 8, 2020.
33 Goldfisher, Alastair. "Unconstrained: Vinod Khosla's Vision for an AI Future." *Medium*, May 20, 2025.
34 Paradis, Tim. "Vinod Khosla Says Universal Basic Income May Be Needed as AI Takes Over Jobs and Drives Wealth Disparity." *Business Insider*, September 23, 2024.
35 Pringle, Eleanor. "Jamie Dimon Says the Next Generation of Employees Will Work 3.5 Days a Week and Live to 100 Years Old." *Fortune*, November 24, 2024.
36 Burleigh, Emma. "Zoom's CEO Agrees with Bill Gates, Jensen Huang, and Jamie Dimon: A 3-Day Workweek Is Coming Soon Thanks to AI." *Fortune*, September 15, 2025.
37 Tremayne-Pengelly, Alexandra. "Anthropic CEO Dario Amodei Thinks Altman and Musk's Inequality Solution Is 'Kind of Dystopian'." *Observer*, June 24, 2024.

38 Frank, Patricia. "Can Philanthropy Cover the Loss of Federal Funding?" *Indiana Philanthropy*, April 15, 2025. https://inphilanthropy.org/news/can-philanthropy-cover-loss-federal-funding
39 Keynes, John Maynard. "Economic Possibilities for Our Grandchildren." *Marxists.org*, 1930. https://www.marxists.org/reference/subject/economics/keynes/1930/our-grandchildren.htm
40 Russell, Bertrand. *In Praise of Idleness and Other Essays*. London: George Allen & Unwin Ltd, 1915, p. 16.
41 Russell. *In Praise of Idleness*.
42 Gorz, Andre. *Farewell to the Working Class: An Essay on Post-Industrial Socialism*. London: Pluto Press, 1982, p. 74.
43 Gorz. *Farewell to the Working Class*, p. 136.
44 Gorz. *Farewell to the Working Class*, p. 72.
45 Barlow, Elizabeth. "The New York Magazine Environmental Teach-In." *New York Magazine*, March 30, 1970, p. 30.
46 Tegmark, Max. *Life 3.0: Being Human in the Age of Artificial Intelligence*. New York: Alfred A. Knopf, 2017, pp. 167–8 [e-book pages].
47 Susskind, Daniel. *A World Without Work*. New York: Metropolitan Books, 2020, pp. 226–30.
48 Bregman, Rutger. *Utopia for Realists: The Case for Universal Basic Income, Open Borders, and a 15-Hour Workweek*. New York: Little, Brown, 2017.
49 Srnicek, Nick, and Alex Williams. *Inventing the Future*. London: Verso, 2015.
50 Bastani, Aaron. *Fully Automated Luxury Communism: A Manifesto*. London: Verso, 2019.
51 Mason, Paul. *PostCapitalism: A Guide to Our Future*. London: Allen Lane, 2015.
52 Truthout. "Myths of Globalization." June 22, 2017. https://chomsky.info/20170705/
53 Widerquist, Karl. "The Deep and Enduring History of Universal Basic Income." *The MIT Press Reader*, March 7, 2024. https://thereader.mitpress.mit.edu/the-deep-and-enduring-history-of-universal-basic-income/
54 Van Parijs, Philippe, and Yannick Vanderborght. *Basic Income: A Radical Proposal for a Free Society and a Sane Economy*. Cambridge: Cambridge University Press, 2019.
55 Lowrey, Annie. *Give People Money*. New York: Penguin, 2018. Stern, Andy, and Lee Kravitz. *Raising the Floor*. New York: Public Affairs, 2016.
56 Widerquist, Karl. "Why Wait Until the Robots Take Our Jobs? We Need a Basic Income Now." *Open Democracy*, September 23, 2024. Liu, Larry. "The Economic Precondition of Voice: How a Universal Basic Income (UBI) Can Promote Workplace Democracy." In *Debating Workplace Democracy*, edited by Christopher Mathieu, 115–34. New York: Palgrave, 2026.
57 Widerquist, Karl. "The Deep and Enduring History of Universal Basic Income."
58 Steelquist, Colleen. "Entrepreneur Andrew Yang Talks to SPU about the Future of Work." *Seattle Pacific University*, October 19, 2020. Yang, Andrew. *The War on Normal People*. New York: Hachette, 2018.
59 DeCiccio, Emily. "NYC Mayoral Candidate Andrew Yang Wants MSG, Tax Exempt Landlords to Pay for His Universal Basic Income Plan." *CNBC*, March 15, 2021.
60 Treisman, Rachel. "California Program Giving $500 No-Strings-Attached Stipends Pays Off, Study Finds." *NPR*, March 4, 2021.
61 Wellington, Darryl Lorenzo. "Cities Can Fight Back with Guaranteed Income Programs." *Source NM*, July 15, 2025.
62 Kottke, Jason. "The Robots Are Coming for Our Jobs (Thank God)." *Kottke.org*, March 11, 2019.
63 Relman, Eliza. "Alexandria Ocasio-Cortez Demands the Government Distribute a Universal Basic Income and Implement 'Medicare For All' to Fight the Coronavirus." *Business Insider*, March 12, 2020.

64 Shakesprere, Jessica, and Demetra Smith Nightingale. "Envisioning an Effective Federal Job Guarantee." *Urban Institute*, October 22, 2019.
65 Veal, A. J. "The 4-Day Work-Week: The New Leisure Society?" *Leisure Studies* 42, no. 2 (2023): 172–87.
66 Lee, Sophia. "The History & Evolution of the 40-Hour Work Week." *Culture Amp*, February 26, 2019. https://www.cultureamp.com/blog/40-hour-work-week
67 Sawhill, Isabel V. "Time for a Shorter Work Week?" *Brookings*, May 13, 2016.
68 Insights Newsroom. "*How Layoffs Impact Culture, Team Dynamics and Those Left Behind.*" N.d. https://blog.insights.com/en-us/blog/the-ripple-effect-how-layoffs-impact-company-culture-team-dynamics-and-those-left-behind
69 Silberling, Amanda. "Bernie Sanders Says That If AI Makes Us So Productive, We Should Get a 4-Day Workweek." *TechCrunch*, June 25, 2025.
70 Takano, Mark. "Rep. Mark Takano – Thirty-Two Hour Workweek Act." n.d. https://takano.house.gov/imo/media/doc/32-hour_workweek_act_one_pager.pdf
71 Zahn, Max. "Will Bernie Sanders' Proposed 32-Hour Workweek Pass Congress?" *ABC News*, March 16, 2024.
72 Isidore, Chris. "The 4-Day Workweek Was a Longshot. The UAW Isn't Giving Up." *CNN*, December 16, 2023.
73 CGT. "Un remède aux suppressions d'emplois annoncées par la révolution numérique." June 11, 2018. https://www.cgt.fr/actualites/un-remede-aux-suppressions-demplois-annoncees-par-la-revolution-numerique
74 Pugh, Marie-Reine. "Workplace Flexibility: Promising Research Supports a 4-Day Work Week." *Bamboo HR*, November 22, 2024.
75 Hjálmtýsdóttir, María. "Iceland's Shorter Working Week Has Been a Huge Success – And It's Changed My Family's Life." *Guardian*, May 21, 2024.
76 Burleigh, Emma. "Forget 40 Hours: The Dutch Get Their Work Done in Just 32 Hours a Week—and Women Made It Possible." *Fortune*, August 28, 2025.
77 Verma, Navya. "10 Countries Experimenting with a 4-Day Work Week." *Conde Nast Traveler*, February 19, 2025.
78 Blair, Jennifer. "Poland Is Trialing Shorter Workweek Hours." *Jibble*, June 9, 2025. McParlane, Phil. "Portugal." N.d. https://4dayweek.io/country/portugal

References

Barlow, Elizabeth. "The New York Magazine Environmental Teach-In." *New York Magazine*, March 30, 1970.

Bastani, Aaron. *Fully Automated Luxury Communism: A Manifesto.* London: Verso, 2019.

Belvedere, Matthew J. "Facebook Co-founder Hughes: The Digital Economy Is 'Going to Continue to Destroy' Jobs in America." *CNBC*, February 20, 2018.

Blair, Jennifer. "Poland Is Trialing Shorter Workweek Hours." *Jibble*, June 9, 2025.

Bregman, Rutger. *Utopia for Realists: The Case for Universal Basic Income, Open Borders, and a 15-Hour Workweek.* New York: Little, Brown, 2017.

Bull, Chris, Jayne Hoose, and Mike Weed. *An Introduction to Leisure Studies.* Hoboken, NJ: Prentice Hall, 2003.

Burleigh, Emma. "Forget 40 Hours: The Dutch Get Their Work Done in Just 32 Hours a Week—and Women Made It Possible." *Fortune*, August 28, 2025.

Burleigh, Emma. "Zoom's CEO Agrees with Bill Gates, Jensen Huang, and Jamie Dimon: A 3-Day Workweek Is Coming Soon Thanks to AI." *Fortune*, September 15, 2025.

CGT. "Un remède aux suppressions d'emplois annoncées par la révolution numérique." June 11, 2018. https://www.cgt.fr/actualites/un-remede-aux-suppressions-demplois-annoncees-par-la-revolution-numerique.

Clifford, Catherine. "Twitter Billionaire Jack Dorsey: Automation Will Even Put Tech Jobs in Jeopardy." *CNBC*, May 22, 2020.

Clifford, Catherine. "OpenAI's Sam Altman: Artificial Intelligence Will Generate Enough Wealth to Pay Each Adult $13,500 a Year." *CNBC*, March 17, 2021.

DeCiccio, Emily. "NYC Mayoral Candidate Andrew Yang Wants MSG, Tax Exempt Landlords to Pay for His Universal Basic Income Plan." *CNBC*, March 15, 2021.

Economic Security Project. "Guaranteed Income." Accessed March 10, 2026. https://www.economicsecurityproject.org/guaranteedincome/.

Eisenstein, Paul. "Electric Vehicles Pose 'Real Risk' for Autoworkers, with Fewer Parts and Jobs Required." *NBC News*, October 3, 2019.

Frank, Patricia. "Can Philanthropy Cover the Loss of Federal Funding?" *Indiana Philanthropy*, April 15, 2025. https://inphilanthropy.org/news/can-philanthropy-cover-loss-federal-funding.

Gilder, Lucy, and Jake Horton. "How Much Has Elon Musk's Doge Cut from US Government Spending?" *BBC*, April 25, 2025. https://www.bbc.com/news/articles/cn4j33klz33o.

Goldfisher, Alastair. "Unconstrained: Vinod Khosla's Vision for an AI Future." *Medium*, May 20, 2025.

Goldstraw, Simeon. "Marx on Leisure: An Aristotelian Interpretation." *Canadian Journal of Political Science/Revue canadienne de science politique* 57, no. 2 (2024): 325–43.

Gorz, Andre. *Farewell to the Working Class: An Essay on Post-Industrial Socialism*. London: Pluto Press, 1982.

Harvard Gazette. "Mark Zuckerberg's Commencement Address at Harvard." May 25, 2017.

Hjálmtýsdóttir, María. "Iceland's Shorter Working Week Has Been a Huge Success – And It's Changed My Family's Life." *The Guardian*, May 21, 2024.Hui, Xiang, Oren Reshef, and Luofeng Zhou. "Artificial Intelligence and Its Short-Term Effects on Employment." *VoxEU*, December 1, 2023.

Huizinga, Johan. *Homo Ludens: A Study of the Play-Element of Culture*. London: Routledge & Kegan Paul, 1949.

Insights Newsroom. *"How Layoffs Impact Culture, Team Dynamics and Those Left Behind."*N.d. https://blog.insights.com/en-us/blog/the-ripple-effect-how-layoffs-impact-company-culture-team-dynamics-and-those-left-behind

Isidore, Chris. "The 4-Day Workweek Was a Longshot. The UAW Isn't Giving Up." *CNN*, December 16, 2023.

Keynes, John Maynard. "Economic Possibilities for Our Grandchildren." 1930. In *Marxists.org*. https://www.marxists.org/reference/subject/economics/keynes/1930/our-grandchildren.htm.

Konish, Lorie. "Twitter CEO Jack Dorsey Donates $15 Million to Help Cities Provide Guaranteed Income to Their Residents." *CNBC*, December 8, 2020.

Kottenstette, Ryan. "Elon Musk Wasn't Wrong about Automating the Model 3 Assembly Line: He Was Just Ahead of His Time." *TechCrunch*, March 5, 2019.

Kottke, Jason. "The Robots Are Coming for Our Jobs (Thank God)." *Kottke.org*, March 11, 2019.

Lee, Sophia. "The History & Evolution of the 40-Hour Work Week." *Culture Amp*, February 26, 2019. https://www.cultureamp.com/blog/40-hour-work-week.

Liu, Larry. "The Economic Precondition of Voice: How a Universal Basic Income (UBI) Can Promote Workplace Democracy." In *Debating Workplace Democracy*, edited by Christopher Mathieu, 115–34. New York: Palgrave, 2026.

Lowrey, Annie. *Give People Money*. New York: Penguin, 2018.

Mancini, Jeanine. "'There Will Be Universal High Income': Elon Musk Predicts with 80% Certainty That 'None of Us' Will Have Jobs, but Bill Gates Says It's Too Soon." *Benzinga*, June 13, 2025.

Marx, Karl. *Grundrisse: Foundations of the Critique of Political Economy*. Translated by Martin Nicolaus. London: Penguin Books, 1973. https://thenewobjectivity.com/pdf/marx.pdf.

Mason, Paul. *PostCapitalism: A Guide to Our Future*. London: Allen Lane, 2015.

Matthews, Dylan. "Chris Hughes Wants Another Chance." *Vox*, January 22, 2020.

McParlane, Phil. "Portugal." n.d. https://4dayweek.io/country/portugal.

Odell, Jenny. *How to Do Nothing: Resisting the Attention Economy*. New York: Melville House, 2019.

Paradis, Tim. "Vinod Khosla Says Universal Basic Income May Be Needed as AI Takes over Jobs and Drives Wealth Disparity." *Business Insider*, September 23, 2024.

Pringle, Eleanor. "Jamie Dimon Says the Next Generation of Employees Will Work 3.5 Days a Week and Live to 100 Years Old." *Fortune*, November 24, 2024.

Pugh, Marie-Reine. "Workplace Flexibility: Promising Research Supports a 4-Day Work Week." *Bamboo HR*, November 22, 2024.

Rajaratnam, Vaikunthan. "Universal Basic Compute Instead of Universal Basic Income." *LinkedIn*, May 13, 2024.

Relman, Eliza. "Alexandria Ocasio-Cortez Demands the Government Distribute a Universal Basic Income and Implement 'Medicare for All' to Fight the Coronavirus." *Business Insider*, March 12, 2020.

Rosenfield, Eric. "Star Trek into Socialism." *Literate Machine*, April 12, 2023. https://literatemachine.com/2023/04/12/star-trek-into-socialism/.

Rosoff, Matt. "A.I. May Replace Most of Today's Jobs, but This Start-up Investor Sees Global GDP Increasing 50 Percent a Year Within Decades." *CNBC*, February 26, 2019.

Russell, Bertrand. *In Praise of Idleness and Other Essays*. London: George Allen & Unwin Ltd, 1915.

Sawhill, Isabel V. "Time for a Shorter Work Week?" *Brookings*, May 13, 2016.

Schopenhauer, Arthur. *Wisdom of Life*. New York: M. W. Dunne, 1901.

Schrittwieser, Julian. "Failing to Understand the Exponential, Again." *Blog*, September 27, 2025. https://www.julian.ac/blog/2025/09/27/failing-to-understand-the-exponential-again/.

Shakesprere, Jessica, and Demetra Smith Nightingale. "Envisioning an Effective Federal Job Guarantee." *Urban Institute*, October 22, 2019.

Silberling, Amanda. "Bernie Sanders Says That If AI Makes Us So Productive, We Should Get a 4-Day Workweek." *TechCrunch*, June 25, 2025.

Srnicek, Nick, and Alex Williams. *Inventing the Future*. London: Verso, 2015.

Star Trek. "First Contact." 1996. Transcript. https://www.chakoteya.net/movies/movie8.html.

Steelquist, Colleen. "Entrepreneur Andrew Yang Talks to SPU about the Future of Work." *Seattle Pacific University*, October 19, 2020.

Stern, Andy, and Lee Kravitz. *Raising the Floor*. New York: Public Affairs, 2016.

Susskind, Daniel. *A World Without Work*. New York: Metropolitan Books, 2020.

Takano, Mark. "Rep. Mark Takano – Thirty-Two Hour Workweek Act." n.d. https://takano.house.gov/imo/media/doc/32-hour_workweek_act_one_pager.pdf.

Tegmark, Max. *Life 3.0: Being Human in the Age of Artificial Intelligence*. New York: Alfred A. Knopf, 2017.

Treisman, Rachel. "California Program Giving $500 No-Strings-Attached Stipends Pays Off, Study Finds." *NPR*, March 4, 2021.

Tremayne-Pengelly, Alexandra. "Anthropic CEO Dario Amodei Thinks Altman and Musk's Inequality Solution Is 'Kind of Dystopian'." *Observer*, June 24, 2024.

Truthout. "Myths of Globalization." June 22, 2017. https://chomsky.info/20170705/.

Twitter. @elonmusk. "…" April 13, 2018. https://twitter.com/elonmusk/status/984882630947753984.

Twitter. @elonmusk. "…" June 15, 2018. https://twitter.com/elonmusk/status/1007762646182047744.

Twitter. @elonmusk. "…" October 12, 2020. https://twitter.com/elonmusk/status/1315751528511094784.

Van Parijs, Philippe, and Yannick Vanderborght. *Basic Income: A Radical Proposal for a Free Society and a Sane Economy*. Cambridge: Cambridge University Press, 2019.

Veal, A. J. "The Elusive Leisure Society." *University of Technology, Sydney*, Working Paper No. 9, 2009. https://opus.lib.uts.edu.au/bitstream/10453/19821/1/lstwp9.pdf.

Veal, A. J. "The Leisure Society II: The Era of Critique, 1980–2011." *World Leisure Journal* 54, no. 2 (2012): 99–140.

Veal, A. J. "The 4-Day Work-Week: The New Leisure Society?" *Leisure Studies* 42, no. 2 (2023): 172–87.

Veal, A. J. *Whatever Happened to the Leisure Society?* London: Routledge, 2018.

Verma, Navya. "10 Countries Experimenting with a 4-Day Work Week." *Conde Nast Traveler*, February 19, 2025.

Weber, Max. *The Protestant Ethic and the "Spirit" of Capitalism and Other Writings*. London: Penguin, 2002.

Wellington, Darryl Lorenzo. "Cities Can Fight Back with Guaranteed Income Programs." *Source NM*, July 15, 2025.

Widerquist, Karl. "The Deep and Enduring History of Universal Basic Income." *The MIT Press Reader*, March 7, 2024. https://thereader.mitpress.mit.edu/the-deep-and-enduring-history-of-universal-basic-income/.

Widerquist, Karl. "Why Wait Until the Robots Take Our Jobs? We Need a Basic Income Now." *Open Democracy*, September 23, 2024.

Yang, Andrew. *The War on Normal People*. New York: Hachette, 2018.

Zahn, Max. "Will Bernie Sanders' Proposed 32-Hour Workweek Pass Congress?" *ABC News*, March 16, 2024.

CONCLUSION

We humans have invented technologies since the beginning of our existence as a species. Any time we have access to new tools, there is a change in the relations that we have with the labor tasks, and there is a change in the social relations. These social relations involve the production process itself, where Marxists have pointed to the exploitative economic relations that are inherent to feudalist and capitalist systems while mainstream economists see labor and capital/technology as two factors of production that synergistically produce useful economic output. Technological innovation has the capacity to displace segments of the workforce and forces them to obtain new employment. It forces unions, policymakers, academics, businesspeople and other social groups to respond to these bouts of technological displacement. Surely, the steam engine is different from the computer and AI, but is this time different? Are we reaching the end of the line of human wage work in the twenty-first century?

While this book cannot definitively answer this question, I have addressed the question of what the societal discursive frames are on automation and the future of work. The discourse of automation covers; how society responds to the implications, policy preferences, hopes and fears about technological change. This discourse is a sociotechnical imaginary and an expectation of the future of work. It is another form of social relation aside from the production process and workplace itself that is worthy of study and subject to sociological analysis.

This book has established the four major discursive frames in response to technological change. Activists believe in resistance to automation or the active process of shaping it in more favorable terms to the people mostly affected by it; the workers. The job guarantee, collective bargaining and strikes are parts of the activist policy repertoire. It is not surprising that organized labor is the

DOI: 10.4324/9781003780236-8

most vocal in this type of discourse, and they are supported by political leaders; who see their political base in the working class.

The resigned argue that automation produces negative or dystopian effects on society, such as mass unemployment, political polarization, lack of meaning/ social cohesion and psychological disorders, but leave it open, whether ameliorative action can be introduced. Intellectuals, media and artists are behind this technology-critical discourse. The resigned view is socially conservative in a Durkheimian sense, where the technological forces produce anomie and reduce social solidarity. Any action that mitigates anomie is favored by the resigned.

The status quo view suggests that new technologies are an integral part behind capitalism. They produce mainly positive societal effects such as new consumer products and a generally higher standard of living. Job displacements are at most minor inconveniences that can be overcome by offering job training to the newly unemployed. Business leaders, business consultants and bipartisan politicians favor the status quo view of automation. Politicians merely disagree on the role of government in reintegrating displaced workers back into the labor market. The business leaders tend to be the largest beneficiaries of technological change, although some labor unions engage in this job training discourse as well for defensive reasons.

Lastly, futurists present a deeply optimistic vision where technologies have liberated most humans from the drudgery of wage work. While they envision the abolition of wage work over the long term, they advocate for policies like UBI or a shorter work week as milestones in their objective. Silicon Valley leaders, progressive intellectuals and a few political leaders are most likely to engage in futurist discourse. The former seeks to gain short-term legitimacy in front of the public and investors for their automating products they are bringing to market as well as long-term legitimacy, because they are afraid of public discontent; if automation prevents the broad sharing of the AI wealth. The futurist intellectuals envision human liberation that they equate to their own creative and temporal freedoms. Progressive politicians look for popular support for their work-shortening or social security policy demands.

Having laid out the four discourses, a final analytical point that I have left unaddressed is how these discourses view each other and evaluate each other's statements.

How the Four Discourses View Each Other

People that advocate for a particular automation discourse will view the other perspectives critically. Individuals can have a more nuanced perspective in practice. For instance, activist unions might support job training and a shorter work week that is advocated by the status quo and futurists. What I present is a Weberian ideal type of response that each actor might give when exposed to the views of the other actor. This has analytical value for social scientists, as researchers can compare, contrast and better understand the unique and general features of social realities by measuring how closely actual cases align with the pure form of the ideal type. Therefore, the analysis provided below is conceptual rather than empirical.

The activists believe that they have the most agency and have the general critique that the other actors are too technologically determinist (Table C.1)

The resigned view is too pessimistic and does not take into account the ability of workers to strike and collectively bargain to improve their outcomes even if automation is encroaching on more labor tasks. The dystopian results of technological unemployment can be averted if workers, political leaders and the public do something about it, including active resistance or ameliorative policies. Activists dismiss the status quo view that new technologies will automatically generate a lot of employment or that these jobs will provide decent wages and working conditions. The status quo view tends to ignore the rise in income and wealth inequality, where capital owners benefit much more from new technologies than ordinary workers, whose working conditions deteriorate in growing job sectors. Activists do not believe that small technocratic adjustments in job training offerings will do enough to mitigate social inequality, though they would be supportive of it as one among many policies. In contrast, the futurists are too optimistic and disregard the human agency that is required to create utopian outcomes. They cannot be dreamed up in academic books or from technological progress alone but require activism whether from unions, political movements, or civil society. Some activists are in favor of shortening workweeks, while others fear the elimination of wage work that will threaten the identity of many humans.

The resigned believe that the other viewpoints are too optimistic and hopeful about technological change (Table C.2).

TABLE C.1 Activist Critiques of Other Discourses

Viewpoint	*Critique*
Resigned	Too pessimistic, disregards agency to improve workers' lives
Status quo	Produces many losers, ignores inequality rise, job training not enough
Futurist	Too optimistic, disregards agency, and utopia requires human effort, workless future is dystopian

TABLE C.2 Resigned Critique of Other Discourses

Viewpoint	*Critique*
Activist	Unions fight rearguard, defensive battle they are bound to lose
Status quo	Ignore the downsides of automation
Futurist	Workless future is dystopian

The resigned think that the activists, who are attempting to block new technologies or produce more favorable collective bargaining clauses for union workers, are fighting a rearguard, defensive battle that they are bound to lose. In a capitalist system, the company owners are principally free to adopt new technologies, and any favorable labor contract arrangements to slow down technology will ultimately not stop their adoption. The resigned are normatively favorable to the activist goals, because their ability to preserve wage work will reduce anomie. The status quo perspective ignores the downsides of automation, such as political polarization, growing inequality or psychological problems. The status quo can only see the upsides of technology because they focus too much on economic goals like profit or tax revenues. The resigned have the biggest philosophical disagreement with the futurists. For the resigned, a workless future is not a desirable utopia but a dystopia. If people's meaning in life is derived from the structure and objectives in wage work, then reducing work hours is deeply disorienting. No amount of UBI or welfare can replace the dignity provided by stable and good-quality jobs.

The status quo advocates believe that the other perspectives on automation are too radical or too pessimistic, thus delegitimizing the societal benefits that come from new technologies (Table C.3).

An activist demands to block automation, give hiring privileges to existing workers and other costly employment programs. These demands threaten economic and productivity growth. The status quo wants to minimize the number of resources devoted to appeasing displaced workers, which allows for more resources devoted to build new technology, and accelerate progress. The resigned fear of widespread technological unemployment is dismissed outright. These unjustified fears might strengthen the activist demands to put a chill on automating technologies that form the basis for an increase in the variety of cheaper consumer goods and exciting, interesting and engaging new jobs. The status quo is strongly opposed to futurists, whose workless future requires an increase in welfare and redistributive obligations that undermine and disincentivize technological development. The much-feared socialist futurist outlook will not establish a workless future, but instead it will prevent any technological benefits from coming to fruition given that they are tied to the capitalist institutions that the futurists will destroy.

TABLE C.3 Status Quo Critique of Other Discourses

Viewpoint	*Critique*
Activist	Threaten economic growth and productivity growth
Resigned	Technological unemployment was never a serious problem, too pessimistic
Futurist	Welfare/redistribution demands destroy technological benefits

TABLE C.4 Futurist Critiques of Other Discourses

Viewpoint	*Critique*
Activist	Too modest and unimaginative in their demands
Resigned	Ignore the liberating potential of technology
Status quo	Too conservative views on social organization and technology potential

Futurists criticize the other views as being too conservative and not embracing the liberating potential of technology (Table C.4).

Futurists believe that activists are too modest and unimaginative in their political demands. Blocking automation or reassigning union workers to other jobs is about defending union privileges rather than seeing how technologies can be used to reduce the burden of work altogether. Futurists are deeply opposed to a national job guarantee that will keep humans trapped as hamsters in a wheel. Futurists are extremely skeptical of the negative technology views of the resigned. They ignore the liberating potential of technology. Isn't the attachment to jobs and wage work a commitment to human enslavement to self-interested and profit-oriented employers? Futurists recognize the dystopia in the attachment to wage work, while self-determined work without pay and for passion becomes possible once UBI or other redistributive programs are in place. The status quo defenders are too conservative in their views on social organization and the potential of technology. Holding on to the model of scarcity, private property and patenting creates an artificial form of scarcity, where the rising economic output becomes ever more concentrated among the well-off, while forcing the majority of people into jobs they do not want to work in. What is the point of ever rising economic and productivity growth if the general public can't see the fruits of them?

The four perspectives on automation view each other critically, and all of these perspectives are valid in the sense that there are advocates that can be found in each camp. In some cases, it is not so much outright disagreement between these views but rather a difference in emphasis that produces such discourses. For example, the resigned describe the negative automation effects because of the inequality and scarcity model that is embedded in the status quo deployment of technology. But what if the scarcity model was replaced by an abundance model, then the futurist leisure society might sound more attractive. Conversely, if the status quo was disrupted by rising technological unemployment, then activist resistance or a resigned view could strengthen. A useful social science agenda would be to quantify that output in the social discourse and how it evolves over time.

On AI Future(s)

Interest in automation has doubtlessly increased with the Fourth IR, of which AI is the major application. Here, I take the liberty to speculate on the possible AI futures, and how they would impact the broader automation discourse.

On balance, AI is a mixed bag. The upsides of an AI future involve the removal of work as drudgery; the pursuit of creative, individual pursuits; the increase in consumer conveniences, e.g. voice assistants, smart devices, personalized algorithmic recommendations and instant translation tools; the increase in labor productivity and the national economy; the improvement in the quality of life, e.g., personalized medicine, early medical diagnostics, better disease cures; better public safety via crime prevention, disaster response and workplace safety algorithms; and better environmental outcomes via precision agriculture, energy optimization, climate modeling and waste reduction.

The downsides of an AI future involve more bias of algorithms that will disadvantage groups who have historically been disadvantaged, such as racial minorities or people from the Global South; the loss of human skills and autonomy due to the overreliance on AI output; the lack of privacy and a rising surveillance state; technological unemployment; the lack of explainability and accountability and rising misuse of AI systems; rising inequality and concentration of ownership of the AI-generated wealth; the growing power of big countries and corporations that operate or own the AI; rising electricity prices due to the rising energy consumption of AI data centers; faster climate change due to rising energy consumption of AI; and the loss of human control of AI systems.

The prevalence of the upsides of AI assumes less available work. This would strengthen the futurist case the most given that these AI systems will deliver greater wealth with less human labor input. It would also back the case of the resigned in that the reduction of work is not a drudgery but an essential part of human identity. The status quo perspective would be reaffirmed in that the rising labor productivity and economic output would benefit the bottom line of companies, though a futurist orientation with reduced labor demand would pose a major challenge to the status quo. The activists will want to stop their job replacement, and the more successful AI is in replacing jobs, the more on the defensive they will be.

But what if AI turns out to be a disappointment? Some jobs will be replaced, some are created and technological unemployment is as irrelevant for AI as for the steam engine. The prohibitive data center and electricity costs might throttle the speed of the AI rollout. Intensifying geopolitical conflicts over rare earth minerals will hamper model development further. The impact on the four discourses will be reversed. The futurists will face a setback. Broader society will ignore their discourse, and the futurists will have to hold out on a future technology to make their case. The resigned will point to the negative consequences of the workers that have lost their jobs to technology, but their worst fears are not confirmed, so their discourse will ebb and flow in public consciousness in that case. The status quo is reaffirmed in either case: whether AI is deeply disruptive in the labor market or not. A lack of disruption suggests that technocratic adjustments in job training or work tax credits are precisely the right measures to deal with the small labor market shocks. The activists will be reaffirmed because they perceive that it is their effort that preserved jobs in the first place. If the deleterious labor effects of AI can be averted, why could this not happen again in the future?

The Future of Work and the Value of Marx and Weber

No social scientist or forecaster is capable of making accurate forecasts on the future of work, though forecasters will want to orient policymakers, investors and the public on the importance of technological disruption. What we can do is to tie automation back to the major concerns formulated by the founders of sociology. Technology is embedded in the rational capitalist order. It is used not merely to increase consumer comfort and use value, but to increase productivity and by extension profits, dividends, interest, rents and tax revenues.

Marx and Weber were not only astute observers of capitalism but also its most vocal critics. Marx was a lifelong communist, who was inspired by the values of the French Revolution: the realization of freedom, equality and brotherhood in broader society. If technology could only be used by capitalists who are obligated to generate profit it would negatively impact workers by increasing managerial control, degrading worker autonomy at the workplace, and, over the long term, expanding the reserve army of the unemployed due to automation. He normatively favored using technology for human liberation presumably by converting the technology and companies into public or worker ownership. He can be considered a futurist. However, Marx' optimism about human liberation was much stronger in his earlier writings in the 1840s than in his later years when he spent most of his effort to describe and critique capitalism. Nonetheless, he never surrendered his hope for human liberation.

Weber was formally committed to value-free science, in which he suggests that social science can only describe the means to achieve ends, not what the chosen ends are.[1] However, individuals do not only act as social scientists and cannot be 'neutral' or 'objective' on human affairs. Unlike Marx, Weber disliked communism, which he regarded as too bureaucratic and oppressive. Nonetheless, he was normatively committed to human liberty. His observation was that the 'Protestant work ethic' is the ideological basis and technology is the technical basis of capitalism and rationalization. Weber formulated the metaphor of the world being increasingly ruled by rationality and called it an "iron cage." This reveals his normative judgment that the pursuit of rationality in an economic sense for its own sake is undesirable. Human freedom is only possible if technologies are not used in the name of rationality and economic profit. In the future of work paradigm, Weber is part of the resigned discourse.

We should ideally use the tools we create for human liberation, but he didn't hold much hope, and he anticipated that our addiction for wealth would result in the endless burning of fossil fuel, which has been continuously increasing over the last few decades. Most recently, Asians and other people from the Global South aspire to attain the Western standard of living which puts an upward pressure on fossil fuel demand. China is competing directly with the US for AI supremacy, which the US attempts to subvert. Sadly, spreading the gains of modern technology is increasingly at the cost of global warming and a destabilization of the eco-system that sustains civilization. Increasingly, the acquisition of wealth and comforts that meet broadly defined goals of poverty reduction and social justice come at the expense of ecological sustainability, thus challenging the technological and economic system that we have collectively adopted.[2]

Further improvements in robotics would imply the diminution of routine, physical work, while further improvements in AI would imply a reduction in more complex and even creative tasks. This trend will be by no means smooth or linear and contestation at the level of the workplace or in public discourse will continue to exert influence over how new forms of automation will be used. As new forms of automation emerge, there might be an organic market-driven process of creative destruction where we reach a new full employment equilibrium, or there will be an increase in the dependent, non-employed population whose leisure is hidden by being an involuntary part-time worker, pensioner, student, housewife, prisoner or homeless person. I surmise that the break from wage labor as a defining feature for being socially accepted will be hard to attain; and this will be reflected in the public discourse that values jobs and the creation of new industries. The counterpoints are the declining work commitment of Generation- Z, the growing popularity of UBI and the desirability of a leisure society. Regardless of the contours in the future of work and its discourse, social scientists will continue to be able to accompany and study this exciting and worrisome social process.

Notes

1 Blum, Fred H. "Max Weber's Postulate of "Freedom" from Value Judgments." *American Journal of Sociology* 50, no. 1 (1944): 46–52.

2 Saitō, Kōhei. *Slow Down: The Degrowth Manifesto.* Translated by Brian Bergstrom. New York: Astra House, 2024. Foster, John Bellamy. *Marx's Ecology: Materialism and Nature.* New York: Monthly Review Press, 2000.

References

Blum, Fred H. "Max Weber's Postulate of "Freedom" from Value Judgments." *American Journal of Sociology* 50, no. 1 (1944): 46–52.

Foster, John Bellamy. *Marx's Ecology: Materialism and Nature.* New York: Monthly Review Press, 2000.

Saitō, Kōhei. *Slow Down: The Degrowth Manifesto.* Translated by Brian Bergstrom. New York: Astra House, 2024.

INDEX

Note: **Bold** page numbers refer to tables and page numbers followed by 'n' refer to notes.

For Product Safety Concerns and Information please contact our EU
representative GPSR@taylorandfrancis.com
Taylor & Francis Verlag GmbH, Kaufingerstraße 24, 80331 München, Germany

www.ingramcontent.com/pod-product-compliance
Ingram Content Group UK Ltd.
Pitfield, Milton Keynes, MK11 3LW, UK
UKHW020003200926
475702UK00015B/2443
9781041316831